Early praise for *3D Game Programming for Kids*

I was thrilled how much my son got into programming as a result of this book. He spent hours with it and was often surprised when his "screen time" was over because the time just flew by. Although the book doesn't delve into the fundamentals of software programming (how computers store and retrieve data), kids get to see the results of their programming right away—the pictures and animations that they created—and are hooked into wanting to learn more.

➤ **Mark Musante, professional software designer**

I would recommend this book to anyone my age that is interested in coding or technology. It was very helpful and insightful about the basic (and the more complex) parts of standard coding. This book would be great for anyone looking to jump head-first into coding.

➤ **Hana B., age 15**

This is the best book a beginning programmer could get. It teaches programming concepts in fun and entertaining ways. This book is a great start in learning to program!

➤ **Alec M., age 13**

It has been great fun reading this book. It takes me back to when I fell in love with programming. After having spent the past twenty years programming solutions on the server side, I find this 3D book a welcome diversion that offers new concepts and ideas with instant visual feedback! I hope the book finds its way into the hands of an inquisitive child who gets hooked on computer programming like I did.

➤ **Darren Hunt, director of Algorithmic Solutions Limited**

3D Game Programming for Kids

Create Interactive Worlds with JavaScript

Chris Strom

The Pragmatic Bookshelf

Dallas, Texas • Raleigh, North Carolina

Pragmatic Bookshelf

Many of the designations used by manufacturers and sellers to distinguish their products are claimed as trademarks. Where those designations appear in this book, and The Pragmatic Programmers, LLC was aware of a trademark claim, the designations have been printed in initial capital letters or in all capitals. The Pragmatic Starter Kit, The Pragmatic Programmer, Pragmatic Programming, Pragmatic Bookshelf, PragProg and the linking g device are trademarks of The Pragmatic Programmers, LLC.

Every precaution was taken in the preparation of this book. However, the publisher assumes no responsibility for errors or omissions, or for damages that may result from the use of information (including program listings) contained herein.

Our Pragmatic courses, workshops, and other products can help you and your team create better software and have more fun. For more information, as well as the latest Pragmatic titles, please visit us at *http://pragprog.com*.

The team that produced this book includes:

Fahmida Rashid (editor)
Potomac Indexing, LLC (indexer)
Candace Cunningham (copyeditor)
David J Kelly (typesetter)
Janet Furlow (producer)
Juliet Benda (rights)
Ellie Callahan (support)

Printed in the United States of America.
ISBN-13: 978-1-937785-44-4
Printed on acid-free paper.
Book version: P1.0—October, 2013

For Greta, so that she knows she can do anything.

Contents

Acknowledgments

I am nothing without my lovely wife, Robin. Not only does she put up with me disappearing for days on end to write, but she also helps in ways innumerable. She was the primary proofreader for the early versions of the book. She helps to run the kid hackathons (OK, she runs them) that aided in development of this book. And oh, yeah—she's an awesome wife and mother.

Also a big thanks to my son Luke for being the primary guinea pig for the early versions of the book. His no-nonsense feedback made this a better product. Thanks also to my daughter Elora for chiming in with her insights.

And, of course, huge thanks to my technical reviewers. It is a tough task to review a book from a kid's perspective, but my reviewers were more than up to the task. In no particular order, they are Alec M., Hana B., Dave S., Thad K., Maik Schmidt, Silvia Domenech, and Mark Musante.

Special thanks to Sophie H., who provided the inspiration for the game that eventually became *Project: Fruit Hunt*.

This book would not exist without the great work of Ricardo Cabello Miguel, affectionately known as "Mr.doob." Ricardo is the primary programmer behind Three.js, the 3D JavaScript library that we use in this book. He also wrote the original implementation of the ICE Code Editor that we use. This book would be significantly less without his amazing talents. Thanks also to Chandler Prall for his work on the Physijs physics engine, of which we make extensive use. Chandler was also wonderful about answering my many, many questions while I was learning.

Last, but not least, many thanks to the folks at The Pragmatic Programmers for believing in the book and helping me realize its full potential. Special thanks to my editor, Fahmida, for keeping me honest and focused.

Introduction

Welcome to the world of programming!

I won't lie; it can be a frustrating world sometimes (it makes me cry at least once a week). But it's totally worth the pain. You get to make this world do whatever you want. You can share your world with others. You can build things that really make a difference.

This book that you hold in your eager hands is a great way to get started programming. It is chock-full of clear and understandable explanations. Best of all, we get to make some pretty cool games. This is going to be a blast.

How I Learned to Program

When I was a kid, I copied computer-program games out of books. This was a long time ago, so I bought books with nothing but programs, and typed them into computers.

When I first started doing it, I had no idea what I was doing. Eventually, I started to recognize certain things that were done over and over, and I almost understood them.

I started to change things—little things at first—to see what happened. Then I started making bigger changes. Eventually I got pretty good at it. And after a long time, I could write my own programs. I hope that this book will let you do the same, but with one important difference: I'll explain what's going on so you won't have to guess quite as much.

What You Need for This Book

Not all web browsers can generate the cool 3D-gaming objects that we'll build in this book. To get the most out of the book, you should install the Google Chrome (https://www.google.com/chrome/) web browser on your computer. Other web browsers will work, but some of the exercises in this book rely on features available only in Google Chrome. One browser that will definitely *not* work with the exercises is Microsoft Internet Explorer.

For most of the exercises in the book, any computer with Google Chrome installed will be sufficient. Later exercises that make use of interesting lighting, shadows, and 3D materials will require a computer that supports WebGL. You can test your computer's capabilities by visiting the Get WebGL site (http://get.webgl.org/). Don't worry much about WebGL; you'll be able to do a ton of programming even if your computer can't handle the advanced 3D graphics.

What Is JavaScript?

There are many, many programming languages. Some programmers enjoy arguing over which is the *best*, but the truth is that all languages offer unique and worthwhile things.

In this book we'll use the JavaScript programming language. We program in JavaScript because it's the language of the Web. It is the only programming language all web browsers understand without needing any additional software. If you can program in JavaScript, not only can you make the kinds of games that you'll learn in this book, but you can also program just about every website there is.

We're not going to become experts in JavaScript.

We'll cover just enough JavaScript to be able to program the games in this book. That is quite a lot of JavaScript—enough that you'll be able to learn the rest without much difficulty.

How to Read This Book

You'll see two kinds of chapters: project chapters and learning chapters. The project chapters start with "Project" just like Chapter 1, *Project: Creating Simple Shapes*, on page 1. All the others are learning chapters.

If you want to learn programming the way I did, just read the project chapters and follow along with all the exercises. You'll create pretty cool game characters and worlds to play in. You'll make space simulations. You'll make purple monsters. You'll make all sorts of great stuff.

If you have questions about *why* the games are written the way they are, then read the learning chapters. We won't go over *everything* about programming, but there should be enough to help you understand why we do what we do. These are the chapters that I wish I'd had when I was a kid.

Let's Get Started!

Enough introduction—let's jump right into programming!

When you're done with this chapter, you will

- *Know what a code editor is and how to use it to program*
- *Know how to make various 3D shapes*
- *Be able to program simple JavaScript*
- *Understand how to make 3D shapes move*

CHAPTER 1

Project: Creating Simple Shapes

There will be plenty of time for detailed explanations later in this book. For now, let's get started with programming!

1.1 Programming with the ICE Code Editor

In this book, we'll use the ICE Code Editor to do our programming. The ICE Code Editor runs right inside a browser. It lets us type in our programming code and see the results immediately.

To get started, open the ICE Code Editor at http://gamingJS.com/ice using Google's Chrome web browser. It should look something like this:

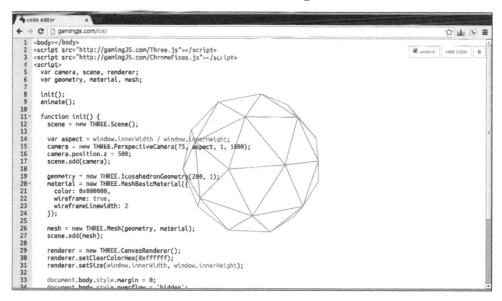

That spinning, multisided thing is a sample of some of the stuff we'll be working on in this book. In this chapter we'll create a new project named Shapes.

To create a new project in the ICE Code Editor, we click on the menu button (the button with three horizontal lines) in the upper-right corner of the screen and select New from the drop-down.

Type the name of the project, Shapes, in the text field and click the Save button. Leave the template set as 3D starter project.

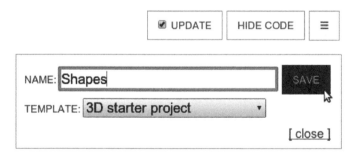

Remember, none of the projects in this book will work if you're using the ICE Code Editor in Internet Explorer. Although some of the exercises will work with Mozilla Firefox, it's easiest to stick with a single browser (Google Chrome) for all our projects.

Coding with the ICE Code Editor

We'll be using the ICE Code Editor throughout this book. You only need web access the first time that you connect to http://gamingJS.com/ice/. After the first visit, ICE is stored in your browser so you can keep working even if you're not connected to the Internet.

When ICE opens a new 3D project, there is already a lot of code in the file. We'll look closely at that code later, but for now let's begin our programming adventure on line 20. Look for the line that says START CODING ON THE NEXT LINE.

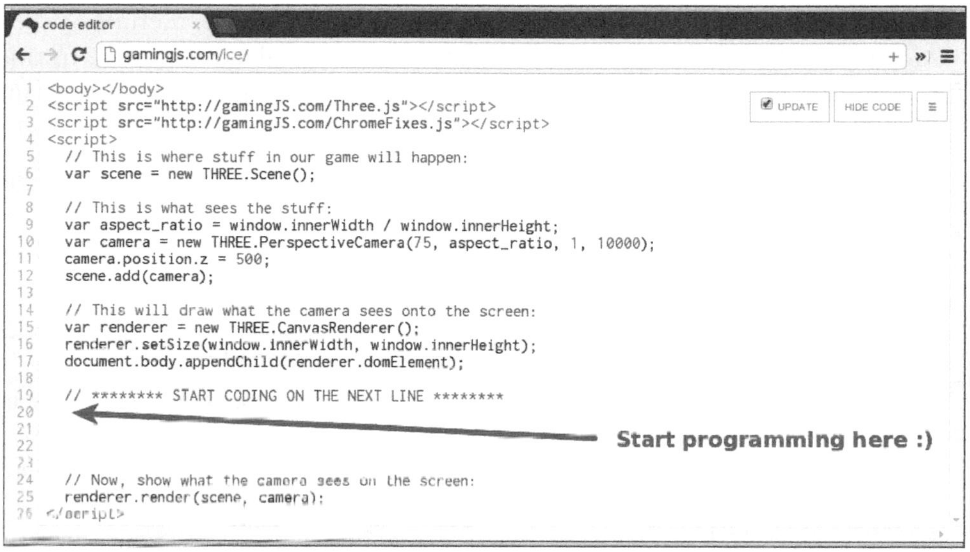

On line 20, type the following:

```
var shape = new THREE.SphereGeometry(100);
var cover = new THREE.MeshNormalMaterial();
var ball = new THREE.Mesh(shape, cover);
scene.add(ball);
```

Once you finish typing that, you should see something cool:

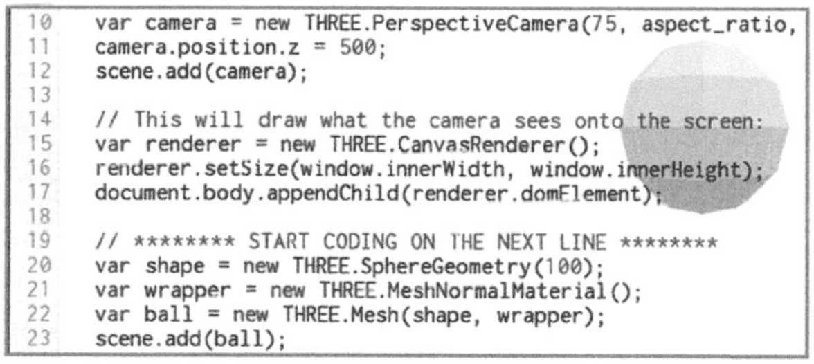

The ball that we typed—the ball that we *programmed*—showed up in ICE. Congratulations! You just wrote your first JavaScript program!

Don't worry about the structure of the code just yet; you'll get familiar with it in *A Closer Look at JavaScript Fundamentals*. For now, let's examine the 3D programming that we just did.

3D things are built from two parts: the shape and something that covers the shape. The combination of these two things, the shape and its cover, is given a special name in 3D programming: *mesh.*

Mesh is a fancy word for a 3D thing. Meshes need shapes (sometimes called *geometry*) and something to cover them (sometimes called *materials*). In this chapter we'll look at different shapes. We won't deal with different covers for our shapes until *Working with Lights and Materials.*

Once we have a mesh, we add it to the *scene.* The scene is where the magic happens in 3D programming. It is the world in which everything takes place. In this case, it's where our ball is hanging out, waiting for some friends. Let's add some other shapes to the scene so that the ball isn't lonely.

Your Work Is Saved Automatically

 Your work is saved automatically, so you don't have to do it yourself. If you want to save the code yourself anyway, click the three-line menu button in ICE and select the Save option from the drop-down. That's it!

1.2 Making Shapes with JavaScript

So far we have seen only one kind of shape: a sphere. Shapes can be simple, like cubes, pyramids, cones, and spheres. Shapes can also be more complex, like faces or cars. In this book we'll stick with simple shapes. When we build things like trees, we'll combine simple shapes, such as spheres and cylinders, to make them.

Creating Spheres

Balls are always called spheres in geometry and in 3D programming. There are two ways to control the shape of a sphere in JavaScript.

Size: SphereGeometry(100)

The first way that we can control a sphere is to describe how big it is. We created a ball whose radius was 100 when we said new THREE.SphereGeometry(100). What happens when you change the radius to 250?

```
❶ var shape = new THREE.SphereGeometry(250);
  var cover = new THREE.MeshNormalMaterial();
  var ball = new THREE.Mesh(shape, cover);
  scene.add(ball);
```

❶ This points to where you should change the sphere's size.

This should make it much bigger:

```
 4  <script>
 5      // This is where stuff in our game will happen:
 6      var scene = new THREE.Scene();
 7
 8      // This is what sees the stuff:
 9      var aspect_ratio = window.innerWidth / window.innerHeight;
10      var camera = new THREE.PerspectiveCamera(75, aspect_ratio, 1, 10000);
11      camera.position.z = 500;
12      scene.add(camera);
13
14      // This will draw what the camera sees onto the screen:
15      var renderer = new THREE.CanvasRenderer();
16      renderer.setSize(window.innerWidth, window.innerHeight);
17      document.body.appendChild(renderer.domElement);
18
19      // ******** START CODING ON THE NEXT LINE ********
20      var shape = new THREE.SphereGeometry(250);
21      var cover = new THREE.MeshNormalMaterial();
22      var ball = new THREE.Mesh(shape, cover);
23      scene.add(ball);
24
25
26      // Now, show what the camera sees on the screen:
27      renderer.render(scene, camera);
28  </script>
```

What happens if you change the 250 to 10? As you probably guessed, it gets much smaller. So that's one way we can control a sphere's shape. What is the other way?

Not Chunky: SphereGeometry(100, 20, 15)

If you click on the Hide Code button in ICE, you may notice that our sphere isn't *really* a smooth ball:

You Can Easily Hide or Show the Code

If you click the white Hide Code button in the upper-right corner of the ICE window, you'll see just the game area and the objects in the game. This is how you'll play games in later chapters. To get your code back, click the white Show Code button within the ICE Code Editor.

Computers can't really make a ball. Instead they fake it by joining a bunch of squares (and sometimes triangles) to make something that looks like a ball. Normally, we'll get the right number of *chunks* so that it's close enough.

Sometimes we want it to look a little smoother. To make it smoother, add some extra numbers to the SphereGeometry() line:

```
var shape = new THREE.SphereGeometry(100, 20, 15);
var cover = new THREE.MeshNormalMaterial();
var ball = new THREE.Mesh(shape, cover);
scene.add(ball);
```

❶ The first number is the size, the second number is the number of chunks around the sphere, and the third number is the number of chunks up and down the sphere.

This should make a sphere that is much smoother:

Play around with the numbers a bit more. You're already learning quite a bit here, and playing with the numbers is a great way to keep learning!

Don't Change the Chunkiness Unless You Have To

The number of chunks that we get without telling SphereGeometry to use more may not seem great, but don't change it unless you must. The more chunks that are in a shape, the harder the computer has to work to draw it. As you'll see in later chapters, it's usually easier for a computer to make things look smooth by choosing a different cover for the shape.

When you're done playing, move the ball out of the way by setting its position:

```
var shape = new THREE.SphereGeometry(100);
var cover = new THREE.MeshNormalMaterial();
var ball = new THREE.Mesh(shape, cover);
scene.add(ball);
ball.position.set(-250,250,-250);
```

❶ The three numbers move the ball to the left, up, and back. Don't worry much about what the numbers do right now—we'll talk about position when we start building game characters in Chapter 3, *Project: Making an Avatar*, on page 25.

Making Boxes with the Cube Shape

Next we'll make a cube, which is another name for a box. There are three ways to change a cube's shape: the width, the height, and the depth.

Size: CubeGeometry(300, 100, 20)

To create a box, we'll write more JavaScript below everything that we used to create our ball. Type the following:

```
var shape = new THREE.CubeGeometry(100, 100, 100);
var cover = new THREE.MeshNormalMaterial();
var box = new THREE.Mesh(shape, cover);
scene.add(box);
```

If you have everything correct, you should see...a square:

Well, that's boring. Why do we see a square instead of a box? The answer is that our *camera*, our perspective, is looking directly at one side of the box. If we want to see more of the box, we need to move the camera or turn the box. Let's turn the box by rotating it:

```
var shape = new THREE.CubeGeometry(100, 100, 100);
var cover = new THREE.MeshNormalMaterial();
var box = new THREE.Mesh(shape, cover);
scene.add(box);
❶ box.rotation.set(0.5, 0.5, 0);
```

❶ These three numbers turn the box down, counterclockwise, and left-right.

In this case, we rotate 0.5 down and 0.5 to the right:

Try This Yourself

Rotating things takes a little getting used to, so play with the numbers. Try smaller and bigger numbers. A full rotation is 6.3 (we'll talk about that number later). Try setting two of the numbers to 0 and another to 0.1, then to 0.25, and finally to 0.5. If you can change the numbers fast enough, it's almost like the cube is spinning!

Setting the box rotation to (0.5, 0.5, 0) should rotate the cube so we can see that it really is a cube:

```
var shape = new THREE.CubeGeometry(100, 100, 100);
var cover = new THREE.MeshNormalMaterial();
var box = new THREE.Mesh(shape, cover);
scene.add(box);
box.rotation.set(0.5, 0.5, 0);
```

Each side of a cube doesn't have to be the same size. Our box so far is 100 wide (from left to right), 100 tall (up and down), and 100 deep (front to back). Let's change it so that it is 300 wide, 100 tall, and only 20 deep:

```
var shape = new THREE.CubeGeometry(300, 100, 20);
var cover = new THREE.MeshNormalMaterial();
var box = new THREE.Mesh(shape, cover);
scene.add(box);
box.rotation.set(0.5, 0.5, 0);
```

This should show something like this:

```
var shape = new THREE.CubeGeometry(300, 100, 20);
var cover = new THREE.MeshNormalMaterial();
var box = new THREE.Mesh(shape, cover);
scene.add(box);
box.rotation.set(0.5, 0.5, 0);
```

Play around with the numbers to get a good feel for what they can do.

Believe it or not, you already know a ton about JavaScript and 3D programming. There is still a lot to learn, of course, but you can already make balls and boxes. You can already move them and turn them. And you only had to write ten lines of JavaScript to do it all—nice!

Let's move our box out of the way so we can play with more shapes:

```
var shape = new THREE.CubeGeometry(300, 100, 20);
var cover = new THREE.MeshNormalMaterial();
var box = new THREE.Mesh(shape, cover);
scene.add(box);
box.rotation.set(0.5, 0.5, 0);
box.position.set(250, 250, -250);
```

Using Cylinders for All Kinds of Shapes

A cylinder, which is also sometimes called a tube, is a surprisingly useful shape in 3D programming. Think about it: cylinders can be used as tree trunks, tin cans, wheels.... Did you know that cylinders can be used to create cones, evergreen trees, and even pyramids? Let's see how!

Size: CylinderGeometry(20, 20, 100)

Below the box code, type in the following to create a cylinder:

```
var shape = new THREE.CylinderGeometry(20, 20, 100);
var cover = new THREE.MeshNormalMaterial();
var tube = new THREE.Mesh(shape, cover);
scene.add(tube);
```

If you rotate that a little (you remember how to do that from the last section, right?), then you might see something like this:

If you were not able to figure out how to rotate the tube, don't worry. Just add this line after the line with scene.add(tube):

```
tube.rotation.set(0.5, 0, 0);
```

When making a cylinder, the first two numbers describe how big the top and bottom of the cylinder is. The last number is how tall the cylinder is. So our cylinder has a top and bottom that are 20 in size and 100 in height.

If you change the first two numbers to 100 and the last number to 20, what happens? What happens if you make the top 1, the bottom 100, and the height 100?

Try This Yourself

  Play with those numbers and see what you can create!

What did you find?

A flat cylinder is a disc:

```
var shape = new THREE.CylinderGeometry(100, 100, 20);
var cover = new THREE.MeshNormalMaterial();
var tube = new THREE.Mesh(shape, cover);
scene.add(tube);
tube.rotation.set(0.5, 0, 0);
```

And a cylinder that has either the top or bottom with a size of 1 is a cone:

```
var shape = new THREE.CylinderGeometry(1, 100, 100);
var cover = new THREE.MeshNormalMaterial();
var tube = new THREE.Mesh(shape, cover);
scene.add(tube);
tube.rotation.set(0.5, 0, 0);
```

It should be clear that you can do a lot with cylinders, but we haven't seen everything yet. We have one trick left.

Pyramids: CylinderGeometry(1, 100, 100, 4)

Did you notice that cylinders look chunky? It should be no surprise then, that you can control the chunkiness of cylinders. If you set the number of chunks to 20, for instance, with the disc, like this:

```
var shape = new THREE.CylinderGeometry(100, 100, 10, 20);
var cover = new THREE.MeshNormalMaterial();
var tube = new THREE.Mesh(shape, cover);
scene.add(tube);
tube.rotation.set(0.5, 0, 0);
```

then you should see something like this:

```
var shape = new THREE.CylinderGeometry(100, 100, 10, 20);
var cover = new THREE.MeshNormalMaterial();
var tube = new THREE.Mesh(shape, cover);
scene.add(tube);
tube.rotation.set(0.5, 0, 0);
```

Just as with spheres, you should use lots of chunks like that only when you really, really need to.

Can you think how you might turn this into a pyramid? You have all of the clues that you need.

Try This Yourself

 Play with different numbers and see what you can create!

Were you able to figure it out? Don't worry if you weren't. The way we'll do it is actually pretty sneaky.

The answer is that you need to *decrease* the number of chunks that you use to make a cone. If you set the top to 1, the bottom to 100, the height to 100, and the number of chunks to 4, then you'll get this:

```
var shape = new THREE.CylinderGeometry(1, 100, 100, 4);
var cover = new THREE.MeshNormalMaterial();
var tube = new THREE.Mesh(shape, cover);
scene.add(tube);
tube.rotation.set(0.5, 0, 0);
```

It might seem like a cheat to do something like this to create a pyramid, but this brings us to a very important tip with any programming:

Cheat Whenever Possible

 You shouldn't cheat in real life, but in programming—especially in 3D programming—you should always look for easier ways of doing things. Even if there is a *usual* way to do something, there may be a *better* way to do it.

You're doing great so far. Move the tube out of the center like we did with the cube and the sphere:

```
tube.position.set(250, -250, -250);
```

Now let's move on to the last two shapes of this chapter.

Building Flat Surfaces with Planes

A plane is a flat surface. Planes are especially useful for the ground, but they can also be handy to mark doors and edges in our games.

PlaneGeometry(100, 100)

Since planes are just flat squares, they are much simpler than the other objects that we've seen. Type in the following:

```
var shape = new THREE.PlaneGeometry(100, 100);
var cover = new THREE.MeshNormalMaterial();
var ground = new THREE.Mesh(shape, cover);
scene.add(ground);
ground.rotation.set(0.5, 0, 0);
```

Don't forget the rotation on the last line. Planes are so thin that you might not see them when looking directly at them.

The numbers when building a plane are the width and depth. A plane that is 300 wide and 100 deep might look like this:

```
var shape = new THREE.PlaneGeometry(300, 100);
var cover = new THREE.MeshNormalMaterial();
var ground = new THREE.Mesh(shape, cover);
scene.add(ground);
ground.rotation.set(0.5, 0, 0);
```

That's pretty much all there is to know about planes. Move our plane out of the way:

```
var shape = new THREE.PlaneGeometry(300, 100);
var cover = new THREE.MeshNormalMaterial();
var ground = new THREE.Mesh(shape, cover);
scene.add(ground);
ground.position.set(-250, -250, -250);
```

Now let's move on to the greatest shape in the world.

Rendering Donuts (Not the Kind You Eat) with Torus

In 3D-programming-speak, a donut is called a *torus*. The simplest torus that we can create needs us to assign two values: one for the distance from the center to the outside edge, and the other for the thickness of the tube.

TorusGeometry(100, 25)

Type the following into ICE:

```
var shape = new THREE.TorusGeometry(100, 25);
var cover = new THREE.MeshNormalMaterial();
var donut = new THREE.Mesh(shape, cover);
scene.add(donut);
```

You should see a very chunky donut, as shown in Figure 1, *A Chunky Donut*, on page 13.

By now you probably know how to make the donut less chunky.

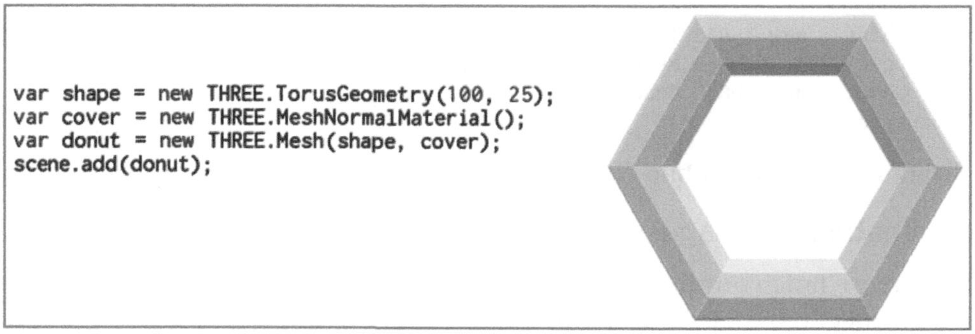

```
var shape = new THREE.TorusGeometry(100, 25);
var cover = new THREE.MeshNormalMaterial();
var donut = new THREE.Mesh(shape, cover);
scene.add(donut);
```

Figure 1—A Chunky Donut

TorusGeometry(100, 25, 8, 25)

Like the sphere, the donut shape is built from chunks. The chunks can be made bigger or smaller around the inner tube, which we can set by including a third number when defining the TorusGeometry. We can also adjust the size of the chunks around the outside of the donut by including a fourth number. Try experimenting with numbers like the following and see what happens.

```
var shape = new THREE.TorusGeometry(100, 25, 8, 25);
var cover = new THREE.MeshNormalMaterial();
var donut = new THREE.Mesh(shape, cover);
scene.add(donut);
```

Now *that* is a good-looking donut:

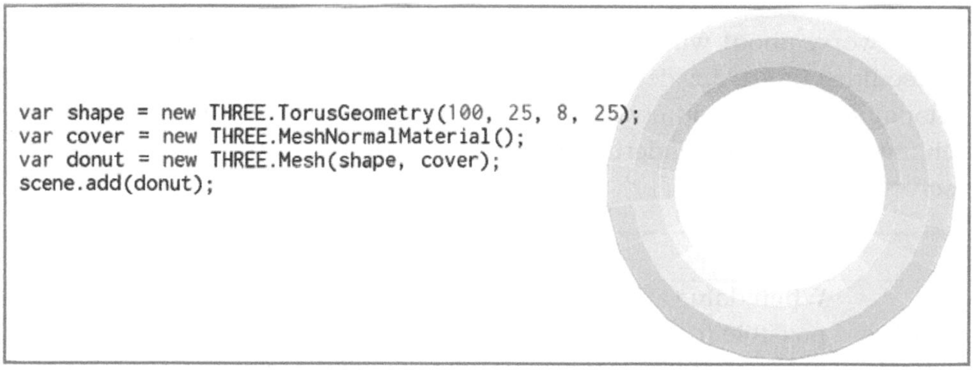

```
var shape = new THREE.TorusGeometry(100, 25, 8, 25);
var cover = new THREE.MeshNormalMaterial();
var donut = new THREE.Mesh(shape, cover);
scene.add(donut);
```

TorusGeometry(100, 25, 8, 25, 3.14)

We can play one other trick with donuts. Try adding another number, 3.14, to the TorusGeometry shape:

```
var shape = new THREE.TorusGeometry(100, 25, 8, 25, 3.14);
var cover = new THREE.MeshNormalMaterial();
var donut = new THREE.Mesh(shape, cover);
scene.add(donut);
```

That should make a half-eaten donut.

1.3 Animating the Shapes

Before we finish our first programming session, let's do something cool. Let's make all of our shapes spin around like crazy.

In ICE, add the following code after all of the shapes:

```
var clock = new THREE.Clock();

function animate() {
  requestAnimationFrame(animate);
  var t = clock.getElapsedTime();

  ball.rotation.set(t, 2*t, 0);
  box.rotation.set(t, 2*t, 0);
  tube.rotation.set(t, 2*t, 0);
  ground.rotation.set(t, 2*t, 0);
  donut.rotation.set(t, 2*t, 0);

  renderer.render(scene, camera);
}

animate();
```

Don't worry about what everything means in that code—we'll look at all of these lines in greater detail later in the book. For now, it's enough to know that at specific time intervals, we're changing the shape's rotation. After each change, we tell the rendering program to redraw the current shapes on the screen.

If ICE Locks Up

When doing animations and other sophisticated programming, it's possible to completely lock up the ICE Code Editor. This is not a big deal. If ICE stops responding, you'll need to undo whatever change you made last. Instructions on how to do that are in *Recovering When ICE Is Broken*.

1.4 The Code So Far

To make things a little easier, the completed version of this project is included as part of Section A1.1, *Code: Creating Simple Shapes*, on page 217. Use that code to double-check your work as you go through the exercises, but do not copy and paste code into ICE. It's impossible to learn and understand programming unless you code it yourself.

1.5 What's Next

Whoa! That was pretty crazy. We learned a ton and we're just getting started!

Already we know how to code projects in the ICE Code Editor. We know how to make a lot of different shapes. We even know how to move and spin things with JavaScript. And best of all, it took us only fifteen lines of code to create a pretty cool animation after making our shapes. That's a good start.

Now that we have a taste of how to do 3D programming, let's talk a little bit about programming in web browsers.

CHAPTER 2

Playing with the Console and Finding What's Broken

When programming within web browsers, it's *extremely* useful to be able to use the browser's JavaScript console. Most modern browsers have a JavaScript console, but here we're using Google Chrome.

Programming Can Be Overwhelming

At times it can make you want to throw your computer against the wall (don't). While doing this stuff, keep these two facts in mind:

- There will be things that you don't know—this is OK.
- Your programs are going to break—this is OK.

Just remember that everyone struggles with this, and you'll be just fine.

2.1 Getting Started

Know the ICE Code Editor

We're still using the ICE Code Editor that we used in Chapter 1, *Project: Creating Simple Shapes*, on page 1. If you haven't already gotten started with ICE, go back to that chapter and familiarize yourself with the editor.

Start a New Project

Any work that you have already done in ICE should be automatically saved, so we can jump right into starting a new project. Click on the menu button and then choose New from the menu:

Let's call the new project Breaking Things.

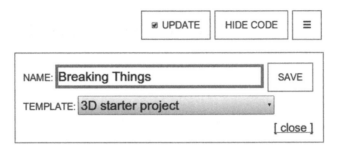

Be sure to leave the template set to 3D starter project.

Now let's open the browser's JavaScript console.

2.2 Opening and Closing the JavaScript Console

The JavaScript console inside the browser is a web programmer's best friend. It tells us where we made our mistakes.

Opening and Closing the JavaScript Console

Ctrl+Shift+J (holding down the Ctrl, Shift, and J keys at the same time) will open and close the JavaScript console.

If you're using an Apple computer, you can use ⌘+Option+J to open and close the console.

Don't worry if you see tons of warnings and errors the first time you open the JavaScript console. It keeps a log of events that happen on a web page or in the ICE Code Editor. If the messages are too much, you can clear the log with the button that has a circle with a line through it.

The same key combination that opens the JavaScript console will close it (but leave it open in this chapter).

Let's start by breaking simple things that the ICE Code Editor can tell us about.

2.3 Debugging in ICE: The Red X

A red X next to your code means ICE sees a problem that will stop your code from running. Let's write some really bad JavaScript to demonstrate this. Enter the following line below START CODING ON THE NEXT LINE.

```
bad()javascript
```

That's some bad JavaScript!

Are you wondering why? It's bad because you should never have a word come after the parentheses. If you write code like this, ICE will show a red X next to the line with the problem to indicate that line has to be fixed. Moving the mouse pointer over the red X will display the actual error message, such as "missing ; before statement."

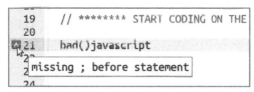

ICE won't tell you that you put words after the parentheses. All it knows is that parentheses should be at the end of the line, and here that wasn't the case. When it detected the line wasn't finished, it triggered an error to warn, "Hey! You forgot the semicolon at the end of the line!" It's up to us to figure out where the line should end.

Some things to check in your code when you see a red X:

- Did you forget a semicolon?

- If you don't see a problem on the red X line, look at the previous line, as well. ICE can't always tell where the problem begins and may be off by one or two lines.

2.4 Debugging in ICE: The Yellow Triangle

Unlike a red X, a yellow triangle showing up to the left of your code is not a show-stopper. Your code will probably run even if lines in your code are marked with yellow triangles, but it may not run *correctly*. It is best to get rid of those triangles as they come up.

Let's put this in action by writing some more bad JavaScript (but not *too* bad). First, remove the bad()javascript line from the previous section, and add the following lines:

```
food;
eat(food);
```

In this case, ICE will tell us via the yellow triangle that the food line is not doing anything.

```
⚠ 21    food;
  22
  23 | Expected an assignment or function call and instead saw
  24 | an expression.
```

We can fix the problem by changing the food line into an assignment, like this:

```
food = 'Cookie';
eat(food);
```

ICE should accept the new food line and no longer display any errors. However, even though ICE may not report any more issues, there is still something wrong with this code.

2.5   Debugging in the Console

This is where the JavaScript console comes in handy, as we get to see what the program is actually doing. Once you open up the console, you'll see an error message that eat() is not defined.

⊗ Uncaught ReferenceError: eat is not defined

When the browser tried to run the bad JavaScript code, it realized there was a problem. In our program, we told the browser to run the eat() function, but we never told the browser *how* to do that. Errors found when trying to run the code are called *run-time* errors.

We'll talk more about functions in Chapter 5, *Functions: Use and Use Again*, on page 49. For now, it's enough to know that a function is a way to write code that can be run again and again.

The errors flagged by ICE with the red X and yellow triangle are called *compile-time* errors. Compile-time errors are caught when the computer is reading the code and deciding what to do with it. Compiling refers to the computer deciding what to do with the code.

The JavaScript console helps us fix run-time errors.

To resolve this problem, let's tell our JavaScript program how to eat food. We do this by adding a function that explains eating after the line with eat(food).

```
food = 'Cookie';
eat(food);

function eat(food) {
  console.log(food + "! Nom. Nom. Nom.");
}
```

At this point, there should be no compile-time errors in ICE, no run-time errors in the JavaScript console, and the message, "Cookie! Nom. Nom. Nom." in the console.

Before we wrap up this chapter, let's look at some common 3D-programming errors. Add the following code after the closing curly brace of the eat() function:

```
var shape = new THREE.SpherGeometry(100);
var cover = new Three.MeshNormalMaterial();
var ball = new THREE.Mesh(shape, cover);
scene.ad(ball);
```

You'll notice that there are no compile-time errors in ICE for this code. The browser reads the JavaScript code and says, "Yup, that looks like perfectly fine JavaScript to me. I'll run it now!" However, problems pop up when the code is actually run, and you'll see run-time errors in the JavaScript console.

Possible Error Message—Undefined Is Not a Function

Let's take a look at what went wrong. First, open the JavaScript console if it's not already open. In there, you should see a very *un*helpful message.

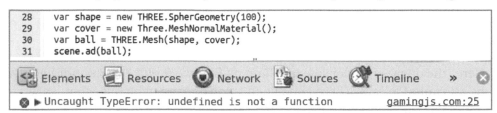

This message is *trying* to tell us that SphereGeometry is spelled incorrectly. Check the code; it turns out we missed an e and typed SpherGeometry instead. The message in the JavaScript console is very poor and unhelpful.

There are two problems to tackle here. First, "undefined is not a function" doesn't really tell us anything and is not easy to understand. Even JavaScript experts get confused by that one.

The second problem is the line number in the error message. In this example, gamingjs.com:25 means the browser thinks the problem happened on line 25 of our program (your line numbers may be slightly different). However, the misspelled word is not on line 25 in ICE. Our problem actually happens on line 28. And yes, JavaScript experts get confused by this as well.

Console Line Numbers Are Not Always Exact

ICE does its best to get the line numbers in the console correct, and sometimes it succeeds—it may even be correct for you now—but other times it can be off by a few lines. Start by looking at the exact line number. If that doesn't seem like it matches the error, then check the next few lines.

Let's get back to the "undefined is not a function" error message that is actually referring to line 28 in ICE. This error means that when the browser tried to run our code, it was looking for a function but found something it knew nothing about. THREE.SpherGeometry was not defined because the actual function was called THREE.SphereGeometry.

Luckily it's easy to fix this problem, as all we have to do is add the e.

Possible Error Message—Three Is Not Defined

However, even after we spell SphereGeometry correctly, a ball doesn't appear on the screen. Something is still wrong with our code.

Looking in the JavaScript console, you should see something like the following.

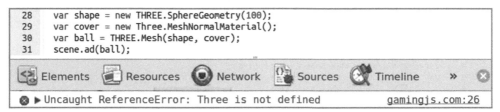

Here, the JavaScript console is telling us that we forgot THREE should always be all capital letters. There is no such thing as Three, which is what we wrote and what the JavaScript console is telling us.

This is a very common mistake when working with the 3D library, so make sure you remember it for the next time you see the error.

We can fix this problem by replacing the Three in the code with THREE.

Possible Error Message—Undefined: No Method

Even with those two issues fixed, the sphere is still not visible and we have another cryptic error message in the console.

```
28    var shape = new THREE.SphereGeometry(100);
29    var cover = new THREE.MeshNormalMaterial();
30    var ball = THREE.Mesh(shape, cover);
31    scene.ad(ball);
```

Elements   Resources   Network   Sources   Timeline   »   ⊗

⊗ ▶ Uncaught TypeError: Object [object Object] has no method 'ad'
                                              gamingjs.com:28
>

Don't worry about the Object [object Object] part of the message, as it's not telling us anything helpful at this point.

In this case, we told the browser that there was a method named ad(), but it was unable to find any information in the file. The fix is the same as in previous examples. The method we should have is add(), not ad(). In other words, we do not want to *ad* the ball to the screen; we want to *add* it.

After fixing that line, you'll finally see a ball and the "Nom. Nom. Nom." message appear in the Javascript console.

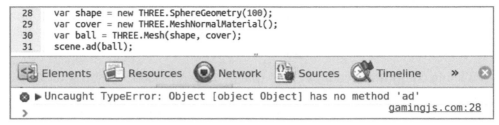

```
19    // ******** START CODING ON THE NEXT LINE ********
20
21    food = 'Cookie';
22    eat(food);
23
24 ▾  function eat(food) {
25      console.log(food + "! Nom. Nom. Nom.");
26    }
27
28    var shape = new THREE.SphereGeometry(100);
29    var cover = new THREE.MeshNormalMaterial();
30    var ball = new THREE.Mesh(shape, cover);
31    scene.add(ball);
32
```

Elements   Resources   Network   {}

Cookie! Nom. Nom. Nom.

2.6 Recovering When ICE Is Broken

It is surprisingly easy to break a web browser. If you create a sphere with a million chunks, the browser will break. If you create a recursive function with no stopping point (we'll talk about those in *Functions: Use and Use Again*), the browser will break.

If the browser is broken, then the ICE Code Editor is broken, right?

Well, yes, but there's an easy way to fix it: add ?e or ?edit-only to the URL so that you're looking at http://gamingjs.com/ice/?e. This is edit-only mode for ICE.

Fix the last thing that you typed to break ICE, and then remove the edit-only question mark from the URL so that you're back at http://gamingjs.com/ice/. Now you should see the preview again.

On some computers, you may find that you need to close the browser tab or window before trying this. Then you can open a new window or tab in which you can enter the ICE edit-only URL. Google Chromebooks, in particular, run edit-only mode better with this procedure.

2.7 What's Next

Now that we know how to make shapes and where to check when things go wrong, let's get started on our first game by building our very own avatar.

When you're done with this chapter, you will

- *Know how to place objects together on the screen*
- *Have an avatar to use in later chapters and in games*

CHAPTER 3

Project: Making an Avatar

Developing games involves building a lot of parts, such as the game area, the players in the game, and things that get in the way of players. In this project chapter we'll create a player that we might use in a game—an avatar. It will end up looking something like this:

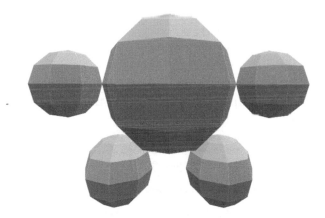

An avatar is who you are within the game world. It shows where you are in the game and what you're doing. Since it's supposed to represent you and me, it should have a good feel to it. We want something better than a plain box to stand for us.

The Difference Between a Player and an Avatar

In this book, we'll use the word "player" to mean the person playing the game. The word "avatar" will be used to describe a player *inside* the game.

3.1 Getting Started

Let's open the ICE Code Editor[1] again and create a new project named My Avatar (check *Start a New Project*, on page 17, if you don't remember how).

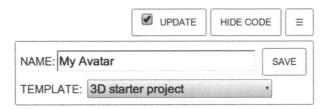

Be sure to leave the template set to 3D starter project. With that, we're ready to start programming on the line following START CODING ON THE NEXT LINE.

3.2 Making a Whole from Parts

From Chapter 1, *Project: Creating Simple Shapes*, on page 1, we already know how to make basic shapes. Let's start building our player avatar by making a sphere for the body.

```
var cover = new THREE.MeshNormalMaterial();
var body = new THREE.SphereGeometry(100);
var avatar = new THREE.Mesh(body, cover);
scene.add(avatar);
```

We already know what happens when we type that in—we get a ball in the center of the scene.

```
// This will draw what the camera sees onto the screen:
var renderer = new THREE.CanvasRenderer();
renderer.setSize(window.innerWidth, window.innerHeight);
document.body.appendChild(renderer.domElement);

// ******** START CODING ON THE NEXT LINE ********
var cover = new THREE.MeshNormalMaterial();
var body = new THREE.SphereGeometry(100);
var avatar = new THREE.Mesh(body, cover);
scene.add(avatar);
```

Let's add a hand next to the body. Add the following lines below the code that you already entered to create the body.

```
var hand = new THREE.SphereGeometry(50);

var right_hand = new THREE.Mesh(hand, cover);
right_hand.position.set(-150, 0, 0);
scene.add(right_hand);
```

1. http://gamingJS.com/ice

Notice that we didn't create a new cover for the hand. Instead we reused the same cover, which we named cover when we used it for the avatar's body. That saves us a bit of typing.

Less typing is a good thing since we're all programmers and programmers are lazy at heart. That reminds me of some programming wisdom I would like to share with you:

Good Programmers Are Lazy

I don't mean that programmers hate doing work. We actually love our jobs and often spend too much time working because we love it so much.

No, what I mean by *lazy* is that we hate doing work that computers are better at. So instead of creating hands and feet individually, we would rather write a single hand/foot and then copy it as many times as necessary.

Being lazy benefits us in two very important ways:

- We type less. Believe it or not, this is a big win. Not only do we have to type less the first time around, but we have to read less when we want to update later.
- If we want to change the way a limb is created, we only have to change one thing. That is, if we want to change the cover or even the shape of a hand in the future, then we only have to make a change in one place.

So let's see if we can be even lazier when we create the left hand for our avatar:

```
var left_hand = new THREE.Mesh(hand, cover);
left_hand.position.set(150, 0, 0);
scene.add(left_hand);
```

Not only did we not make a new cover for the left hand, but we also didn't create a new shape! Instead we just used the same shape for the left hand that we did for the right hand. Now that's lazy!

With that, our avatar should look something like Figure 2, *Avatar with Hands*, on page 28.

OK, I admit that doesn't look much like a body with hands. Bear with me for a bit longer, and you'll see.

```
var hand = new THREE.SphereGeometry(50);

var right_hand = new THREE.Mesh(hand, cover);
right_hand.position.set(-150, 0, 0);
scene.add(right_hand);

var left_hand = new THREE.Mesh(hand, cover);
left_hand.position.set(150, 0, 0);
scene.add(left_hand);
```

Figure 2—Avatar with Hands

3.3 Breaking It Down

Let's take a quick look at why we used those numbers for the hands. If you're impatient, skip ahead to Section 3.4, *Adding Feet for Walking*, on page 29, to keep building our game avatar.

When anything is added to a scene, it starts off in the very center. So when we add the body and a hand, it starts off something like this:

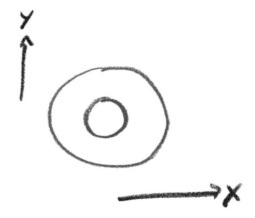

In 3D programming and mathematics, left and right are called the X direction. Up and down are called the Y direction.

This is why we change the X position of the hands:

```
var left_hand = new THREE.Mesh(hand, cover);
left_hand.position.set(150, 0, 0);
scene.add(left_hand);
```

The numbers inside left_hand.position.set(150, 0, 0) are the X, Y, and Z position of the left hand (Z would be forward and backward). We set X to 150 while Y and Z are both 0. This is really the same thing as left_hand.position.x = 150. As we'll see shortly, it can be very convenient to set multiple values on a single line.

But why 150? The answer is that the radius of the body is 100 and the radius of the hand is 50. We need to move the hand 100 + 50, or 150 in the X (left/right) direction:

If we only moved the center of the hand 100, then we would end up with the hand partly inside the body:

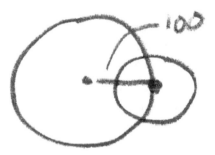

Try This Yourself

If you're not convinced, try it yourself. Change the number for the X position by fiddling with the first number in right_hand.position.set(-150, 0, 0). Try it for both the left and right hand. Don't make them too big, though, or they won't even be on the screen anymore!

3.4 Adding Feet for Walking

For the feet, we'll again use spheres of size 50. I'll leave it up to you to figure out how to add the relevant lines.

Some hints:

- Don't move the feet left/right as far as we did the hands. The feet should be underneath the body.

- You'll have to move them down. The up/down positioning is done with the Y direction instead of the X direction. This is the second number of right_hand.position.set(-150, 0, 0). You may have to use negative numbers to go down—for example, –25.

- Recall that the hand was added before we *rendered* the scene—before the line with renderer.render(scene, camera). The feet should be as well.

Here is how we did the right hand; it might help while you try to figure out the feet:

```
var hand = new THREE.SphereGeometry(50);

var right_hand = new THREE.Mesh(hand, cover);
right_hand.position.set(-150, 0, 0);
scene.add(right_hand);
```

Good luck!

Try This Yourself

Try to place the feet yourself. To move the feet left and right, you change the first number in right_foot.position.set(0, 0, 0). To move it up and down, you change the second number (the third number is forward and backward).

It may take a while to get it right, but believe me—it's good practice. Try for a bit and then continue with the text.

Did you get it?

This is what it might look like:

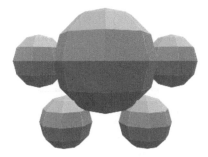

Don't worry if yours is not exactly the same. Yours may even be better!

If you're having difficulty, refer to the code that was used to make the avatar:

```
var cover = new THREE.MeshNormalMaterial();
var body = new THREE.SphereGeometry(100);
var avatar = new THREE.Mesh(body, cover);
scene.add(avatar);

var hand = new THREE.SphereGeometry(50);

var right_hand = new THREE.Mesh(hand, cover);
right_hand.position.set(-150, 0, 0);
scene.add(right_hand);

var left_hand = new THREE.Mesh(hand, cover);
left_hand.position.set(150, 0, 0);
scene.add(left_hand);

var foot = new THREE.SphereGeometry(50);

var right_foot = new THREE.Mesh(foot, cover);
right_foot.position.set(-75, -125, 0);
scene.add(right_foot);

var left_foot = new THREE.Mesh(foot, cover);
left_foot.position.set(75, -125, 0);
scene.add(left_foot);
```

This is everything after START CODING ON THE NEXT LINE.

3.5 Challenge: Make the Avatar Your Own

If you're up for a challenge, see if you can create an avatar that looks something like this:

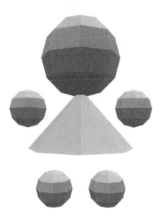

To make this, you need to replace the body with one of the shapes from Chapter 1, *Project: Creating Simple Shapes*, on page 1, and add a head. Don't worry about arms and legs to connect the hands and feet to the body—that would make it harder in later chapters.

And, of course, you can make whatever kind of avatar you like. *Just remember to make one with hands and feet*—we'll need them in later chapters.

3.6 Doing Cartwheels

We'll add controls to our avatar later. But before moving on to the next lesson, let's make the avatar do some flips and cartwheels.

Just like we did at the end of Chapter 1, *Project: Creating Simple Shapes*, on page 1, we start by changing the very last line of the code (which is just above the </script>) tag at the end of the editor. Instead of telling the browser to show the scene one time, we animate the scene as follows.

```
// Now, animate what the camera sees on the screen:
function animate() {
  requestAnimationFrame(animate);
  avatar.rotation.z = avatar.rotation.z + 0.05;
  renderer.render(scene, camera);
}
animate();
```

If you typed everything correctly, you might notice something odd. Just the head is spinning, not the whole avatar.

That might be a cool effect, but it's not what we wanted. So how do we go about spinning the whole avatar?

If you guessed that we add rotation.z changes to the hands and feet, you made a good guess. But that won't work. The hands and feet would spin in place just like the head.

The answer to this problem is a very powerful 3D-programming technique. We group all of the body parts together and spin the group. It is a simple idea, but, as you'll find later, it's surprisingly powerful.

To group the body parts together, we add the parts to the avatar instead of the scene.

If you look back up to the right hand, you'll see that we added it to the scene. We'll change that line.

```
var right_hand = new THREE.Mesh(hand, cover);
right_hand.position.set(-150, 0, 0);
scene.add(right_hand);
```
❶

❶ Change this line.

Instead of adding the hand to the scene, we add it to the avatar:

```
var right_hand = new THREE.Mesh(hand, cover);
right_hand.position.set(-150, 0, 0);
avatar.add(right_hand);
```
❶

❶ This line now adds the right hand to the avatar instead of the scene.

After doing the same for the left_hand, the right_foot, and the left_foot, your avatar should be doing cartwheels—*without* losing any parts!

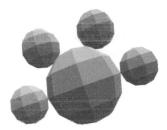

Sometimes we might not want our avatar to do cartwheels. Let's add a line to control that.

```
var is_cartwheeling = false;
function animate() {
  requestAnimationFrame(animate);
  if (is_cartwheeling) {
    avatar.rotation.z = avatar.rotation.z + 0.05;
  }
  renderer.render(scene, camera);
}
animate();
```
❶
❷

❶ This is where we say if our avatar is doing cartwheels or not. If we set this to true, then our avatar is doing cartwheels. If we set it to false (like we've done here), then our avatar won't do cartwheels.

❷ Wrap the avatar.rotation in an if, as shown. Don't forget the curly braces on this line and after the avatar.rotation line.

Change the value of is_cartwheeling from false to true. Does the avatar start cartwheeling again?

Make Our Avatar Flip!

Now that you have the avatar cartwheeling, try to make the avatar flip, as well. You should use a value like is_flipping to control the flipping. *Hint:* instead of avatar.rotation.z, try avatar.rotation.x or avatar.rotation.y. Did you get it? If not, it's OK. We'll cover more of this in later chapters.

3.7 The Code So Far

The entirety of the code will look something like the code in Section A1.3, *Code: Making an Avatar*, on page 219.

Don't worry if yours is not exactly like that code. Your code may be better or just different.

3.8 What's Next

We have a pretty cool-looking avatar. It might be nice for it to have a face or clothes. But you know what would be even better? If we could move our avatar with the keyboard. And that is just what we'll do in Chapter 4, *Project: Moving Avatars*, on page 35.

For now, take some time to play with the size, positioning, and rotation of the parts that make up your avatar.

When you're done with this chapter, you will

- *Know how to move the avatar with your keyboard*
- *Begin to understand JavaScript events*
- *Be able to move the camera with an avatar*

CHAPTER 4

Project: Moving Avatars

In Chapter 3, *Project: Making an Avatar*, on page 25, we covered how to build a game avatar. An avatar that we cannot move is pretty dull. So in this chapter you'll learn how to make the avatar move in different directions. We'll also give it a little forest to move around in. It will end up looking something like this:

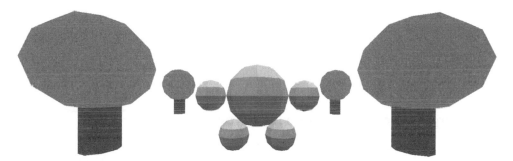

4.1 Getting Started

This chapter builds on the work that we did in *Project: Making an Avatar*. If you haven't already done the exercises in that chapter, go back and do them before proceeding. In particular, you need to go over the animate() exercise at the end of that chapter.

Let's make a copy of the previous chapter's avatar project. That way, if we ever want to go back to see our simple spinning and cartwheeling avatar, we can. To make a copy of that project, click the menu button and choose Make a Copy from the menu. (See Figure 3, *Selecting Make a Copy*, on page 36. Let's call this project My Avatar: Keyboard Controls, as shown in Figure 4, *Naming the Project*, on page 36.

With that, we're ready to add keyboard controls.

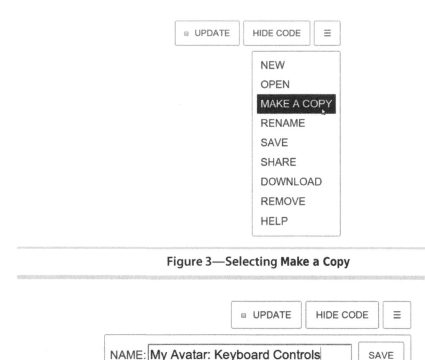

Figure 3—Selecting **Make a Copy**

Figure 4—Naming the Project

4.2 Building Interactive Systems with Keyboard Events

So far in this book, our code has been very linear—it follows a straight line. First we made a cover, a shape, and a mesh, and then we added the objects to the scene. Then we moved to the next mesh, which was also added to the scene. Although it is possible to write a lot of JavaScript that looks like this, most JavaScript programs tend to be quite different.

That's because JavaScript usually runs in a web browser. In a web browser, JavaScript code has to respond to events. A key being pressed on the keyboard, a mouse button being clicked, and the mouse pointer moving around the page are all events in the web browser. A crazy number of events can potentially happen on every web page, and for the most part, these events are ignored.

But we're not going to ignore key presses. We'll *listen* for events with something called—you guessed it—an *event listener*. Let's add the following at the very bottom of our code, below the animate() line that we added in Chapter 3, *Project: Making an Avatar*, on page 25.

```
// Listen for keypress events
document.addEventListener('keydown', function(event) {
  alert(event.keyCode);
});
```

This adds an event listener to the entire page. It listens for keydown events. When our code notices a keydown, it will alert us with the *keycode* of the event that just occurred.

What is a keycode? To answer that, let's try it out! Click the Hide Code button in the toolbar at the top of the page, then press the A key on your keyboard. You should see something like this alert dialog.

What is this 65? Keep in mind that computers store everything, even letters, as numbers. The computer converts that number into a letter when displaying the correct letter to us humans. When we think of the letter a, a computer is thinking 65.

Why do we need to know this? Click the OK button on the alert if you haven't already done so. Then repeat for the left, up, right, and down arrow keys on your keyboard. For the left arrow, you should discover that the computer thinks 37. For the up arrow, the computer thinks 38. For the right arrow, the computer detects the key as 39. For the down arrow, the computer thinks 40.

Let's use those keycodes to move our avatar!

4.3 Converting Keyboard Events into Avatar Movement

By playing with the keyboard event listener, we now know the numbers that correspond to each of the four arrow keys. We convert those arrow keys and numbers into avatar movement like this:

Arrow Key	Computer Number	Avatar Direction
Left	37	Left
Up	38	Forward
Right	39	Right
Down	40	Back

So let's make this happen. Remove the alert(event.keyCode) line inside the document.addEventListener(). Replace it with the following code, starting with the var code statement.

```
document.addEventListener('keydown', function(event) {
  var code = event.keyCode;
  if (code == 37) avatar.position.x = avatar.position.x-5; // left
  if (code == 38) avatar.position.z = avatar.position.z-5; // up
  if (code == 39) avatar.position.x = avatar.position.x+5; // right
  if (code == 40) avatar.position.z = avatar.position.z+5; // down
});
```

We saw the if statement in *Project: Making an Avatar*. In this case, we're checking *if* the keycode is equal to one of the arrow-key computer numbers. If the key code is 37 (left arrow key), then we change the avatar's X position by subtracting 5.

A double equals (==) in JavaScript checks if something is equal to something else—a single equal (=) makes a value equal to something else. In our preceding code example, we make code equal to event.keyCode. Then we check to see if it is equal to the different arrow-key values.

Give It a Try!

Press the Hide Code button and give it a try. Use the arrow keys to move the avatar around. Does it work like you expect?

Remember: If something goes wrong, check the JavaScript console!

If everything is working correctly, then you should be able to move your avatar far away, up close, all the way to the left or right, and even off the screen.

You learned how to make sure the avatar's hands and feet move with the body when we added the ability to do cartwheels back in Section 3.6, *Doing Cartwheels*, on page 32. Since the hands and feet were added to the avatar object instead of the scene, moving the avatar means that the hands and feet go along with it.

Let's see what happens if one of the legs is not attached to the avatar. In this case, we'll change the left_foot so that it's added to the scene instead of the avatar.

```
var left_foot = new THREE.Mesh(foot, cover);
left_foot.position.set(75, -125, 0);
scene.add(left_foot);
```

Run this, and the left foot goes missing.

Don't underestimate the power of this concept. We'll do some crazy things with it later. For now, don't forget to fix your left foot to the avatar!

4.4 Challenge: Start/Stop Animation

Remember the is_cartwheeling and is_flipping values from when we built the avatar in Chapter 3, *Project: Making an Avatar*, on page 25? Let's add two more if statements to the keyboard event listener. If the C key, which the computer thinks is the number 67, is pressed, then the avatar should either start or stop cartwheeling. If the F key, which the computer thinks is 70, is pressed, then the flip routine should start or stop.

Hint: switch between true and false with the not operator. In JavaScript, the not operator is an exclamation point, !. You can use this not operator to assign the value of is_cartwheeling to the opposite of its original value with something like is_cartwheeling = !is_cartwheeling. We'll see this again in *Booleans*.

Hopefully, you were able to get it working yourself. Here is the animate() function that handles the cartwheeling and flipping.

```
var is_cartwheeling = false;
var is_flipping = false;
function animate() {
  requestAnimationFrame(animate);
  if (is_cartwheeling) {
    avatar.rotation.z = avatar.rotation.z + 0.05;
  }
```

```
  if (is_flipping) {
    avatar.rotation.x = avatar.rotation.x + 0.05;
  }
  renderer.render(scene, camera);
}
animate();
```

Here is the complete keyboard event listener for moving, flipping, and cartwheeling our avatar.

```
document.addEventListener('keydown', function(event) {
  var code = event.keyCode;
  if (code == 37) avatar.position.x = avatar.position.x-5; // left
  if (code == 38) avatar.position.z = avatar.position.z-5; // up
  if (code == 39) avatar.position.x = avatar.position.x+5; // right
  if (code == 40) avatar.position.z = avatar.position.z+5; // down

  if (code == 67) is_cartwheeling = !is_cartwheeling;       // C
  if (code == 70) is_flipping = !is_flipping;               // F
});
```

If you've got it right, you should be able to make the avatar do flips and cartwheels as it moves off the screen.

Actually, it's pretty crazy that the avatar can leave the screen. We'll fix that in a bit, but first let's add some trees for our avatar to walk through.

4.5 Building a Forest with Functions

We'll need a lot of trees for our forest. We could build them one at a time, but we're not going to do that. Instead, let's add the following JavaScript after all of the avatar body parts:

```
makeTreeAt( 500,    0);
makeTreeAt(-500,    0);
makeTreeAt( 750, -1000);
makeTreeAt(-750, -1000);
```

```
function makeTreeAt(x, z) {
  var trunk = new THREE.Mesh(
    new THREE.CylinderGeometry(50, 50, 200),
    new THREE.MeshBasicMaterial({color: 0xA0522D})
  );

  var top = new THREE.Mesh(
    new THREE.SphereGeometry(150),
    new THREE.MeshBasicMaterial({color: 0x228B22})
  );
  top.position.y = 175;
  trunk.add(top);

  trunk.position.set(x, -75, z);
  scene.add(trunk);
}
```

If you entered all that code correctly, you'll see the avatar standing in front
of a forest of four trees.

That's pretty cool, but how did we do that?

Breaking It Down

The first part of the forest-building is pretty easy to follow. We add trees at
different X and Z coordinates (remember that Y is up and down) around the
scene.

```
makeTreeAt( 500,    0);
makeTreeAt(-500,    0);
makeTreeAt( 750, -1000);
makeTreeAt(-750, -1000);
```

That's easy enough, but how does that makeTreeAt() thing work?

As we'll see in Chapter 5, *Functions: Use and Use Again*, on page 49, a Java-
Script function is a way to run the same code over and over. In this case, we

do all of the repetitive work of building the trunk and treetop in the function named makeTreeAt(). We could have named it anything, but we give it a name that tells us what it does—in this case, it makes a tree at the coordinates that we defined.

We should be familiar with most of the things going on inside this function.

```
function makeTreeAt(x, z) {
  var trunk = new THREE.Mesh(
    new THREE.CylinderGeometry(50, 50, 200),
    new THREE.MeshBasicMaterial({color: 0xA0522D})
  );

  var top = new THREE.Mesh(
    new THREE.SphereGeometry(150),
    new THREE.MeshBasicMaterial({color: 0x228B22})
  );
  top.position.y = 175;
  trunk.add(top);

  trunk.position.set(x, -75, z);
  scene.add(trunk);
}
```

❶ Make a trunk out of a cylinder.

❷ Make a treetop out of a sphere.

❸ Move the treetop up (remember Y is up and down) to the top of the trunk.

❹ Add the treetop to the trunk.

❺ Set the position of the trunk to the x and z that the function was called with—makeTreeAt(500,0)). The Y value of -75 moves the trunk down enough to look like a tree trunk.

❻ Add the trunk to the scene.

It's important to remember that we have to add the treetop to the trunk and *not* the scene. If we added the treetop to the scene, then when we try to move the tree, only the trunk will be moved and not the treetop. We would also have to set the treetop position if we added it to the scene—adding it to the trunk means that the treetop's position is the same as the trunk's.

By now we're getting good at building objects from shapes and materials and placing them on the screen. You could probably make four trees without too much effort. For one tree you need a THREE.CylinderGeometry for the trunk and a THREE.SphereGeometry for the top of the tree. If you add the green leaves to the top of the tree, then you move both parts together.

And then you would have to repeat the same thing three more times to make a total of four trees. Four trees would be a lot of typing. Don't forget: we programmers don't like typing. Always remember that we're lazy. And the thing that lets us be lazy this time is a *function*.

Also new here is color. We picked those colors from the Wikipedia list of color names at http://en.wikipedia.org/wiki/X11_color_names. The tree trunk is the color sienna. You can try your own colors if you like. The color comes from the first column on that web page, but we need to replace the # symbol on the web page with 0x so that JavaScript can read it. Thus, #A0522D becomes 0xA0522D.

Now that we have a forest, let's see if we can make the camera move with the avatar as it travels through the scene.

4.6 Moving the Camera with the Avatar

Remember that to get the hands and feet to move along with our avatar, we added them to the avatar's body instead of adding them to the scene. That is exactly what we need to do with the camera. First let's find the line that says scene.add(camera) and delete it. Then, below the line where the avatar is added to the scene, and above the makeTreeAt() function, let's add the camera to the avatar:

```
var left_foot = new THREE.Mesh(foot, cover);
left_foot.position.set(75, -125, 0);
avatar.add(left_foot);

❶ avatar.add(camera);
```

❶ Add this line.

After hiding the code, you'll see that when the avatar is moved, the camera stays right in front of the avatar.

It's always 500 units in front of the avatar (camera.position.z = 500). The camera is always at the same height as the avatar since we never defined the camera's height with position.y. The camera is always right in front since we haven't yet set the left-right position with position.x.

It might help to think of the camera being attached to the avatar with an invisible chain.

Wherever the avatar goes, the camera goes as well.

Pretty cool, right? Well, there is a major problem with this approach. What happens if the avatar starts cartwheeling or flipping (remember that we're using the C and F keys for this)? Try it yourself!

The avatar appears to stay still, but everything else starts spinning! (See Figure 5, *Everything Starts Spinning!*, on page 45.)

This is because the camera is stuck on the invisible chain that's attached to the avatar. If the avatar spins, the camera spins right along with it. (See Figure 6, *The Camera Spinning with the Avatar*, on page 45.)

That's not quite what we want. Instead of locking the camera on the avatar, what we really want is to lock the camera on the avatar's *position*.

In 3D programming there is no easy way to reliably lock something to just the position of another thing. But all is not lost.

Figure 5—Everything Starts Spinning!

Figure 6—The Camera Spinning with the Avatar

We'll add an avatar position marker to the game.

If we lock both the camera and the avatar to this marker, then moving the marker moves both the avatar and the camera.

But, more importantly, when the avatar does cartwheels, the camera doesn't move. The avatar is cartwheeling, but the marker doesn't spin. Since the marker is not spinning, the camera doesn't spin either.

In 3D programming, this marker is just a marker. It should be invisible. So we don't want to use meshes or geometries for this. Instead we use Object3D. Let's add the following code before the avatar-generated code, just after START CODING ON THE NEXT LINE.

```
var marker = new THREE.Object3D();
scene.add(marker);
```

Now we change the avatar so that it is added to the marker instead of adding it to the scene:

```
var avatar = new THREE.Mesh(body, cover);
marker.add(avatar);
```

We also need to change how the camera is added. Instead of adding the camera to the avatar, we add it to the marker.

```
marker.add(camera);
```

The last thing we need to change is the keyboard event listener. Instead of changing the position of the avatar, we have to change the position of the marker.

```
document.addEventListener('keydown', function(event) {
  var code = event.keyCode;
  if (code == 37) marker.position.x = marker.position.x-5; // left
  if (code == 38) marker.position.z = marker.position.z-5; // up
  if (code == 39) marker.position.x = marker.position.x+5; // right
  if (code == 40) marker.position.z = marker.position.z+5; // down

  if (code == 67) is_cartwheeling = !is_cartwheeling;      // C
  if (code == 70) is_flipping = !is_flipping;              // F
});
```

With that, we can move the avatar's position with the keyboard, but when we flip or cartwheel, the camera stays upright.

4.7   The Code So Far

If you would like to double-check your code so far, compare it to the code in Section A1.4, *Code: Moving Avatars*, on page 220.

4.8   What's Next

We covered a very important skill in this chapter. We'll group objects like this over and over as our gaming skills improve. Grouping simplifies moving things together, as well as twisting, turning, growing, and shrinking things together.

Before adding even more stuff to our avatar, let's take a break so that we can explore JavaScript functions a bit more. We're already using them to make a forest, to animate, and to listen for events. There's even more cool stuff that we can do with them.

When you're done with this chapter, you will

- *Understand a superpowerful tool (functions)*
  for programmers
- *Know two reasons to use functions*
- *Recognize some common JavaScript errors*
  and know how to fix them

CHAPTER 5

Functions: Use and Use Again

We've come across functions more than once. Most recently we saw them in Chapter 4, *Project: Moving Avatars*, on page 35, where we used them to make a forest. If you were paying close attention, you may have noticed that we also used a function to build the keyboard event listener in the same chapter.

Although we have used functions already, we haven't talked much about them. You may already have a sense that they are pretty powerful, so let's take a closer look now.

We're not going to talk about every aspect of functions—they can get quite complicated. We'll talk about them just enough to be able to understand the functions that we use throughout the book.

5.1 Getting Started

Create a new project in the ICE Code Editor. Use the Empty project template and call it Functions.

After the opening <script> tag, delete the line that says "Your code goes here," and enter the following JavaScript.

```
var log = document.createElement('div');
log.style.height = '75px';
log.style.width = '450px';
log.style.overflow = 'auto';
log.style.border = '1px solid #666';
log.style.backgroundColor = '#ccc';
log.style.padding = '8px';
log.style.position = 'absolute';
log.style.bottom = '10px';
log.style.right = '20px';
document.body.appendChild(log);
```

```
var message = document.createElement('div');
message.textContent = 'Hello, JavaScript functions!';
log.appendChild(message);

message = document.createElement('div');
message.textContent = 'My name is Chris.';
log.appendChild(message);

message = document.createElement('div');
message.textContent = 'I like popcorn.';
log.appendChild(message);
```

The first chunk of that code creates a place within the browser to log messages.
The last three blocks of code write three different messages to that log. If you
have everything typed in correctly, you should see the three messages printed
at the bottom right of the page.

```
19  message = document.createElement('div');
20  message.textContent = 'My name is Chris.';
21  log.appendChild(message);
22                                              Hello, JavaScript functions!
23  message = document.createElement('div');    My name is Chris.
24  message.textContent = 'I like popcorn.';    I like popcorn.
25  log.appendChild(message);
26  </script>
```

Back in Chapter 3, *Project: Making an Avatar*, on page 25, we used a function
to avoid having to repeat the same process for creating a tree four times. So
you can probably guess the first thing that we'll change here. Let's change
the way we log those three messages.

Start by deleting everything from the first var message line all the way through
the last log.appendChild line. Where that code was, add the following.

```
logMessage('Hello, JavaScript functions!', log);
logMessage('My name is Chris.', log);
logMessage('I like popcorn.', log);

function logMessage(message, log) {
  var holder = document.createElement('div');
  holder.textContent = message;
  log.appendChild(holder);
}
```

When we write that code, a surprising thing happens—it gets easier to read.
Even nonprogrammers could read those first three lines and figure out that
they send a message to the log. This is a *huge* win for programmers like us.

If we decide later that we want to add the time before each message, now it's
much easier to figure out where to make that change.

Readable Code Is Easier to Change Later

 One of the skills that separates great programmers from good programmers is the ability to change working code. And great programmers know that it's easier to make changes when the code is easy to read.

Obviously we need to change something inside the function. Before, it would have taken us some time to figure out that those three code blocks were writing log messages, and how to change them.

This also brings up a very important rule.

Keep Your Code DRY—Don't Repeat Yourself

 This book was published by the same people behind a famous book called *The Pragmatic Programmer*. If you keep programming, you'll read that book one day. It contains a fantastic tip that programmers should keep their code DRY—that they follow the rule known as Don't Repeat Yourself (DRY for short).

When we first wrote our code, we repeated three things:

1. Creating a holder for the message
2. Adding a text message to the holder
3. Adding the message holder to the log

It was easy to see that we were repeating ourselves since the code in each of the three chunks was identical except for the message. This is another opportunity for us to be lazy. If we add more than three messages, we only have to type one more line, not three.

And of course, if we have to change something about the log message, we only have to change one function, not three different blocks of code.

We're not quite finished using functions here. If you look at all of the code, you'll notice that it takes a long time to get to the important stuff. (See Figure 7, *A Lot of Junk Before the Function*, on page 52.)

The important work—writing the messages—doesn't start until line 15. Before we write messages to the log we need a log, but all of that other stuff is just noise.

To fix that, let's move the noise into a function below the logMessage() lines. Add a new function named makeLog() in between the three lines that call logMessage() and where we defined the logMessage() function. The "noise" of

```
 1  <body></body>
 2  <script>
 3  var log = document.createElement('div');
 4  log.style.height = '75px';
 5  log.style.width = '450px';
 6  log.style.overflow = 'auto';
 7  log.style.border = '1px solid #666';
 8  log.style.backgroundColor = '#ccc';
 9  log.style.padding = '8px';
10  log.style.position = 'absolute';
11  log.style.bottom = '10px';
12  log.style.right = '20px';
13  document.body.appendChild(log);
14
15  logMessage('Hello, JavaScript functions!', log);
16  logMessage('My name is Chris.', log);
17  logMessage('I like popcorn.', log);
18
19  function logMessage(message, log) {
20    var holder = document.createElement('div');
21    holder.textContent = message;
22    log.appendChild(holder);
23  }
24  </script>
```

☑ UPDATE   HIDE CODE   ☰

Hello, JavaScript functions!
My name is Chris.
I like popcorn.

Figure 7—A Lot of Junk Before the Function

creating the log holder that goes in makeLog() starts with the line that says var log = document.createElement('div'); and ends with the line document.body.appendChild(holder). Move those lines and everything in between into makeLogM():

```
function makeLog() {
  var holder = document.createElement('div');
  holder.style.height = '75px';
  holder.style.width = '450px';
  holder.style.overflow = 'auto';
  holder.style.border = '1px solid #666';
  holder.style.backgroundColor = '#ccc';
  holder.style.padding = '8px';
  holder.style.position = 'absolute';
  holder.style.bottom = '10px';
  holder.style.right = '20px';
  document.body.appendChild(holder);

  return holder;
}
```

Note that we have changed log to holder. Also, don't forget the last line, which returns holder so that we can do something else with it.

We can create our log with this function. Our first four lines after the opening <script> tag become the following:

```
var log = makeLog();
logMessage('Hello, JavaScript functions!', log);
logMessage('My name is Chris.', log);
logMessage('I like popcorn.', log);
```

That is some very easy-to-read code!

It's more difficult to write code like that than you would think. Really good programmers know not to use functions until there's a good reason for them. In other words, great programmers do exactly what we've done here: write working code, then look for ways to make it better.

Always Start with Ugly Code

You are a very smart person. You have to be to have made it this far. So you must be thinking, "Oh, I can just write readable code to begin with."

 Believe me when I say that you can't. Programmers know this so well that we have a special name for trying it: *premature generalization.* That's a fancy way to say it's a mistake to guess how functions are going to be used before you write *ugly* code. Programmers have fancy names for mistakes that we make a lot.

5.2 Understanding Simple Functions

So far we have looked at reasons why we want to use functions. Now let's see how functions work.

Remove the three logMessage() lines from the code. Write the following after the var log = makeLog line.

```
logMessage(hello('President Obama'), log);
logMessage(hello('Mom'), log);
logMessage(hello('Your Name'), log);

function hello(name) {
  return 'Hello, ' + name + '! You look very pretty today :)';
}
```

The result of this hello() function would be to first return the phrase "Hello, President Obama! You look very pretty today :)." Logging these phrases should look something like this:

> Hello, President Obama! You look very pretty today
> :)
> Hello, Mom! You look very pretty today :)
> Hello, Purple Fruit Monster! You look very pretty

There is a lot going on in the hello function to make that work, so let's break down the function into smaller pieces.

```
❶ function hello(name) {
❷   return 'Hello, ' + name + '! You look very pretty today :)';
  }
```

The pieces of a function are as follows:

❶ The word function, which tells JavaScript that we're making a function.

The name of the function—hello in this case.

Function *arguments*. In this case, we're accepting one argument (name) that we'll use inside the function body. When we call the function with an argument—hello(Fred)—we're telling the function that any time it uses the name argument, it is the same as using Fred.

The body of the function starts with an open curly brace, {, and ends with a closing curly brace, }. You may never have used curly braces when writing English. You'll use them a lot when writing JavaScript.

❷ The word return tells JavaScript what we want the result of the function to be. It can be anything: numbers, letters, words, dates, and even more-interesting things.

JavaScript lines, even those inside functions, should end with a semicolon.

Letters, Words, and Sentences Are Strings

Things inside quotes, like 'Hello', are called *strings*. Even in other programming languages, letters, words, and sentences are usually called strings.

Always be sure to close your quotes. If you forget, you'll get very weird errors that are hard to fix.

Next, let's try to break it intentionally so that we get an idea of what to do when things go wrong.

5.3 When Things Go Wrong

Let's put our hacker hats on and try to break some functions.

Although it's easy to do something wrong with JavaScript functions, it's not always easy to figure out what you did wrong. The most common mistakes that programmers make generate weird errors. Let's take a look so that you'll be better prepared.

Hack, Don't Crack

Don't worry! We won't really break anything. Breaking something would be *cracking*, not hacking. Hacking is a good thing. You'll often hear nonprogrammers using the word *hack* wrongly. Since you're a programmer now, you need to know what the word means and how to use it correctly. Hacking means that we are playing around with code, an application, or a website. We play with it to learn, not to cause damage. And sometimes we try to break our own code—but only to better understand it.

Hack always. *Never* crack.

Unexpected Errors

The most common thing to do is forget a curly brace:

```
// Missing a curly brace - this won't work!
function hello(name)
  return 'Hello, ' + name + '! You look very pretty today :)';
}
```

This is a compile-time error in JavaScript—one of the errors that JavaScript can detect when it's trying to read, compile, and run—that we encountered in Section 2.5, *Debugging in the Console,* on page 20. Since it's a compile-time error, the ICE Code Editor will tell us about the problem.

```
 9  // Missing a curly brace - this won't work!
10  function hello(name)
11  return 'Hello, ' + name + '! You look very pretty today :)';
12  Expected '{' and instead saw 'return'.
13
```

What happens if we put the curly brace back, but remove the curly brace after the return statement?

```
// Missing a curly brace - this won't work!
function hello(name) {
  return 'Hello, ' + name + '! You look very pretty today :)';
```

There are no errors in our hello function, but there is an error at the very bottom of our code.

```
 8
 9  Unmatched '{'.  urly brace - this won't work!
10  function hello(name) {
11    return 'Hello, ' + name + '! You look very pretty today :)';
12
13
```

This can be a tough error to fix. Often programmers will type many lines and possibly several functions before they realize that they have done something wrong. Then it takes time to figure out where you meant to add a curly brace.

Challenge

Try to figure out the following broken code on your own. Where do the errors show up? *Hint:* as in Section 2.5, *Debugging in the Console*, on page 20, some of these may be run-time errors.

Forgot the parentheses around the argument:

```
function hello name {
  return 'Hello, ' + name + '! You look very pretty today :)';
}
```

Forgot the function's argument:

```
function hello() {
  return 'Hello, ' + name + '! You look very pretty today :)';
}
```

Wrong variable name inside the function:

```
function hello(name) {
  return 'Hello, ' + person + '! You look very pretty today :)';
}
```

Function called with the wrong name:

```
logMessage(helo('President Obama'), log);

function hello(name) {
  return 'Hello, ' + name + '! You look very pretty today :)';
}
```

Wow! There sure are a lot of ways to break functions. And believe me when I tell you that you'll break functions in these and many other ways as you get to be a great programmer.

Great Programmers Break Things All the Time

 Because they break things so much, they are *really* good at fixing things. This is another skill that makes great programmers great.

Don't ever be upset at yourself if you break code. Broken code is a chance to learn. And don't forget to use the JavaScript console like you learned in *Playing with the Console and Finding What's Broken* to help troubleshoot!

5.4   Weird Tricks with Functions

Functions are so special in JavaScript that you can do all sorts of crazy things to them. Whole books have been written on "functional" JavaScript, but let's take a look at one trick that we will use later.

Recursion

Change the hello like this:

```
function hello(name) {
  var ret = 'Hello, ' + name + '! ' + 'You look very pretty today :)';
  if (!name.match(/again/)) {
    ret = ret + ' /// ' + hello(name + ' (again)');
  }
  return ret;
}
```

❶ Look closely here. Inside the body of the function hello, we're calling the function hello!

This will log the hello messages twice.

Hello, President Obama! You look very pretty today
:) /// Hello, President Obama (again)! You look very
pretty today :)
Hello, Mom! You look very pretty today :) /// Hello,

A function that calls itself like this is actually not crazy. It is so common that it has a special name: a *recursive function.*

Be careful with recursive functions! If there is nothing that stops the recursive function from calling itself over and over, you'll lock your browser and have to go into edit-only mode to fix it, as described in Section 2.6, *Recovering When ICE Is Broken*, on page 23.

In this case, we stop the recursion by calling the hello function again only if the name variable doesn't match the again. If name doesn't match again, then we call hello() with name + '(again)' so that the next call will include again.

Recursion can be a tough concept, but you have a great example in the name of your code editor:

- What does the I in ICE Code Editor stand for?
- It stands for ICE Code Editor.
- What does the I in ICE Code Editor stand for?

- It stands for ICE Code Editor.
- What does the I in ICE Code Editor stand for?
- ...

You could go on asking that question forever, but eventually you'll get sick of it. Computers don't get sick of asking, so you have to tell them when to stop.

5.5 The Code So Far

In case you would like to double-check the code in this chapter, it's included in Section A1.5, *Code: Functions: Use and Use Again*, on page 222.

5.6 What's Next

Functions are very powerful tools for JavaScript programmers. As we saw, the two main reasons to use a function are for reuse and for making code easier to read. We created a logMessage() function so that we could use its functionality over and over again. We created the makeLog() function to move a whole bunch of messy code out of the way of more important code. We even took a peek at some of the crazy things that we can do with functions, like recursion.

And we're still just scratching the surface!

As you'll see shortly, we'll use functions a lot in the upcoming chapters. Let's get started in the next chapter as we teach our avatar how to move its hands and feet!

When you're done with this chapter, you will

- *Understand some important math for 3D games*
- *Know how to swing objects back and forth*
- *Have an avatar that looks like it's walking*

CHAPTER 6

Project: Moving Hands and Feet

When we last saw our avatar in Chapter 4, *Project: Moving Avatars*, on page 35, it was moving around pretty well, but it was a little stiff. Even when the body moved, the hands and the feet stayed still. In this chapter we'll make our avatar more lively.

6.1 Getting Started

In this chapter we're again building on work from previous chapters. Since we did so much work to get the avatar moving in *Project: Moving Avatars*, let's make a copy of that project to work on in this chapter.

If it's not already open in the ICE Code Editor, open the project that we named My Avatar: Keyboard Controls. Make a copy of it by clicking the menu button and choosing Make a Copy from the menu.

Name the project My Avatar: Moving Hands and Feet and click the Save button.

With that, we're ready to start adding life to our avatar!

6.2 Moving a Hand

Let's start with a hand. Recall from previous chapters that hands and feet are just balls that stick out from the head. We built the right hand in Java-Script with this:

```
var right_hand = new THREE.Mesh(hand, cover);
right_hand.position.set(-150, 0, 0);
avatar.add(right_hand);
```

As you know, the three numbers we use to set the position of the hand are the X position (left/right), the Y position (up/down), and the Z position (in/out). In the case of the right hand, we have placed it −150 from the center of the avatar.

In addition to setting all three numbers for the position, we can change just one of the positions by updating position.x, position.y, or position.z. To move the right hand forward (toward the viewer), add the position.z line shown.

```
var right_hand = new THREE.Mesh(hand, cover);
right_hand.position.set(-150, 0, 0);
avatar.add(right_hand);
right_hand.position.z = 100;
```

Change the value of position.z from 100 to -100. What happens? What happens if you keep changing between 100 and -100?

When z is 100, the hand is moved forward.

```
var right_hand = new THREE.Mesh(hand, cover);
right_hand.position.set(-150, 0, 0);
player.add(right_hand);
right_hand.position.z = 100;

var left_hand = new THREE.Mesh(hand, cover);
left_hand.position.set(150, 0, 0);
```

When z is -100, the hand has moved backward so that we almost cannot see the hand behind the body.

```
var right_hand = new THREE.Mesh(hand, cover);
right_hand.position.set(-150, 0, 0);
player.add(right_hand);
right_hand.position.z = -100;

var left_hand = new THREE.Mesh(hand, cover);
left_hand.position.set(150, 0, 0);
```

And when you change position.z back and forth between -100 and 100, it's almost like the hand is swinging back and forth. Congrats! You just learned a famous animation technique!

In some games, it's enough to move a thing from one place to another place to make it seem like it's moving. But we can do better in our game.

Start by removing the line that sets the position.z. We don't want to set it once. We want to animate it. So, after removing that line, move to the animate() function. After Chapter 4, *Project: Moving Avatars*, on page 35, we're already animating cartwheels and flips.

```
var is_cartwheeling = false;
var is_flipping = false;
function animate() {
  requestAnimationFrame(animate);
  if (is_cartwheeling) {
    avatar.rotation.z = avatar.rotation.z + 0.05;
  }
```

```
  if (is_flipping) {
    avatar.rotation.x = avatar.rotation.x + 0.05;
  }
  renderer.render(scene, camera);
}
animate();
```

There is a lot happening in our animate() function. We know from Chapter 5, *Functions: Use and Use Again*, on page 49, that this "noise" can make it hard to read our code. We'll be adding even more stuff to animate(). Unless we do something, that animate() function is going to get really, really big.

So, let's create an acrobatics() function that does the flipping and cartwheeling. We might as well move the is_cartwheeling and is_flipping variables with it. Then we can call acrobatics() from within animate(), making it easier to read.

```
function animate() {
  requestAnimationFrame(animate);
  acrobatics();
  renderer.render(scene, camera);
}
animate();
var is_cartwheeling = false;
var is_flipping = false;
function acrobatics() {
  if (is_cartwheeling) {
    avatar.rotation.z = avatar.rotation.z + 0.05;
  }
  if (is_flipping) {
    avatar.rotation.x = avatar.rotation.x + 0.05;
  }
}
```

Take a moment to make sure everything still works. If something has gone wrong, check the JavaScript console!

Now let's add three things to the animate() function.

```
❶ var clock = new THREE.Clock(true);
  function animate() {
    requestAnimationFrame(animate);
❷   walk();
    acrobatics();
    renderer.render(scene, camera);
  }
  animate();
❸ function walk() {
    var position = Math.sin(clock.getElapsedTime()*10) * 100;
    right_hand.position.z = position;
  }
```

❶ We'll use this 3D clock as a timer for our animation.

❷ In addition to performing acrobatics, now we'll also walk.

❸ This is the function that moves the hands and feet.

As you might guess from the name, Math.sin() has something to do with math. In fact, it's a pretty amazing mathematical something called a *sine* that has all sorts of uses. Here we're making use of the fact that Math.sin() will generate a number between –1 and 1 as time passes.

Multiplying 100 times Math.sin() means that position will be a number between –100 and 100. In JavaScript, the asterisk character (*) is used for multiplication.

We'll talk more about how we work with math in *A Closer Look at JavaScript Fundamentals*.

If you've typed in everything correctly, you should see the right hand of the avatar jiggling back:

and forth:

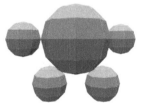

And it should be moving pretty quickly.

Try This Yourself

Experiment with the number inside animate(). If you change the 10 to 100, what happens? If you change the 100 to 1000, what happens? Try doing a position.x or position.y instead of position.z. Try doing position.y and position.z at the same time.

Once you have a feel for those numbers, try doing the other hand and the feet.

6.3   Swinging Hands and Feet Together

How did it work? Were you able to get all of the hands and feet swinging back and forth? Did you run into any problems?

If you tried moving the hands and feet in the same way, you might have noticed that our avatar is moving awfully strangely. Both feet and both hands move forward at the same time. And then both feet and both hands swing back at the same time. No one walks like that in real life.

When you walk, one foot is in front and the other is behind. In avatar terms, one foot is in the positive Z direction while the other is in the negative Z direction:

```
var position = Math.sin(clock.getElapsedTime()*5) * 50;
right_foot.position.z = -position;
left_foot.position.z = position;
```

People also usually move their right hand forward when their *left* foot is forward. And if the right hand is forward, then the left hand should be back. We can make our avatar do this with the following.

```
function walk() {
  var position = Math.sin(clock.getElapsedTime()*5) * 50;
  right_hand.position.z = position;
  left_hand.position.z = -position;
  right_foot.position.z = -position;
  left_foot.position.z = position;
}
```

With that, our hands and feet should be swinging back and forth in a nice walking motion.

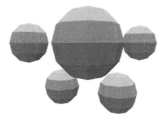

6.4   Walking When Moving

Right now, our avatar is constantly walking—even when we're not controlling it with our controls from Chapter 4, *Project: Moving Avatars*, on page 35. Let's fix this problem.

First we add one line to our walk() function.

```
function walk() {
  if (!isWalking()) return;
  var position = Math.sin(clock.getElapsedTime()*5) * 50;
  right_hand.position.z = position;
  left_hand.position.z = -position;
  right_foot.position.z = -position;
  left_foot.position.z = position;
}
```

Did you notice the first line of the function? This line of code means *if the avatar is not walking, then return immediately from the function.* Calling return means that we leave the function immediately and that nothing else in the function is run. That is, *if the avatar is not walking, then leave the walk() function without running any of the code that makes the avatar look like it is walking.*

If you've been paying very close attention, you might wonder what that isWalking() thing is. It's a function that we'll write now!

We'll add this code before the keydown event listener.

```
var is_moving_right, is_moving_left, is_moving_forward, is_moving_back;
function isWalking() {
  if (is_moving_right) return true;
  if (is_moving_left) return true;
  if (is_moving_forward) return true;
  if (is_moving_back) return true;
  return false;
}
```

Immediately before the isWalking() function, we declare "is moving" variables that will be used soon. We use a JavaScript shortcut—a comma-separated list—for all four variables on a single line and with only one var.

Inside the function, we use the return keyword to exit immediately from the function. This time we return a true or false value. If any of the movement properties of the avatar controls are true, then isWalking() will return true. In other words, if any of the movement properties of the controls say that the avatar is moving, then the avatar isWalking().

The very last line of the function isWalking() that returns false, will be reached only if none of the movement controls are true. If none of the movement properties of the avatar controls are on, then we return false to let it be known that the avatar is not walking.

Now we need to turn those movement controls on and off. We do this in the event listener, where we're already moving the avatar depending on the key being pressed. Add the lines shown.

```
document.addEventListener('keydown', function(event) {
  var code = event.keyCode;
  if (code == 37) {                                  // left
    marker.position.x = marker.position.x-5;
    is_moving_left = true;
  }
  if (code == 38) {                                  // up
    marker.position.z = marker.position.z-5;
    is_moving_forward = true;
  }
  if (code == 39) {                                  // right
    marker.position.x = marker.position.x+5;
    is_moving_right = true;
  }
  if (code == 40) {                                  // down
    marker.position.z = marker.position.z+5;
    is_moving_back = true;
  }
  if (code == 67) is_cartwheeling = !is_cartwheeling; // C
  if (code == 70) is_flipping = !is_flipping;        // F
});
```

❶ The avatar is moving left.

❷ The avatar is moving forward.

❸ The avatar is moving right.

❹ The avatar is moving backward.

This turns the movement controls on, but we still need to be able to turn them off. Since we used keydown to decide when a key is being pressed, you can probably guess how we'll decide when a key is let go.

After the last line of the keydown event-listener code—after the }); line—add the following keyup event-listener code.

```
document.addEventListener('keyup', function(event) {
  var code = event.keyCode;

  if (code == 37) is_moving_left = false;
  if (code == 38) is_moving_forward = false;
  if (code == 39) is_moving_right = false;
  if (code == 40) is_moving_back = false;
});
```

With that, we should be able to move our avatar with the arrow keys and see the avatar's hands and feet swing back and forth. When we let go of those keys, the avatar's walking should stop.

Cool!

Challenge: Better Acrobatics Controls

If you're up for a challenge, let's aim for better acrobatics controls.

Since we have code to listen for keydown and keyup events, try to make the cartwheels and flips start when the C or F key is pressed and stop when the C or F key is let go. Do you think the controls are better this way? If so, leave them in there—it's your game!

6.5 The Code So Far

If you would like to double-check the code in this chapter, turn to Section A1.6, *Code: Moving Hands and Feet*, on page 223.

6.6 What's Next

We now have a new way to bring our avatars to life. Back in Chapter 4, *Project: Moving Avatars*, on page 35, we were able to move the avatar around the scene and perform flips and cartwheels. In this chapter we were able to make parts of the avatar move—making the avatar seem much more alive.

The big concept in this chapter was not a JavaScript thing or even a 3D thing. It was a math thing: sine. Even if you've learned about those in math class, I bet that you didn't learn to use them like we did here!

One thing that our avatar still lacks is the ability to turn. Even when the avatar moves to the left or right, it continues to face forward. That's a bit odd, right? In Chapter 8, *Project: Turning Our Avatar*, on page 79, we'll cover how to rotate the entire avatar.

But first it's time for a quick break to look a little more closely at JavaScript.

When you're done with this chapter, you will

- *Know what many of those JavaScript things, like var, are*
- *Be able to write code that does things only when you want it to*

CHAPTER 7

A Closer Look at JavaScript Fundamentals

Before we go further, let's take a closer look at JavaScript. Like any other programming language, JavaScript was built so that both computers and people could understand it.

JavaScript programming can be thought of as describing things and what those things do, just like English and other languages. When we built our avatar, we used JavaScript to describe its head, hands, and feet. We also described how the 3D renderer should draw the scene in our browser. To put it all together, JavaScript has *keywords* that both computers and humans can understand.

Let's have a look.

7.1 Getting Started

Instead of drawing and moving shapes in this chapter, we're going explore the JavaScript programming language. We can do a lot of this in the JavaScript console, so start by opening that. Refer back to Section 2.2, *Opening and Closing the JavaScript Console*, on page 18, if you do not remember how.

Some of the JavaScript that we'll look at is too big for the JavaScript console. For that, we need to create a new project in the ICE Code Editor. Use the 3D starter project template and call it Just JavaScript.

Code in the JavaScript Console.

We're just introducing things in the beginning of this chapter, so it's easiest to play with it in the JavaScript console. Be sure to experiment!

7.2 Describing a Thing in JavaScript

Have you noticed how we introduce new things in JavaScript?

```
// You don't need to type this in:
var head_shape = new THREE.SphereGeometry(100);
```

The var keyword declares new things in JavaScript. It tells both the computer and humans reading the code, "Get ready—something new is coming!"

There are lots of different kinds of things in JavaScript. In the little bit of code you just saw, we're making a new 3D sphere shape. Things can also be numbers:

```
var my_height = 1.5;
```

They can be words:

```
var title = "3D Game Programming for Kids";
```

Programmers usually call the things inside quotation marks strings. Here the title item is a string that holds the title of this book.

Strings Are Easy to Break

 Always be sure to close your quotes. If you forget, you'll get very weird errors that are hard to fix.

They can be true things:

```
var am_i_cool = true;
var am_i_dumb = false;
```

They can even be weird JavaScript things that mean nothing:

```
var i_mean_nothing = null;
var i_also_mean_nothing = undefined;
```

What Are These null and undefined Things?

 You generally don't have to worry about undefined or null things. It doesn't make much sense to create such things. If you see them at all, it will be in a function—usually indicating that nothing was found or created by the function.

Why var?

The var keyword is short for *variable*. A variable is a thing that can change:

```
var game = "started";
// do some work here
game = "over";
```

At first we're not done with the game. Then, some time later, we are. If we wrote code where it says, // do some work here, that code would think that the game is still in progress. Being able to update variables will come in handy shortly.

About that line that starts with two slashes...

Comments

Double slashes indicate comments. The computer knows it's supposed to ignore everything on the line that follows //. In other words, comments are for people only:

```
// This returns today's date
var today = new Date();

// This is January 1, 2013
var jan1 = new Date(2013, 1, 1);
```

You Don't Need to Type the Comments

The comments you see in this book are meant to give you helpful hints. You don't need to type them in, but you should. Comments will help you to remember why you did things when you open your code later to make a change.

Really, you should be adding your own comments as well.

7.3 Changing Things

We know that we can change things, but how can each kind of variable change in JavaScript? Let's take them one at a time.

Numbers

You can use standard math symbols to add and subtract numbers in JavaScript. Try the following in the JavaScript console:

```
5 + 2;
10 - 9.5;
23 - 46;
84 + -42;
```

You should get back the following answers (the answer is shown in the comments below the math problem).

```
5 + 2;
// 7
```

```
10 - 9.5;
// 0.5

23 - 46;
// -23

84 + -42;
// 42
```

So it even works with negative numbers. Remember this; negative numbers will be handy as we play with 3D graphics.

OK, so adding and subtracting are pretty easy in JavaScript. What about multiplication and division? There are plus and minus signs on most keyboards, but there aren't × and ÷ keys.

For multiplication, use the asterisk (*) character:

```
3 * 7;
// 21

2 * 2.5;
// 5

-2 * 4;
// -8

7 * 6;
// 42
```

Division is done with the slash (/) character:

```
45 / 9;
// 5

100 / 8;
// 12.5

84 / 2;
// 42
```

One other thing to know about numbers is that when doing a lot of arithmetic at the same time, you can use parentheses to group things. The math inside parentheses is always calculated first:

```
5 * (2 + 4);
// 30

(5 * 2) + 4;
// 14
```

What happens without the parentheses? Can you guess why?[1]

Geometry

We're working on 3D game concepts in this book, which means geometry. We'll discuss geometry in more detail as part of the various project chapters that need it. For now let's consider two geometric functions: sine and cosine. If you don't know them, don't worry—you'll get to know them in the games.

Just remember that in JavaScript, we do not use degrees. Instead we use radians. What are radians? Instead of saying that we turned 180° when we spin half way around a circle, we would say that we turned pi radians around.

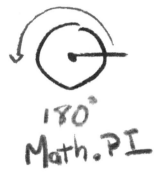

Pi is a special number in math. Its value is about 3.14159. You will often see the symbol π used for pi. We'll call it pi since JavaScript calls it Math.PI.

Going around a full circle is twice as much as 180° turn—more commonly called a 360° turn, this is two pi radians, or 2 × pi.

By the way, 2 × pi is the 6.3 that we said was a full rotation way back when we first started talking about rotation in *Making Boxes with the Cube Shape*, on page 6. Since the number value of pi is about 3.15, then 2 × pi is 2 × 3.15, or 6.3.

---

1. Without parentheses, multiplication is done first, then division. Remember the "order of operations" from your math class!

In JavaScript, pi is called Math.PI. So 360° would be 2*Math.PI. A handy conversion table follows:

Degrees	Radians	JavaScript
0°	0	0
45°	pi ÷ 4	Math.PI/4
90°	pi ÷ 2	Math.PI/2
180°	pi	Math.PI
360°	2 × pi	2*Math.PI
720°	4 × pi	4*Math.PI

Geometric functions are also available in JavaScript's Math module. An example is the sine that we saw in Chapter 6, *Project: Moving Hands and Feet*, on page 59. JavaScript shortens both sine and its companion, cosine, to sin and cos:

```
Math.sin(0);
// 0

Math.sin(2*Math.PI);
// 0

Math.cos(0);
// 1
```

Really, Really Close to Zero

Depending on your computer, when you tried Math.sin(2*Math.PI) in the JavaScript console, you may not have gotten the right answer. The sine of 2 × pi is zero, but you may have seen something like -2.4492127076447545e-16 instead. This shows that computers are not perfect. Sometimes their math can be off by a tiny amount.

When JavaScript has e-16 at the end of number, it means that it's a decimal number with the 16 places to the left. In other words, -2.45e-16 is the same thing as writing -0.000000000000000245. That is a really, really small number—you would have to add it more than two million times to get 1.

We won't need these Math. functions often. They will pop up now and again as we progress. For the most part, we can make do with the simple arithmetic operators for addition, subtraction, multiplication, and division.

Strings

Strings in JavaScript are kind of boring. You can really only join two strings into larger strings. What *is* interesting is that the plus operator is what joins them together. Try the following in the JavaScript console.

```
var str1 = "Howdy";
var str2 = "Bob";

str1 + " " + str2;
// "Howdy Bob"
```

Pretty crazy, isn't it? Given that there are no multiplication and division keys on most keyboards, there definitely are no stick-two-strings-together keys. So JavaScript gets lazy and uses the plus sign again.

What do you suppose happens if you try to join a string and a number? Well, give it a try:

```
var str = "The answer to 7 + 4 is ";
var answer = 7 + 4;

str + answer;
```

Try This Yourself

 Do this and check it in the JavaScript console!

The result is that, when combining a string and a number, JavaScript will treat the number as a string:

```
var str = "The answer to 7 + 4 is ";
var answer = 7 + 4;

str + answer;
// "The answer to 7 + 4 is 11"
```

Booleans

There is not much to a Boolean. It is either true or false. It is possible to convert Booleans with the not operator. In JavaScript, the exclamation point is the not operator:

```
var yes = true;
var the_opposite = !yes;
var the_opposite_of_the_opposite = !!yes;
yes;
// true
```

```
the_opposite;
// false

the_opposite_of_the_opposite;
// true
```

We won't use Booleans directly like this very often. We'll usually see comparison operators that make Booleans:

```
// The > symbol checks for values greater than others
var is_ten_greater_than_six = 10 > 6;
is_ten_greater_than_six;
// true

// Two equal signs check if values are equal
var is_twelve_the_same_as_eleven = 12 == 11;
is_twelve_the_same_as_eleven;
// false
```

Double Equal Sign vs. Single Equal Sign

A double equal sign (==) in JavaScript checks if something is equal to something else. It makes no changes to anything—it only checks values and produces a Boolean.

As we have seen throughout the book, a single equal sign (=) *makes* a value equal to something else. Often called the assignment operator, a single equal sign does change a value—it updates a variable or assigns it for the first time.

You might be wondering if it's wise to have two very different operators look so similar. It isn't. It's a very common source of mistakes —even for people who've been programming for years. But, since it has been around for so long, it probably won't be changing any time soon. So be on the lookout for these kinds of mistakes.

We'll see these kinds of Booleans a lot. In fact, they are in the very next section.

7.4 Repeating and Skipping Code with while and if

Normally JavaScript code is run from top to bottom. The lines of code at the top of a program are run first. Once the computer is done running those lines, it moves on to the next lines. This happens all the way to the bottom of a program file.

But sometimes we don't want all of the code to run. And other times we want to run code more than once. For these times, we use *control keywords*. The keywords that we'll see the most in this book are while and if.

Code in ICE, Check in the Console

The code in the rest of this chapter is too large for the JavaScript console, so add it in ICE after the START CODING line. Be sure to keep the JavaScript console open—even though we're not typing code in there, we'll still use it to show messages.

While

If a section of code, which we call a *block*, starts with while, then the block is run again and again until something changes. The something that needs to change goes in parentheses after the while keyword:

```
var i = 0;
while (i < 5) {
  console.log("i is now: " + i);
  i = i + 1;
}
```

If you try this and check in the JavaScript console, you'll see something like the following:

```
i is now: 0
i is now: 1
i is now: 2
i is now: 3
i is now: 4
```

Each time through the code block, we log the variable i to the JavaScript console. We also do a little math. We add 1 to the old value of i. Then the computer will run the while block again—as long as i is less than 5 (that < symbol means *less than*). As soon as i is equal to 5, the computer stops rerunning the while block and moves on to the next lines.

Try This Yourself

What happens if you run the following?

```
var i = 0;
while (i < 5) {
  console.log("Chris is awesome!!!!");
  i = i + 1;
}
```

Be sure to try your own name!

Running Code Only If Something Is True

Sometimes we want to skip over code entirely. For these times, we use the if keyword. Just like while, the if keyword does something with a block of code:

```
var game = "started";
// More code here that might change the variable "game"
// to something else...

if (game == "over") {
  console.log("Game Over!!!");
}
```

The if keyword lets us write JavaScript code that runs only *if* some condition is true. In this case, we check if game is equal to the string over, using the double equals (==) operator to do so.

We can also extend an if statement with else if and else. Consider the following code, which we'll use to turn and move a raft in Chapter 20, *Project: River Rafting*, on page 185:

```
document.addEventListener("keydown", function(event) {
  var code = event.keyCode;
❶  if (code == 32) pushRaft();      // space
❷  else if (code == 37) rotateRaft(-1); // left
❸  else if (code == 39) rotateRaft(1);  // right
❹  else { // Something else
    console.log(code);
  }
});
```

We'll talk more about the code in the project chapters, but we see that

❶ if the code is a space bar code, then we push the raft forward

❷ otherwise, if the code is for the left arrow key, then we turn the raft to the left

❸ otherwise, if the code is for the right arrow key, then we turn to the right

❹ otherwise, some strange key is pressed and we just log the code to the JavaScript console

---

Don't Overuse Ifs

If, else if, and else are very powerful, but can be used too much. We'll talk about better approaches in some of the project chapters.

7.5 Listing Things

At times it's quite handy to be able to describe a list of things. In JavaScript, lists are made with square brackets. A list of amazing movies might look something like this:

```
var amazing_movies = [
  'Star Wars',
  'The Empire Strikes Back',
  'Indiana Jones and the Raiders of the Lost Ark'
];
```

The things in the list can be any of the kinds of things that we have talked about so far: strings, numbers, Booleans. It is even possible to make a list with various types of things:

```
// Don't do this:
var useless_list = [
  true,
  3.14,
  'OK'
];
```

But don't do that. It's silly. Just like in real life, computer lists should contain the same kinds of things. It wouldn't make sense to include your favorite color, the time your friend is coming over, or the score of last night's game on a grocery list. A list of things to buy at the store should include only items that are at the store.

There are lots of ways to use lists, but the one we'll use the most in this book is to call a function for each item in the list:

```
var amazing_movies = [
  'Star Wars',
  'The Empire Strikes Back',
  'Indiana Jones and the Raiders of the Lost Ark'
];

amazing_movies.forEach(function(movie) {
  console.log("GREAT: " + movie);
});
```

Think of the forEach() function as a way of saying that "for each" thing in our list,

- give it a nickname—we call it movie in the preceding code
- do stuff with it inside the function—we log it as "GREAT"

If you type this and check the JavaScript console, you'll get back this output:

```
GREAT: Star Wars
GREAT: The Empire Strikes Back
GREAT: Indiana Jones and the Raiders of the Lost Ark
```

We'll see lists again in some of the later chapters.

7.6 What Makes JavaScript Different

Many things make JavaScript different from other languages, but the most important for us is that it's meant to be run in a browser. This means it can do a lot of web work very easily. As we saw in Chapter 4, *Project: Moving Avatars*, on page 35, JavaScript can open browser alert dialogs:

```
alert('Stop what you are doing and shout "Yay!"');
```

JavaScript is also really good at making changes in web pages. We won't change web pages much in this book, although we will cover the topic when we make scoreboards in some of our games.

7.7 What's Next

There is a lot of information in this chapter. Don't worry if not all of it makes sense yet. When you work through the later chapters, come back here if you have questions. More and more of this will begin to make sense as you progress.

The basics that we've covered here are like the nouns of the JavaScript language. The functions we saw in Chapter 5, *Functions: Use and Use Again*, on page 49, are like the verbs—they tell the basics what they need to do in order to make things happen.

Speaking of making things happen, let's get back to adding cool stuff to our avatar!

When you're done with this chapter, you will

- *Know even more fun math for 3D programming*
- *Know how to rotate something to face a specific direction*
- *Be able to make smooth animations*

CHAPTER **8**

Project: Turning Our Avatar

We're nearly finished animating our avatar. In Chapter 4, *Project: Moving Avatars*, on page 35, we learned how to make our avatar move. In Chapter 6, *Project: Moving Hands and Feet*, on page 59, we made the avatar look like it was walking. Now we need to make it look as though it can turn when we switch directions. Turning, or rotating, is not new to us—we already make the avatar turn when flipping and cartwheeling. But this time we want to make our avatar face a particular direction.

8.1 Getting Started

If it's not already open in the ICE Code Editor, open the project that we named My Avatar: Moving Hands and Feet (from *Project: Moving Hands and Feet*). Make a copy of it by clicking the menu button and choosing Make a Copy from the menu.

Name the project My Avatar: Turning and click the Save button.

8.2 Facing the Proper Direction

Getting the avatar to face the proper direction is fairly easy—especially with all that we already know. Just as we did when we added the walking motion of the hands and feet, we'll write a new function to turn our avatar. We'll call this function turn(), so let's add a call to this function in the animate() function.

```
function animate() {
  requestAnimationFrame(animate);
  walk();
  turn();
  acrobatics();
  renderer.render(scene, camera);
}
animate();
```

Next write the function turn(). JavaScript doesn't care where you put this function, but since we call it after walk() in the animate() function, we might as well put it after the walk() function. Type the following after the closing curly brace of the walk() function:

```
function turn() {
  var direction = 0;
  if (is_moving_forward) direction = Math.PI;
  if (is_moving_back) direction = 0;
  if (is_moving_right) direction = Math.PI/2;
  if (is_moving_left) direction =  -Math.PI/2;

  avatar.rotation.y = direction;
}
```

With that, when we walk left or right, the avatar now faces the direction in which it's moving:

That is pretty amazing. You have now made a complicated game avatar. Think about what you've accomplished:

- Given the avatar a body, hands, and feet

- Made the avatar move so that all the pieces move with it

- Made the avatar do cartwheels and flips

- Stuck the camera to the avatar

- Stuck the camera to the avatar's position so that flips and cartwheels don't make us dizzy

- Made the hands and feet swing back and forth when the avatar walks

- Made the hands stop moving when the avatar is not moving

- Made the avatar face the direction that it's walking

That is an incredible amount of JavaScript 3D programming. You have done very well to make it this far, but we can do more.

First let's take a closer look at that turn() function so we're sure we understand what's going on there.

8.3 Breaking It Down

In the turn() function, why do we set the direction to values like Math.PI and -Math.PI/2?

Recall from *Geometry*, on page 71, that angles, the amount of rotation, use radians instead of degrees. The avatar starts facing backward, toward the camera. So 0° of rotation is 0 radians of rotation, which means facing backward. And 180° is pi radians, which means facing forward into the screen. The following table is the complete list we're using in the turn() function.

Direction	Degrees	Radians	JavaScript
Forward	180°	pi	Math.PI
Right	90°	pi ÷ 2	Math.PI/2
Left	-90°	-pi ÷ 2	-Math.PI/2
Backward	0°	0	0

Why rotation.y?

So that explains the number that we use for the direction variable in the function turn(), but why do we set rotation.y? Why not rotation.z or rotation.x?

Well, for one thing, we already change rotation.x when we do cartwheels and rotation.z when we flip.

We set the rotation.y because we want to spin the avatar around the y-axis. Recall that, in 3D, the y-axis is pointing up and down. If you imagine a pole sticking right up the middle of the avatar, that is the avatar's y-axis:

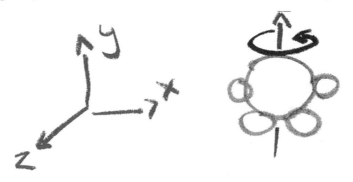

Spinning the avatar around this pole is what it means to rotate the avatar around the y-axis.

Don't Forget About avatar.rotation!

If you tried turning marker.rotation instead of avatar.rotation, you may have noticed that not only did the avatar spin, but everything else seemed to spin as well. This is because we attached the camera to the avatar's marker:

```
var marker = new THREE.Object3D();
scene.add(marker);

marker.add(camera);
```

Think of the marker as an invisible box that holds the avatar's parts. By adding the camera to the marker, we're sticking it to one side of the marker. If we spin the box, then the camera has to go along with it:

This is also why we added the hands and feet to the avatar's head instead of to the avatar's marker. When we turn the avatar inside the marker, its hands and feet need to move with it—not stay still with the marker.

8.4 Animating the Spin

When we turn our avatar, it's immediately facing the new direction. Let's make it a little more realistic by animating a turn to the new direction. For that, we'll need a new JavaScript library. This library will help us animate between different positions and rotations. The library is called Tween.

For this, go to the top of your code (the very top, not just to the START CODING ON THE NEXT LINE line). Add the <script> tag for Tween.js, as shown:

```
<body></body>
<script src="http://gamingJS.com/Three.js"></script>
<script src="http://gamingJS.com/Tween.js"></script>
<script src="http://gamingJS.com/ChromeFixes.js"></script>
```

The Tween library animates changes between a start and end. Here we want to animate starting with one rotation and moving to an ending rotation.

The first step in using Tween is to add its update() function to our animate() function:

```
function animate() {
  requestAnimationFrame(animate);
  TWEEN.update();
  walk();
  turn();
  acrobatics();
  renderer.render(scene, camera);
}
animate();
```

Next we need to change the function turn() that we just wrote. Instead of setting the direction right away, we'll call a new function that will spin the avatar in the new direction. Change the last line of the function turn() to call spinAvatar():

```
function turn() {
  var direction = 0;
  if (is_moving_forward) direction = Math.PI;
  if (is_moving_back) direction = 0;
  if (is_moving_right) direction = Math.PI/2;
  if (is_moving_left) direction =  -Math.PI/2;

  spinAvatar(direction);
}
```

Last, we need to write the code for the spinAvatar() function. The Tween code might seem a little strange at first. When reading it, keep in mind that we want to start the spin where the avatar's head is currently facing (avatar.rotation.y). We want to end in the new direction that is sent into spinAvatar() as the direction argument.

Write the following spinAvatar() function after the turn() function:

```
function spinAvatar(direction) {
  new TWEEN.
    Tween({y: avatar.rotation.y}).
    to({y: direction}, 100).
    onUpdate(function () {
      avatar.rotation.y = this.y;
    }).
    start();
}
```

Reading from top to bottom in that function, the new Tween starts with a Y rotation value of avatar.rotation.y—the direction the avatar is already facing. We then tell the Tween that we want to rotate *to* the new Y rotation passed to the spinAvatar() function. Every time the animation runs, the stuff inside onUpdate() is what happens. The rotation of the avatar's head is updated to the Y rotation of the Tween. The last line starts it all.

The periods at the end of each line in that function represent *method chaining*. In JavaScript, a semicolon ends a "sentence" of code. The period in JavaScript, unlike in English, indicates that we want to do something else with the current code—that the code sentence is not over yet.

We could have put all of that code on a single line, but it can be easier for humans to read code split across lines (computers don't care). Method chaining works with only certain JavaScript objects, like Tweens. It is a somewhat common practice in JavaScript, though we won't be using it much ourselves.

Try This Yourself

We told the Tween library that it will run from start to finish in 100 milliseconds. This number was at the end of the line that started with to.

It would take 1000 milliseconds to make one second, so 100 milliseconds is less than a second. The spin of the avatar takes less than a second. Experiment with that number to get it the way that you like. Is 1000 too long? Is 10 too short? You decide!

8.5 The Code So Far

If you would like to double-check the code in this chapter, turn to Section A1.8, *Code: Turning Our Avatar*, on page 226.

8.6 What's Next

Wow! Our simple avatar simulation is getting quite sophisticated, isn't it? We've already put quite a bit of work into our avatar, but you may have noticed that it can pass right through our trees. In the next project chapter we'll talk about collision detection, and use it to make our avatar stop when it collides with a tree.

But first it's time to take a closer look at all of that JavaScript code that was added for us when we started this project.

When you're done with this chapter, you will

- *Know a little about making web pages*
- *Understand the starter code*
- *Be comfortable changing the starter code*

CHAPTER 9

What's All That Other Code?

When we create a new project from the 3D starter template, there is a lot of code already in there. In this chapter we'll see what it all means.

9.1 Getting Started

Create a new project from the 3D Starter template in the ICE Code Editor. Name the project All that other code.

9.2 A Quick Introduction to HTML

At the very top of our code is the following HTML:

```
<body></body>
```

HTML is not a programming language. So what's it doing messing up our beautiful JavaScript code?

HTML is the Hypertext Markup Language. It is used to build web pages, not to make web pages do interesting things.

Even though it's not a programming language, we still need HTML for Java-Script. Since JavaScript is a web programming language, we need a web page where we can program—even if it is just a simple page.

The very first line contains an opening and closing <body> tag. In between those two tags, HTML authors would normally put writing—links to images and other pages. We're not putting anything in there because we're programming, not making web pages.

To get a sense of what HTML does, add the following HTML in between the two <body> tags, as shown:

```
<body>
  <h1>Hello!</h1>
  <p>
    You can make <b>bold</b> words,
    <i>italic</i> words,
    even <u>underlined</u> words.
  </p>
  <p>
    You can link to
    <a href="http://gamingJS.com">other pages</a>.
    You can also add images from web servers:
    <img src="/images/purple_fruit_monster.png">
  </p>
</body>
```

Ignore ICE Warnings for HTML

 Your HTML code may get red X warnings. These can be safely
ignored. ICE is meant to edit JavaScript, not HTML, so it can get
confused.

If you hide the code in the ICE Code Editor, you'll see something like this:

This is a JavaScript book, not an HTML book, but you already see some of
what's possible with HTML.

After the <body> tags come two <script> tags. Just like the <body> tags, these
<script> tags are HTML, but these load JavaScript from elsewhere on the Web
so that we can use it on the current page.

```
<script src="http://gamingJS.com/Three.js"></script>
<script src="http://gamingJS.com/ChromeFixes.js"></script>
```

These two lines tell the browser to load two libraries. In this case, we're
loading a 3D JavaScript library named Three.js and a small library that fixes
some ICE Code Editor bugs in the Chrome web browser.

JavaScript doesn't have to come from other locations. For most of this book, we're coding *inside* an HTML web page.

9.3 Setting the Scene

To do anything in 3D programming, we need a scene. Think of the scene as the universe in which all of the action is going to take place. For something so important, it's really easy to create. The following code in ICE does just that:

```
// This is where stuff in our game will happen:
var scene = new THREE.Scene();
```

Scenes are really simple to work with. We've been adding objects to them throughout the book. Once things have been added to a scene, it's the scene's job to keep track of everything. In fact, that's pretty much all we need to know about scenes—after creating one, we add lots of stuff to it and the scene takes care of the rest.

9.4 Using Cameras to Capture the Scene

Scenes do a great job of keeping track of everything, but they don't show us what's happening. To see anything in the scene, we need a camera. Notice the following code in ICE:

```
// This is what sees the stuff:
var aspect_ratio = window.innerWidth / window.innerHeight;
var camera = new THREE.PerspectiveCamera(75, aspect_ratio, 1, 10000);
camera.position.z = 500;
scene.add(camera);
```

The purpose of the aspect_ratio is to determine the shape of the browser. This is the same thing as aspect ratios for movie screens and TV sets. A large TV with a 4:3 aspect ratio might be four meters wide and three meters tall (OK that's a *really* large TV). An even larger 4:3 screen might be twelve meters wide and nine meters tall (multiply both the 4 and 3 in 4:3 by 3 to get 12:9). Most movies today are made at an aspect ratio of 16:9, which would mean a nine-meter-tall screen would be sixteen meters wide—four extra meters when compared with the same-height 4:3 aspect ratio.

Why does this matter for us? If you try to project a movie made in 16:9 onto a 4:3 screen, a lot of squishing has to be done. Similarly, a 4:3 movie would need to be stretched to be shown on a 16:9 screen. Instead of stretching or squishing, most movies are chopped so that you miss those four meters of action. Our Three.js library doesn't chop—it stretches or squishes. In other words, it's pretty important to get the aspect ratio right.

After we build a new camera, we need to add it to the scene. Like anything else in 3D programming, the camera is placed at the center of the scene to which we add it. We move it 500 units away from the center in the Z direction ("out" of the screen) so that we have a good view of what's going on back at the center of the scene.

9.5 Using a Renderer to Project What the Camera Sees

The scene and the camera are enough to describe how the scene looks and from where we're viewing it, but one more thing is required to show it on the web page. This is the job of the *renderer*. It shows, or renders, the scene as the camera sees it:

```
// This will draw what the camera sees onto the screen:
var renderer = new THREE.CanvasRenderer();
renderer.setSize(window.innerWidth, window.innerHeight);
document.body.appendChild(renderer.domElement);
```

We have to tell the renderer the size of the screen to which it will be drawing. We set the size of the view to take up the whole browser (window.innerWidth and window.innerHeight).

To include the renderer in the web page, we use its domElement property. A domElement is another name for an HTML tag like those we added earlier in the chapter. Instead of holding a title or paragraph, this domElement holds our amazing 3D worlds.

We add that domElement to the document.body—which is the same <body> tag that held the HTML from earlier. The appendChild() function takes care of adding the domElement to the document body. If you're wondering why we have names like appendChild() and domElement, all I can tell you is to be glad you are a 3D-game programmer, not a web programmer. Web programmers have to use silly (and hard-to-remember) names like this all the time.

At this point, the renderer *can* draw to the screen, but we still need to tell it to render before anything will show up. This is where renderer.render() comes into play at the end of your current code.

```
// Now, show what the camera sees on the screen:
renderer.render(scene, camera);
```

It might seem as though the renderer is an obnoxious younger brother or sister, doing the right thing only when we're extremely specific in our instructions. In a sense this is true, but in another sense all programming is like this. Until we tell the computer in exactly the right way to do something, it often does something completely unexpected.

In the case of the renderer, we can already see why it's nice to have this kind of control. In some of our experiments, we rendered just a single time. But in many of our projects, we render repeatedly inside an animate() function. Without this kind of control, it would be much harder to pick and choose the right rendering style.

9.6 Exploring Different Cameras and Renderers

You may have noticed that we call our camera a PerspectiveCamera and our renderer a CanvasRenderer. If these names seem oddly specific, that's because there are other kinds of cameras and renderers. We've been using these because most browsers and hardware support them. As we'll see in Chapter 12, *Working with Lights and Materials*, on page 109, some cool effects that we might want to add to our 3D games require different cameras and renderers that work only on relatively new computers.

You Don't Have to Do These Examples

Some computers will not be able to run the examples in the rest of the chapter. This is because they rely on a technology called WebGL, which we will talk about in more detail in Chapter 12, *Working with Lights and Materials*, on page 109. Since your computer might not support WebGL, you don't have to follow along in the ICE Code Editor in this section.

Introducing the WebGL Renderer

The other important renderer is the WebGLRenderer. We use it exactly the same way that we use the CanvasRenderer. We only need to change the name:

```
// This will draw what the camera sees onto the screen:
var renderer = new THREE.WebGLRenderer();
renderer.setSize(window.innerWidth, window.innerHeight);
document.body.appendChild(renderer.domElement);
```

WebGL is a fairly new technology that allows programmers to perform interesting 3D-programming techniques like lighting, shadows, and fog. It also runs animations much faster than is possible with the CanvasRenderer. We'll explore it more in *Working with Lights and Materials*.

A Quick Peek at a Weirdly Named Camera

The other kind of camera is called *orthographic*. To understand what an orthographic camera does, we can add a red road on which the purple fruit monster can travel. Add the following after START CODING ON THE NEXT LINE.

```
var shape = new THREE.CubeGeometry(200, 1000, 10);
var cover = new THREE.MeshBasicMaterial({color:0x990000});
var road = new THREE.Mesh(shape, cover);
scene.add(road);
road.position.set(0, 400, 0);
road.rotation.set(-Math.PI/4, 0, 0);
```

Our perspective camera makes the road look something like this:

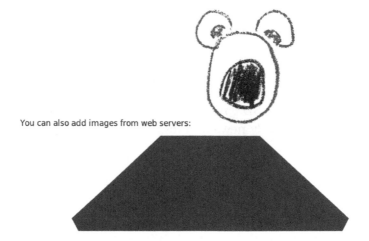

You can also add images from web servers:

This is a rectangular road, but it doesn't *look* rectangular. It looks as though it's getting smaller the farther away it gets. The perspective camera does this for us:

```
var aspect_ratio = window.innerWidth / window.innerHeight;
var camera = new THREE.PerspectiveCamera(75, aspect_ratio, 1, 10000);
```

If we use an orthographic camera, on the other hand, everything looks flat:

You can also add images from web servers:

That is the same road from the previous image. We've only replaced the two lines that create the perspective camera with the following:

```
var width = window.innerWidth,
    height = window.innerHeight;
var camera = new THREE.OrthographicCamera(
  -width/2, width/2, height/2, -height/2, 1, 10000
);
```

As you might imagine, the perspective camera that gives everything a three-dimensional feel is very handy in 3D games. Why would you want to use an orthographic camera?

Orthographic cameras are useful in two cases. The first is when you want to make a flat, 2D game. Using a 3D camera for a flat game just looks weird—especially at the edges of the screen. The other is when we make games with really, really long distances, such as space games. In fact, we can use orthographic cameras in some of the space simulations we'll do in a little while.

9.7 What's Next

Now that we understand all about cameras, scenes, and JavaScript libraries, we'll change them more and more. But first let's teach our game avatar to *not* walk through trees.

When you're done with this chapter, you will

- *Be able to stop game elements from moving through each other*
- *Understand collisions, which are important in gaming*
- *Have game boundaries for your avatar*

CHAPTER 10

Project: Collisions

We have a pretty slick game avatar. It moves, it walks, it even turns. But you may have noticed something odd about our avatar. It can walk through trees.

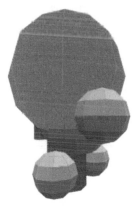

In this chapter we'll use tools that are built into our Three.js 3D JavaScript library to prevent the avatar-in-a-tree effect. (As we'll see in other chapters, there are other ways to do the same thing.)

10.1 Getting Started

If it's not already open in the ICE Code Editor, open the project from *Project: Turning Our Avatar* that we named My Avatar: Turning.

Make a copy of our avatar project. From the menu in the ICE Code Editor, select Make a Copy and enter My Avatar: Collisions as the new project name.

10.2 Rays and Intersections

The way we prevent our avatar from walking through trees is actually quite simple. Imagine an arrow pointing down from our avatar.

In geometry, we call an arrow point a *ray*. A ray is what you get when you start in one place and point in a direction. In this case, the place is where our avatar is and the direction is down. Sometimes giving names to such simple ideas seems silly, but it's important for programmers to know these names.

Programmers Like to Give Fancy Names to Simple Ideas

 Knowing the names for simple concepts makes it easier to talk to other people doing the same work. Programmers call these names *patterns*.

Now that we have our ray pointing down, imagine circles on the ground around our trees.

Here is the crazy-simple way that we prevent our avatar from running into a tree: we don't! Instead, we prevent the avatar's ray from pointing through the tree's circle.

If, at any time, we find that the next movement would place the avatar's ray so that it points through the circle, we stop the avatar from moving. That's all there is to it!

Star Trek II: The Wrath of Khan

It may seem strange, but watching certain science-fiction movies will make your life easier as a programmer. Sometimes programmers say odd things that turn out to be quotes from movies. It is not a requirement to watch or even like these movies, but it can help.

One such quote is from the classic *Star Trek II: The Wrath of Khan*. The quote is "He is intelligent, but not experienced. His pattern indicates two-dimensional thinking."

 The bad guy in the movie was not accustomed to thinking in three dimensions, and this was used against him. In this case, we *want* to think about collisions in only two dimensions even though we are building a three-dimensional game. We're thinking about collisions only in two dimensions (X and Z), completely ignoring the up-and-down Y dimension.

This is yet another example of cheating whenever possible. *Real* 3D collisions are difficult and require new JavaScript libraries. But we can cheat and get the same effect in many cases using easier tricks.

At this point, a picture of what to do next should be forming in your mind. We'll need a list of these tree-circle boundaries that our avatar won't be allowed to enter. We'll need to build those circle boundaries when we build the trees, and detect when the avatar is about to enter a circle boundary. Last, we need to stop the avatar from entering these forbidden areas.

Let's establish the list that will hold all forbidden boundaries. Just below the
START CODING ON THE NEXT LINE line, add the following.

```
var not_allowed = [];
```

Recall from Section 7.5, *Listing Things*, on page 77, that square brackets are
JavaScript's way of making lists. Here, our empty square brackets create an
empty list. The not_allowed variable is an empty list of spaces in which the
avatar is not allowed.

Next, find where makeTreeAt() is defined. When we make our tree, we'll make
the boundaries as well. Add the following code after the line that adds the
treetop to the trunk, and before the line that sets the trunk position.

```
var boundary = new THREE.Mesh(
  new THREE.CircleGeometry(300),
  new THREE.MeshNormalMaterial()
);
boundary.position.y = -100;
boundary.rotation.x = -Math.PI/2;
trunk.add(boundary);

not_allowed.push(boundary);
```

There's nothing superfancy there. We create our usual 3D mesh—this time
with a simple circle geometry. We rotate it so that it lays flat and position it
below the tree. And, of course, we finish by adding it to the tree.

But we're not quite done with our boundary mesh. At the end, we push it
onto the list of disallowed spaces. Now every time we make a tree with the
makeTreeAt() function, we're building up this list. Let's do something with that
list.

At the very bottom of our code, just above the </script> tag, add the following
code to detect collisions.

```
function detectCollisions() {
  var vector = new THREE.Vector3(0, -1, 0);
  var ray = new THREE.Ray(marker.position, vector);
  var intersects = ray.intersectObjects(not_allowed);
  if (intersects.length > 0) return true;
  return false;
}
```

This function returns a Boolean—a yes-or-no answer—depending on whether
the avatar is colliding with a boundary. This is where we make our ray to see
if it points through anything. As described earlier, a ray is the combination
of a direction, or *vector* (down in our case), and a point (in this case, the

avatar's marker.position). We then ask that ray if it goes through (intersects) any of the not_allowed objects. If the ray does intersect one of those objects, then the intersects variable will have a length that is greater than zero. In that case, we have detected a collision and we return true. Otherwise, there is no collision and we return false.

Collisions are a tough problem to solve in many situations, so you're doing great by following along with this. But we're not quite finished. We can now detect when an avatar is colliding with a boundary, but we haven't actually stopped the avatar yet. Let's do this in the keydown listener.

In the keydown listener, if an arrow key is pressed, we change the avatar's position.

```
if (code == 37) {                                    // left
  marker.position.x = marker.position.x-5;
  is_moving_left = true;
}
```

Such a change might mean that the avatar is now in the boundary. If so, we have to undo the move right away. Add the following code at the bottom of the keydown event listener (just after the if (code == 70)).

```
if (detectCollisions()) {
  if (is_moving_left) marker.position.x = marker.position.x+5;
  if (is_moving_right) marker.position.x = marker.position.x-5;
  if (is_moving_forward) marker.position.z = marker.position.z+5;
  if (is_moving_back) marker.position.z = marker.position.z-5;
}
```

Read through these lines to make sure you understand them. That bit of code says *if we detect a collision, then check the direction in which we're moving. If we're moving left, then reverse the movement that the avatar just did—go back in the opposite direction the same amount.*

With that, our avatar can walk up to the tree boundaries, but go no farther.

Yay! That might seem like some pretty easy code, but you just solved a very hard problem in game programming.

10.3 The Code So Far

In case you would like to double-check the code in this chapter, it's included in Section A1.10, *Code: Collisions*, on page 230.

10.4 What's Next

Collision detection in games is a really tricky problem to solve, so congratulations on getting this far. It gets even tougher once you have to worry about moving up and down in addition to left, right, back, and forward. But the concept is the same. Usually we rely on code libraries written by other people to help us with those cases. In some of the games we'll experiment with shortly, we'll use just such a code library.

But first we'll put the finishing touch on our avatar game. In the next chapter we'll add sounds and scoring. Let's get to it!

When you're done with this chapter, you will

- *Be able to add sounds to games*
- *Be able to add simple scoring to a game*
- *Have a silly game to play*

CHAPTER 11

Project: Fruit Hunt

We have an avatar. We have trees. Let's make a game in which our avatar has to get stuff out of those trees. The trees are hiding yummy fruit that the avatar wants. And if the avatar can get to the fruit in time, points will be added to the scoreboard.

It will end up looking something like this:

Congratulations to fellow game programmer Sophie H. for coming up with the winning game concept used in this chapter!

11.1 Getting Started

To make this game, we need the avatar, the trees, and the collision-detection functions that we've been working on throughout this book. After Chapter 10, *Project: Collisions*, on page 93, we have everything that we need to get started on this project. So let's make a copy of that project we've been working on.

From the menu in the ICE Code Editor, select Make a Copy and enter Fruit Hunt! as the new project name.

To keep score in this game, we'll need something new—a scoreboard. There is a fairly nice scoreboard built into the ICE Code Editor, but we have to load the library first. In Chapter 9, *What's All That Other Code?*, on page 85, we looked at the libraries that are loaded with the <script> tags at the very top of the code. We need to add another one.

Similarly, to make sounds in our game, we need the sounds library. So let's add a second <script> tag at the top of the code.

We make these changes by starting a new line after the three <script> tags at the top of the page with src attributes. The new line should be on line 5. Add the following <script> tags to pull in the scoreboard and sound libraries:

```
<script src="http://gamingJS.com/Scoreboard.js"></script>
<script src="http://gamingJS.com/Sounds.js"></script>
```

Since this is just the "getting started" section of our program, those lines won't actually change anything in the game. To see the scoreboard, we need to configure it and turn it on. Let's do that next.

11.2 Starting a Scoreboard at Zero

The rest of the code in this chapter will go below the START CODING ON THE NEXT LINE line.

To add a scoreboard to our game, we create a new one using the new keyword. Then we tell the scoreboard to start a countdown timer, show the score, and add a help message. To do all of that, we first enter the following code after the line that introduces the not_allowed variable:

```
var scoreboard = new Scoreboard();
scoreboard.countdown(45);
scoreboard.score();
scoreboard.help(
  'Arrow keys to move. ' +
  'Space bar to jump for fruit. ' +
  'Watch for shaking trees with fruit.' +
  'Get near the tree and jump before the fruit is gone!'
);
```

These lines add a nifty-looking scoreboard to our screen, complete with the time remaining in the game (45 seconds), the current score (zero), and a hint to players that they can press the question mark (?) key to get some help.

The scoreboard should look like the following:

Before making the game behave the way the help text says it should, we need to teach the game what to do when time runs out. To do so, add the following on the line after all of the scoreboard code:

```
var game_over = false;
scoreboard.onTimeExpired(function() {
  scoreboard.message("Game Over!");
  game_over = true;
});
```

This tells the scoreboard that when time expires, it should run the function that sets the scoreboard message to Game Over! and that the game_over variable should be set to true.

That's all there is to build the scoreboard. Now, let's figure out a way for the player to add points to the scoreboard.

11.3 Giving Trees a Little Wiggle

The goal of this game will be to find fruit, which we'll call treasure, in the trees. At any given time, only one tree will have treasure. To show which tree it is, we'll give it a little shake. But first we need a list of trees.

Find the code that created the forest—there should be four lines that make different makeTree() calls. We added this way back in Chapter 4, *Project: Moving Avatars*, on page 35. We need to make a little change to the part of the code that adds the trees to the scene.

We start by adding two variables. The first is tree_with_treasure, which you might have guessed will point to the tree that currently has treasure. The second variable is a list containing all the trees, which we'll call trees. We then push into this list all the trees that will make up our forest. Change your four makeTreeAt() lines to the following:

```
var tree_with_treasure;
var trees = [];
trees.push(makeTreeAt( 500,    0));
trees.push(makeTreeAt(-500,    0));
trees.push(makeTreeAt( 750, -1000));
trees.push(makeTreeAt(-750, -1000));
```

To make this bit work, we need to change the makeTreeAt() function so that it returns something. If makeTreeAt() doesn't return anything, then we would be pushing nothing onto our list of trees. Add the following line to the very bottom of the makeTreeAt() function before the last curly brace:

```
function makeTreeAt(x, z) {
  // Don't change any code at the start...

  // ... but add the following line to the end:
  return top;
}
```

With that, the treetop (the green ball/leaves) is returned to be added to the list of trees. We could have returned the trunk or even the collision boundary that we added in *Project: Collisions*. The top of the tree is what we need to work with the most (as that is where the treasure will be hidden), so it makes sense to return it so that it can be pushed into the list of trees.

Now that we have a list of trees, we can hide treasure in one and shake it. After the makeTreeAt() function, add the following function *and* function call:

```
function shakeTree() {
  tree_with_treasure = Math.floor(Math.random() * trees.length);

  new TWEEN
    .Tween({x: 0})
    .to({x: 2*Math.PI}, 200)
    .repeat(20)
    .onUpdate(function () {
      trees[tree_with_treasure].position.x = 75 * Math.sin(this.x);
    })
    .start();

  setTimeout(shakeTree, 12*1000);
}
```

```
shakeTree();
```

We'll talk about Math.floor() and Math.random() in Chapter 20, *Project: River Rafting*, on page 185. For now, let's leave it that the first line in shakeTree() picks a random tree.

We've already met the Tween library, which moves things from one value to another. In this case, we again move along a sine curve. Sines and cosines are great because they start and end at the same value when moving from zero to 360° (2*Math.PI). We use the sine.

As the value of the Tween moves from 0 to 2*Math.PI, the value of Math.sin() goes from 0 to 1, then back to 0, then to -1, and finally back to 0. In other words, it's perfect to make things wiggle a little.

The last part of shakeTree() sets a timeout for 12 seconds. After 12 seconds have passed, this timeout calls the shakeTree() function again and assigns a new tree with the treasure.

After this code, a different tree should be wiggling uncontrollably telling the player that there is treasure to be collected. Let's give the avatar a way to grab that treasure.

11.4 Jumping for Points

In this game, the avatar needs to jump next to the current treasure-filled tree. We'll do two things when this happens: the avatar will score some points and we'll make a nice little animation of the treasure and play a sound.

But first we need a key that will start a jump. We do this by adding the following if statement to the keydown() listener:

```
if (code == 32) jump();                              // space
```

You can add that if code just above the other if statements that turn the avatar.

Now we add the jump() function that the case statement calls. This function can go after the detectCollisions() function. It checks for treasure and animates the jump on our screen:

```
function jump() {
  checkForTreasure();
  animateJump();
}
```

To check whether the avatar is close enough to grab treasure, add the following function at the bottom of the code (just above the last <script/> tag):

```
function checkForTreasure() {
  if (tree_with_treasure == undefined) return;

  var treasure_tree = trees[tree_with_treasure],
      p1 = treasure_tree.parent.position,
      p2 = marker.position;

  var distance = Math.sqrt(
    (p1.x - p2.x)*(p1.x - p2.x) +
    (p1.z - p2.z)*(p1.z - p2.z)
  );

  if (distance < 500) {
    scorePoints();
  }
}
```

The checkForTreasure() function does three things:

- If there is no active tree—if it is undefined, as described in *Describing a Thing in JavaScript*—then it returns immediately and does nothing else.

- If there is an active tree near the avatar, then checkForTreasure() calculates the distance between the tree and the avatar.

- If the distance is less than 500, then the scorePoints() function is called.

Pythagorean Theorem Alert

 If you have already learned a little bit of trigonometry, you may have recognized the Pythagorean theorem in the checkForTreasure() function. We used it to find the distance between two points: the avatar and the active tree.

For now, we'll keep the scorePoints() function very simple. Add it after the checkForTreasure() function. We'll use it only to add points to the scoreboard:

```
function scorePoints() {
  if (scoreboard.getTimeRemaining() === 0) return;
  scoreboard.addPoints(10);
}
```

Be sure to add the first line in that function; otherwise players can get points after time has expired!

The last thing we need to do is animate the jump so we can see it on the screen. We combine two things that we've seen before: Tweens and a sine function. Let's add the animateJump() function next:

```
function animateJump() {
  new TWEEN
    .Tween({jump: 0})
    .to({jump: Math.PI}, 500)
    .onUpdate(function () {
      marker.position.y = 200* Math.sin(this.jump);
    })
    .start();
}
```

That should do it! If you hide the code, you can now move about, find the active tree, and jump to get treasure out of it. If you are very fast, you can even jump multiple times next to the active tree to get multiple points.

This is already a fun game, but we can add a few tweaks to make it even better.

11.5 Making Our Games Even Better

We've spent a good deal of time in this book adding animations to our avatar. We do this partly to understand important concepts like grouping objects, but also because this is a lot of what 3D-game programmers do.

Our avatar doesn't *really* need to have hands and feet that move as in real life, but this animation helps make the game seem more real. In this example, the gameplay is pretty simple: press the `space bar` near the treasure to get points.

What makes the game compelling and fun enough that players keep coming back is a combination of interesting gameplay and the occasional glimpses of realism.

Adding Animation and Sound

How many tweaks you add is up to you, the game programmer. But for this chapter let's add two together: we see an animation and hear a sound when the avatar gets the treasure-fruit. Adding sound to the game is the easier of the two, so we'll tackle that first.

First we add Sounds.bubble.play() to the scorePoints() function:

```
function scorePoints() {
  if (scoreboard.getTimeRemaining() === 0) return;
  scoreboard.addPoints(10);
  Sounds.bubble.play();
}
```

You can find more information on the Sounds.js library in Section A2.5, *Sounds.js*, on page 277. The library has a fairly small number of sounds to pick from, but there should be enough to get started writing games.

With that line added, we can score points and hear sound when the avatar jumps up to grab treasure-fruit. But we're not actually getting any of that golden fruit out of the tree.

To animate the fruit, we need to add the fruit to the avatar's frame of reference, then Tween it. The Tween will be a little different than those we have done so far, as it will animate *two* things. It will rise above the avatar and it will spin. The following code, which we can add after the scorePoints() function, will do all of that:

```
var fruit;
function animateFruit() {
  if (fruit) return;
```

```
  fruit = new THREE.Mesh(
    new THREE.CylinderGeometry(25, 25, 5, 25),
    new THREE.MeshBasicMaterial({color: 0xFFD700})
  );
  fruit.rotation.x = Math.PI/2;

  marker.add(fruit);

  new TWEEN.
    Tween({
      height: 150,
      spin: 0
    }).
    to({
      height: 250,
      spin: 4
    }, 500).
    onUpdate(function () {
      fruit.position.y = this.height;
      fruit.rotation.z = this.spin;
    }).
    onComplete(function() {
      marker.remove(fruit);
      fruit = undefined;
    }).
    start();
}
```

We'll talk more about the properties inside the curly braces when we reach Chapter 17, *Project: Learning about JavaScript Objects*, on page 159. For now, it's enough to know that we're setting two different number properties: the spin and the height of the fruit. The spin starts at zero and rotates around four times over the course of the entire animation. The fruit also rises from the position 150 to 250 on the screen over the course of the animation.

Of course, the animateFruit() function needs to be called before it will do anything. Add a call to it at the bottom of the scorePoints() function so that it looks like this:

```
function scorePoints() {
  if (scoreboard.getTimeRemaining() === 0) return;
  scoreboard.addPoints(10);
  Sounds.bubble.play();
  animateFruit();
}
```

The result is a nice animation that plays as the avatar collects fruit.

Yay! Score!

What Else Can We Add?

This is it for our avatar that we built from scratch starting all the way back in Chapter 3, *Project: Making an Avatar*, on page 25. That doesn't mean you can't make this game even better, though!

It is really easy to grab the fruit from a tree in this game. Perhaps you can add a tweak where the avatar is allowed only one piece of fruit from a tree? It might also be nice to penalize a player—think subtractPoints()—if the avatar jumps when the tree is not active and wiggling. If you think the player is moving too fast or too slow, maybe look in the keydown listener for ways to improve that. You can build the game to have all sorts of nooks and crannies and prizes.

This is the job of the game designer, which happens to be you. Make a copy of the code so far and see what you can add to make the game work the way you want it to. How are you going to make this game great?

11.6 The Code So Far

If you would like to double-check the code in this chapter, turn to Section A1.11, *Code: Fruit Hunt*, on page 234.

11.7 What's Next

This may be it for our avatar projects, but there is still plenty to do. Next we'll explore more of the small touches that go into 3D programming, starting with lights, materials, and shadows.

When you're done with this chapter, you will

- *Understand how to make different colors*
- *Be able to make shapes shiny or hard to see*
- *Know how to make shadows in 3D games*

CHAPTER 12

Working with Lights and Materials

In this chapter we'll cover how to build interesting shapes and materials that look like this:

Back in Chapter 1, *Project: Creating Simple Shapes*, on page 1, we discussed shapes in our 3D library. Here we'll talk about different kinds of covers for those shapes. We cannot learn about covers without also learning about lighting. Even in the real world, material and lights go together. If a material is shiny, then it means it reflects light better. If a material is dark and not shiny, then a very bright light might be needed in order to see it.

The MeshNormalMaterial that we have used so far is helpful when we're first building games, but it's not a good choice for real games. There is no control over the color, the shininess, or anything. Let's look at a couple of materials that will let us change that.

12.1 Getting Started

Start a new project in ICE. Choose the 3D starter project template from the menu, then save it with the name Lights and Materials.

12.2 Changing Color

Add the following below START CODING ON THE NEXT LINE:

```
var shape = new THREE.SphereGeometry(100);
var cover = new THREE.MeshBasicMaterial();
cover.color.setRGB(1, 0, 0);
var ball = new THREE.Mesh(shape, cover);
scene.add(ball);
```

MeshBasicMaterial

Notice that, instead of the MeshNormalMaterial that we have used to wrap things so far, we're now using a MeshBasicMaterial. Since it's a basic cover, there's not much we can do with it. But we *can* change the color, which is new.

You should see a red ball on the screen:

```
// ******** START CODING ON THE NEXT LINE ********
var shape = new THREE.SphereGeometry(100);
var cover = new THREE.MeshBasicMaterial();
cover.color.setRGB(1, 0, 0);
var ball = new THREE.Mesh(shape, cover);
scene.add(ball);

// Now, show what the camera sees on the screen:
renderer.render(scene, camera);
```

Colors in computer programs are written as *RGB numbers*, which describe how much red (R) green (G), and blue (B) is used. Believe it or not, you can make just about every color there is by combining those three colors. Combining RGB colors may not work quite like you would expect—for instance, you make yellow by combining red and green: cover.color.setRGB(1,1,0).

Wikipedia Has a Very Nice List of Colors

The Wikipedia list at http://en.wikipedia.org/wiki/List_of_colors includes RGB percentages, which you would need to write as decimals. For instance, one of the first colors on that list is "Air Force blue (RAF)" which has the following RGB percentages: 36%, 54%, 66%. To make our ball that color, use this: cover.color.setRGB(0.36, 0.54, 0.66).

This *basic* material is a little more useful in real games than the MeshNormalMaterial that we've used so far. It's particularly helpful for backgrounds and flat surfaces. Even so, it's not the most realistic-looking material that we can choose. The color always looks the same no matter what light is shining on it. It won't reflect light or have shadows. That said, use it wherever possible—it's easy for the computer to draw.

Now let's look at a more interesting material. But first, move the basic red ball out of the way:

```
ball.position.set(500, 0, 0);
```

12.3 Realism: Shininess

The first thing we need to do for this exercise is switch renderers. We talked about renderers in Chapter 9, *What's All That Other Code?*, on page 85. Remember that the renderer is the thing that draws our games on our computer screens. We briefly discussed different kinds of renderers in that chapter. Now we'll use them. The one that we have been using, the CanvasRenderer, will work with most computers but cannot perform some of the cool effects that we might want in our games.

This May Not Work on Your Computer!

To achieve realism, your computer must be WebGL-capable. If your computer cannot do WebGL, then you should just read through the rest of this chapter, but not type any of it in since it won't work. It's nice to be able to see these effects, but not necessary for most of the games that we'll work with.

The easiest way to tell if your computer and browser can do WebGL is to visit http://get.webgl.org/. If you see the spinning cube on that page, then you have WebGL.

To switch to the WebGLRenderer, find the renderer code (it should be near line 15) and change the CanvasRenderer to WebGLRenderer so that the code looks like this:

```
// This will draw what the camera sees onto the screen:
var renderer = new THREE.WebGLRenderer();
```

If you still see the ball to the right, then everything is OK and your computer can do WebGL. If not, switch back to the CanvasRenderer and read through this chapter without making the changes described.

Below the code for the ball, let's create a donut with the Phong material:

```
var shape = new THREE.TorusGeometry(100, 50, 8, 20);
var cover = new THREE.MeshPhongMaterial();
cover.emissive.setRGB(0.8, 0.1, 0.1);
var donut = new THREE.Mesh(shape, cover);
scene.add(donut);
```

If you have done everything correctly, then you should see a very dull red donut. You might be thinking, "that's it?" Well, of course that's not it!

What's missing is light. When something is shiny in real life, that means that a light—the sunlight, a flashlight, etc.—shines brightly off of it. The same holds true in computer games. So let's add a light.

Below the donut code, add some sunlight:

```
var sunlight = new THREE.DirectionalLight();
sunlight.intensity = 0.5;
sunlight.position.set(100, 100, 100);
scene.add(sunlight);
```

We're positioning the sunlight to the right, above, and in front of the donut. The result should be a pretty cool-looking donut:

Emissive

Unlike with the MeshBasicMaterial cover—where we adjusted the color attribute—with MeshPhongMaterial we adjust the emissive attribute to describe the color:

```
cover.emissive.setRGB(0.8, 0.1, 0.1);
```

We can't just use color because we need to adjust a number of color-related attributes when working with a MeshPhongMaterial. The emissive attribute describes the color that the cover "emits"—the color that it is.

Specular

Specular is another color attribute we can adjust. The specular attribute describes the color of the shiny parts of the object. If we do not set this value, it's not very bright. Let's make it bright.

Add the specular line below the line on which we set the emissive color:

```
var shape = new THREE.TorusGeometry(100, 50, 8, 20);
var cover = new THREE.MeshPhongMaterial();
cover.emissive.setRGB(0.8, 0.1, 0.1);
cover.specular.setRGB(0.9, 0.9, 0.9);
var donut = new THREE.Mesh(shape, cover);
scene.add(donut);
```

If all of the RGB colors are the same value, then we'll see black, white, or some shade of gray. All zeros would be black. All ones would be white. Anything in between is gray. In this case we set the specular color—the color of the shine—to three 0.9 values, which is pretty close to all 1.0 values that would make white.

In other words, we see a little more of the shine:

Always Use Gray or White for Specular Colors

It's possible to use any color you like for the specular attribute. Normally, however, it's best to stick with gray or white. For instance, the sunlight that we're shining on our donut is white, but it's still possible to make the specular color yellow (change the last number to 0.0). But that is just weird—white light creating a yellow shine.

We've covered emissive and specular; there are two other color-related properties that we can set on Phong materials: ambient and plain-old color. The ambient color applies only when using an "ambient" light—a light that is everywhere. The color property is used only when there are no strong lights nearby. We'll stick with emissive and specular in this book—they make cooler-looking objects.

12.4 Shadows

We're shining a light on our donut, and yet there is no shadow. You can usually skip rendering shadows, but sometimes they really help.

Don't Overuse Shadows

It requires a lot of work for the computer to be able to draw shadows, so use them only in spots that they really help. This is a tough choice to make because shadows almost always make games look better. But, as we'll see, it makes the computer work harder on something besides the main game and it's a bit of a pain to set up correctly.

First, we need to tell the renderer to expect shadows. Add the line setting the shadowMapEnabled attribute just below the WebGL renderer line:

```
// This will draw what the camera sees onto the screen:
var renderer = new THREE.WebGLRenderer();
renderer.shadowMapEnabled = true;
```

It might seem like that's enough—we told the renderer that it should draw shadows, and it should take care of everything else. But shadows require a lot of work by the computer. If every light makes shadows and every object casts a shadow and every object can have a shadow fall on it...well, then the computer is going to use all of its power drawing shadows and have nothing left for the user to actually play games.

The next step is to mark the donut as making shadows. To do this, we set the castShadow attribute after adding the donut to the scene. Add the donut.castShadow line after scene.add(donut):

```
var shape = new THREE.TorusGeometry(100, 50, 8, 20);
var cover = new THREE.MeshPhongMaterial();
cover.emissive.setRGB(0.8, 0.1, 0.1);
cover.specular.setRGB(0.9, 0.9, 0.9);
var donut = new THREE.Mesh(shape, cover);
scene.add(donut);
donut.castShadow = true;
```

Now tell the sunlight that it makes shadows by setting castShadow on it, as well. Again, add the sunlight.castShadow line after scene.add(sunlight):

```
var sunlight = new THREE.DirectionalLight();
sunlight.intensity = 0.5;
sunlight.position.set(100, 100, 100);
scene.add(sunlight);
sunlight.castShadow = true;
```

Last, we need a place for the shadow to fall. In real life, we see a shadow on a building or the ground. Let's create some ground below the donut for the shadow to fall on:

```
var shape = new THREE.PlaneGeometry(1000, 1000);
var cover = new THREE.MeshBasicMaterial();
var ground = new THREE.Mesh(shape, cover);
scene.add(ground);
ground.position.set(0, -200, 0);
ground.rotation.set(-Math.PI/2, 0, 0);
ground.receiveShadow = true;
```

Notice that we're using a plane and a basic material for this. Always use the simplest object you can.

With this, you should see that our awesome donut is casting a shadow:

```
var sunlight = new THREE.DirectionalLight();
sunlight.intensity = 0.5;
sunlight.position.set(100, 100, 100);
scene.add(sunlight);
sunlight.castShadow = true;

var shape = new THREE.PlaneGeometry(1000, 1000);
var cover = new THREE.MeshBasicMaterial();
var ground = new THREE.Mesh(shape, cover);
scene.add(ground);
ground.position.set(0, -200, 0);
ground.rotation.set(-Math.PI/2, 0, 0);
ground.receiveShadow = true;
```

12.5 Let's Animate!

That is all pretty cool, but you know what's even cooler than a shiny donut casting a shadow? A shiny donut casting a shadow and spinning!

Replace the renderer.render() at the bottom of our code:

```
var clock = new THREE.Clock();
function animate() {
  requestAnimationFrame(animate);

  var time = clock.getElapsedTime();
  donut.rotation.set(time, 2*time, 0);

  renderer.render(scene, camera);
}
animate();
```

We've seen a lot of that code before, but now is a good time to explain it. Our 3D library provides the clock. It is extremely useful for finding out how much time has gone by since the animation began. This "elapsed time" is useful for animating all sort of things.

In this code, we use it to set the rotation of the donut around the x-axis and the y-axis. As the seconds tick by, the donut's rotation will go from zero to 0.5, to 1, and eventually to 2 × pi (a full rotation). And then it keeps on rotating another spin to 4 × pi, then 6 × pi, and on and on forever (or until the computer can no longer count that high). We spin around the y-axis twice as fast as the x-axis to give it a crazy, wobbly motion.

It's a little weird using the number of seconds for the amount of rotation. Then again, they are both just numbers. The clock.getElapsedTime() call gives us the number of seconds and we use the same number to be the number of radians the donut has turned.

The other interesting thing happening in the animate() function is requestAnimationFrame(). This is a function that is built into modern web browsers, which are very good about knowing just the right time to draw things. By using the requestAnimationFrame() function, we get very smooth animations.

What's really interesting about requestAnimationFrame() is that we give it another function—the very animate() function that's currently running. We don't add the parentheses at the end of animate because that would call the animate() function. By giving requestAnimationFrame() a reference to animate(), we tell the web browser that the next time it is ready to do some drawing, which should be in a few milliseconds, it should call this animate function again.

With that, you just made a donut from nothing and sent it spinning around wildly.

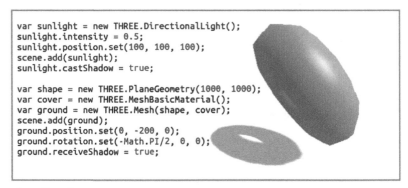

```
var sunlight = new THREE.DirectionalLight();
sunlight.intensity = 0.5;
sunlight.position.set(100, 100, 100);
scene.add(sunlight);
sunlight.castShadow = true;

var shape = new THREE.PlaneGeometry(1000, 1000);
var cover = new THREE.MeshBasicMaterial();
var ground = new THREE.Mesh(shape, cover);
scene.add(ground);
ground.position.set(0, -200, 0);
ground.rotation.set(-Math.PI/2, 0, 0);
ground.receiveShadow = true;
```

How cool is that?

12.6 The Code So Far

If you would like to double-check the code in this chapter, flip to Section A1.12, *Code: Working with Lights and Materials*, on page 240.

12.7 What's Next

Lights and materials are advanced topics and we have only scratched the surface of what's possible. There are many settings that take a lot of getting used to. Just setting colors with red, green, and blue values is a little strange at first. But that's not why these are advanced topics. Lights and materials are incredibly cool, but you must realize that you shouldn't *always* use them. This is an important lesson in any kind of programming, not just JavaScript gaming: just because you *can* doesn't mean you *should*. The best programmers in the world know this rule well. And now you do, too!

Let's put our new lighting skills to good use in the next chapter as we build a simulation of our solar system.

When you're done with this chapter, you will

- *Know how to move things in circles*
- *Understand how to make a sun light source*
- *Be able to switch between two cameras in the same scene*
- *Understand a mystery that took humans thousands of years to solve*

CHAPTER 13

Project: Build Your Own Solar System

Let's take a break from our avatar to do something different, but just as cool: animate the solar system. It will end up looking like this:

No, this isn't a game, but it's still fun.

13.1 Getting Started

Start a new project in ICE. Choose the 3D starter project template and name this project Planets.

13.2 The Sun, Earth, and Mars

Since we're dealing with space, we need to adjust the usual camera and switch the renderer. We make these changes to the code that is *above* START CODING ON THE NEXT LINE.

Create the camera so that it can see as far away as 1e6, which is a short way of writing 1 with six zeros following it, or 1,000,000. Also, move the camera 1000 away from the center of the screen.

```
// This is what sees the stuff:
var aspect_ratio = window.innerWidth / window.innerHeight;
var camera = new THREE.PerspectiveCamera(75, aspect_ratio, 1, 1e6);
camera.position.z = 1000;
scene.add(camera);
```

One other change that we'll make is to switch to the WebGLRenderer like we did in Chapter 12, *Working with Lights and Materials*, on page 109.

```
// This will draw what the camera sees onto the screen:
var renderer = new THREE.WebGLRenderer();
renderer.setSize(window.innerWidth, window.innerHeight);
document.body.appendChild(renderer.domElement);
```

If the **WebGLRenderer** Doesn't Work on Your Computer

If the WebGLRenderer didn't work for your computer when you tested it in Chapter 12, *Working with Lights and Materials*, on page 109, you can still do most of this chapter. You'll need to keep the CanvasRenderer here. In the following code, replace the MeshPhongMaterial references with MeshBasicMaterial. The simulation won't look as cool—and you won't be able to do the last bit—but most of it will still work.

Now we start coding after START CODING ON THE NEXT LINE.

First, let's do something important for a space simulation. Let's make space black.

```
document.body.style.backgroundColor = 'black';
```

Now add the sun to our simulation.

```
var surface = new THREE.MeshPhongMaterial({ambient: 0xFFD700});
var star = new THREE.SphereGeometry(50, 28, 21);
var sun = new THREE.Mesh(star, surface);
scene.add(sun);

var ambient = new THREE.AmbientLight(0xffffff);
scene.add(ambient);

var sunlight = new THREE.PointLight(0xffffff, 5, 1000);
sun.add(sunlight);
```

The color of the sun is gold from http://en.wikipedia.org/wiki/List_of_colors (recall that we replace the # on that page with 0x when making JavaScript colors). We make this the ambient color because there won't be other lights shining on the sun. This is the color it gets just by being there.

For the ambient color to work, we need an ambient light, which we add. For the sun to give light to the planets in our solar system, we need to add a *point light* in the middle of the sun. A point light shines light in all directions from a single point, much like the sun.

With that, let's create our planets and place them a little away from the sun (obviously not to scale!).

```
var surface = new THREE.MeshPhongMaterial({ambient: 0x1a1a1a, color: 0x0000cd});
var planet = new THREE.SphereGeometry(20, 20, 15);
var earth = new THREE.Mesh(planet, surface);
earth.position.set(250, 0, 0);
scene.add(earth);

var surface = new THREE.MeshPhongMaterial({ambient: 0x1a1a1a, color: 0xb22222});
var planet = new THREE.SphereGeometry(20, 20, 15);
var mars = new THREE.Mesh(planet, surface);
mars.position.set(500, 0, 0);
scene.add(mars);
```

That should give us our sun, Earth, and Mars. So far, they are not doing anything. Let's fix that by changing the last line of code from a single render to an animate() function.

```
clock = new THREE.Clock();

function animate() {
  requestAnimationFrame(animate);

  var time = clock.getElapsedTime();

  var e_angle = time * 0.8;
  earth.position.set(250* Math.cos(e_angle), 250* Math.sin(e_angle), 0);

  var m_angle = time * 0.3;
  mars.position.set(500* Math.cos(m_angle), 500* Math.sin(m_angle), 0);

  // Now, show what the camera sees on the screen:
  renderer.render(scene, camera);
}

animate();
```

We've already used the 3D clock timer, back in Chapter 6, *Project: Moving Hands and Feet*, on page 59, when we wanted to move our avatar's hands and feet back and forth. To make the hands and feet move back and forth, we didn't use JavaScript—we used math. Specifically, we used sine. For our planets, we are again using sine, but we are also using a new function, cosine.

If we just used a sine, our planets would move back and forth through the sun, just like our avatar hands and feet moved back and forth. But we want our planets to move up and down as well. This is what the cosine is for. When the sine function would move the planet through the sun, the cosine pushes it away in the other direction. Over time, this makes a perfect circle.

With that, we should have our planets moving around the sun! In real life, the planets don't move in perfect circles, but this is pretty cool anyway, right?

Our space simulation is still missing something: stars. To make stars, we'll use a *particle system*. Be careful while adding the particle system with the following code (see the warning that follows).

```
var stars = new THREE.Geometry();
while (stars.vertices.length < 1e4) {
  var lat = Math.PI * Math.random() - Math.PI/2;
  var lon = 2*Math.PI * Math.random();

  stars.vertices.push(new THREE.Vector3(
    1e5 * Math.cos(lon) * Math.cos(lat),
    1e5 * Math.sin(lon) * Math.cos(lat),
    1e5 * Math.sin(lat)
  ));
}
var star_stuff = new THREE.ParticleBasicMaterial({size: 500});
var star_system = new THREE.ParticleSystem(stars, star_stuff);
scene.add(star_system);
```

Be Careful Adding while Statements in ICE

A while statement will continue to run until something stops it. If nothing stops it, then the browser will lock up. When that happens in ICE, your only option is to switch to edit-only mode (see *Recovering When ICE Is Broken*).

To prevent freezes, you can comment out the while statement until you have typed the entire code block. That is, you can put the double slashes for a comment before the while and type everything else in the code block. Then go back and remove the double slashes to see the results of the while onscreen.

We're not going to worry much about the details of a particle system. In essence, particle systems are a way of adding a whole lot of things to a simulation in a way that doesn't make the computer work very hard. In this case, we add a whole lot of stars to the scene.

13.3 Earth-Cam!

Let's add the ability to watch the planet Mars from Earth. As you watch Mars from Earth over several months, Mars's position in the sky changes in a pretty strange way. It's so strange that ancient astronomers couldn't explain it. But we'll be able to.

To watch Mars from Earth, we'll need another camera besides the one looking down on our solar system. So the first thing we need to do is give our above-the-solar-system camera a better name. Let's call it above_cam. Change camera to above_cam at the top of your code:

```
// This is what sees the stuff:
var aspect_ratio = window.innerWidth / window.innerHeight;
var above_cam = new THREE.PerspectiveCamera(75, aspect_ratio, 1, 1e6);
above_cam.position.z = 1000;
scene.add(above_cam);
```

Next let's add a new camera named earth_cam.

```
var earth_cam = new THREE.PerspectiveCamera(75, aspect_ratio, 1, 1e6);
scene.add(earth_cam);
```

The rest of our code expects a camera named camera, so let's give it just that. To start, let's make camera mean the same thing as above_cam.

```
var camera = above_cam;
```

Next we need to add earth_cam to Earth and rotate it so that it points to Mars. We do that inside the animate() function. Add the following after the line that sets Mars's position and before the renderer.render line.

```
var y_diff = mars.position.y - earth.position.y,
    x_diff = mars.position.x - earth.position.x,
    angle = Math.atan2(x_diff, y_diff);

earth_cam.rotation.set(Math.PI/2, -angle, 0);
earth_cam.position.set(earth.position.x, earth.position.y, 22);
```

If you know the difference between the X and Y coordinates of two objects, you can again use math to figure out the rotation between the two things. This is what we're doing with the x_diff and y_diff variables—we are calculating how far apart Mars's and Earth's X and Y positions are. This is what the Math.atan2() tells us.

Declaring a Bunch of Variables with One var

You may have noticed that we used only one var keyword to build the list of variables in the preceding code. JavaScript programmers often find this a nice way to group a bunch of variables that are related—in this case, two points and the angle between them. It's especially common to do this at the start of functions.

Once we know the rotation, we can place the camera at the same position as Earth and then rotate it so it's facing Mars.

Last, we need to add the ability to use the keyboard to switch between our two cameras. Let's use A to switch to the above_cam and E to switch to earth_cam. The computer code for A is 65 and the computer code for E is 69. So, at the very bottom of our code, before the ending <script> tag, add the following event listener.

```
document.addEventListener("keydown", function(event) {
  var code = event.keyCode;

  if (code == 65) { // A
    camera = above_cam;
  }
  if (code == 69) { // E
    camera = earth_cam;
  }
});
```

That should do it! Now if you hide the code, you should be able to switch back and forth between "Earth-cam" and "above-solar-system-cam." Watching from

Earth, you should notice something strange (but only if you're using the WebGL renderer, unfortunately). Mars normally seems to be moving to the left as time passes. But every now and then, it stops and seems to go backward for a little while.

If you go outside and observe where Mars is in the sky for several months, you'll see the same phenomenon. Ancient astronomers called this "retrograde motion." Because they thought Earth was at the center of the universe, they had no good explanation for why retrograde motion happened. Oh, some of them came up with crazy explanations, but nothing as simple as we just simulated.

But we know what's going on, don't we? If you switch to above_cam just as Mars starts going backward, you'll see that retrograde motion happens when Earth catches up with Mars and passes it. It's sort of like a fast car passing a slower car—the slower car (Mars) almost looks like it's going backward.

It took you just a hundred lines of JavaScript to solve a question that the greatest minds in the world couldn't solve for thousands of years. Awesome!

13.4 The Code So Far

If you would like to double-check the code in this chapter, turn to Section A1.13, *Code: Build Your Own Solar System*, on page 241.

13.5 What's Next

We have a pretty incredible view of the solar system here, which is not bad for a quick, single-chapter project! Not only did you solve a mystery that has perplexed great minds, but you learned some pretty useful things about 3D programming along the way. You now know how to move objects in circular motion. Even cooler, you can add multiple cameras to a 3D scene, move the cameras around, and switch back and forth between them.

We'll build on this project in the next chapter to do something that every 3D programmer has to do at some point: simulate the phases of the moon as it revolves around Earth.

CHAPTER 14

Project: Phases of the Moon

The retrograde-motion chapter was pretty amazing, but in this chapter we'll cover something every 3D programmer must learn at some point: how to visualize the moon and its phases. It'll end up looking like this:

Why is it important to simulate the moon's phases? First, it's a simple enough problem—the sun shines on the moon, which revolves around Earth—that lets us use our knowledge of lights and materials. It also lets us play the relative-positioning tricks that we practiced with an avatar's hands and feet previously.

If you still think it's not important, go watch *Toy Story*. It was the first full-length computer-animated movie, and the programmers behind the project made sure they got it right—a waxing crescent moon is visible behind Woody and Buzz when they argue after being left by Andy at the gas station. If it was important enough for those movie-makers, it's important enough for us!

14.1 Getting Started

We'll do something a little different in this chapter. Instead of starting anew, let's make a copy of our Mars project. From the menu in the ICE Code Editor, choose Make a Copy.

In the usual project dialog that comes up, call this project Moon Phases.

14.2 Change Mars into the Moon

The first thing we need to do is rename every instance of mars to moon. Do this before anything else and be sure that no mars variables remain (there should be six changes).

Once you've done this, you'll still have a red planet revolving around the sun. Naming it differently doesn't change how it looks or behaves—we'll need to change our code for that.

This is an important first step. We didn't try to change everything, just the name of one thing in our code. Once everything is behaving as before, we're ready for the next step. Never try to change everything at once—you'll almost always end up breaking everything. The worst thing that we could have done with our first step is make the animation disappear because we missed a mars somewhere, which is an easy thing to find and correct. Small steps always win.

With that, let's change how the moon looks. Change the color property of the moon to all white: 0xffffff. We should also make the moon a little smaller than Earth and, while we're at it, let's make it less chunky. The size should be 15 and it should have 30 up-and-down chunks and 25 chunks going around.

```
var surface = new THREE.MeshPhongMaterial({ambient: 0x1a1a1a, color: 0xffffff});
var planet = new THREE.SphereGeometry(15, 30, 25);
var moon = new THREE.Mesh(planet, surface);
```

Next we need to make the moon behave a bit more like a moon. Instead of orbiting around the sun, we need to make it orbit around Earth. So delete the lines that set the moon's position, and add it to the scene. Since the moon is no longer added to the scene, it will disappear—this is OK. We'll add it back in a second.

But first, let's remove the code that moves the moon around. Inside the curly braces of the animate() function, delete the lines that calculate y_diff, x_diff, and angle. Also delete the two lines that set the earth_cam rotation and position.

Finally, remove the line that sets the moon's position with the sine and cosines, the line just under var m_angle. We still need to do that for Earth, but we'll try something new to move the moon around.

Now that we have removed everything that made the moon behave like Mars, we're ready to make it do what the moon should—mainly, revolve around Earth. To accomplish this, we'll do something really sneaky.

14.3 The Coolest Trick: Frame of Reference

Just after we create the moon, we create the moon's orbit, which is just an empty 3D object—similar to what we did back in Chapter 3, *Project: Making an Avatar*, on page 25. Then we add the orbit to Earth:

```
var moon_orbit = new THREE.Object3D();
earth.add(moon_orbit);
```

Adding the moon_orbit to Earth like that means that it's centered on Earth. And, no matter where Earth goes, this moon_orbit object stays with Earth.

It probably doesn't seem like it, but this is a crazily important trick in 3D programming. So important, in fact, that it gets a fancy name: *frame of reference*. Our moon_orbit is a new frame of reference. To see the power of frame-of-reference thinking, we add the moon to the moon_orbit and move it 100 units away from the center:

```
moon_orbit.add(moon);
moon.position.set(0, 100, 0);
```

With that, we should again see the moon, only now it's stuck next to Earth as Earth travels around the sun.

Since the moon_orbit frame of reference is always centered on Earth, the moon is now always 100 units away from Earth. We still need to make the moon revolve around Earth. We add Earth's camera to the moon_orbit frame of reference and rotate it to face the moon:

```
moon_orbit.add(earth_cam);
earth_cam.rotation.set(Math.PI/2, 0, 0);
```

Now comes the really cool part of frame of reference. Back inside the animate() function, we'll animate the rotation of the moon_orbit. Add the second line and change the m_angle—the amount by which the moon's orbit is changed—to be as follows:

```
var m_angle = time * 4;
moon_orbit.rotation.set(0, 0, m_angle);
```

With that, the moon should be traveling around Earth!

If you look closely, you'll notice that we're not moving the moon. Instead, we're rotating the *moon's orbit*—that is, we're rotating the moon's frame of reference. If you hide the code and press the E key to switch to Earth-cam, you'll see that, since we added the camera to the moon's frame of reference, it spins to point at the moon at all times.

You can think of this frame of reference as a plate to which we glue the camera and the moon:

When we spin the plate, the moon and camera spin along with it:

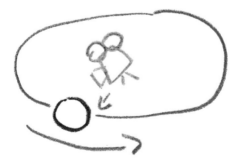

The result is that we had to do very little work to orbit the moon or keep Earth-cam pointed at it. With Mars, we had to do all sorts of crazy sines and cosines and distance calculations. We had to position Earth and Mars *and* the camera with the animate() sequence. With frame of reference, we just rotate one thing.

Laziness is a wonderful thing.

Oh, you might be wondering: why don't we use the same trick for Earth? I'm glad you asked.

14.4 Challenge: Create an Earth Orbit Frame of Reference

You can do this. Just follow the steps that we took for the moon:

- Create a 3D object to hold Earth, and add it to the sun.
- Add Earth to the new orbit frame of reference instead of the scene.
- Delete the animate() code that sets Earth's position.
- Rotate Earth's orbit.

Once you do that, you have a very complex astronomical simulation that is built using nothing but simple frame of reference—no complicated sines or cosines anywhere!

14.5 Pausing the Simulation

It's pretty neat to see the moon revolve around Earth while Earth revolves around the sun. But to really understand the moon's phases we need to be able to see the moon from Earth—like we would see it in the night sky. It would also be helpful to pause everything so that we can switch back and forth between above-cam and Earth-cam.

To pause, we need to make some changes to the animate() function. When the simulation is paused, we still need to perform animation and render the scene, but we shouldn't update the position of Earth or the moon. This means we have to move the renderer.render() call up in the animate() function—it will need to render before we check if the simulation is paused. We also need to come up with a different way of keeping time in the simulation. The THREE.Clock() that we have been using cannot be paused.

So remove the clock = THREE.Clock statement above the animate() function. Replace it with the three variables shown (time, speed, and pause):

```
var time = 0,
    speed = 1,
    pause = false;
```

```
function animate() {
  requestAnimationFrame(animate);
  renderer.render(scene, camera);

  if (pause) return;
  time = time + speed;
  var e_angle = time * 0.001;
  earth.position.set(250* Math.cos(e_angle), 250* Math.sin(e_angle), 0);
  var m_angle = time * 0.02;
  moon_orbit.rotation.set(0, 0, m_angle);
}
animate();
```

There are other changes in there, as well:

- The renderer.render() line is no longer at the bottom. It is now the second line in animate().
- We added a return statement if pause is true.
- We increased the time by adding speed to it each time.
- The number by which time is multiplied to calculate e_angle and m_angle has gotten smaller.

Once you have all of those changes made, the simulation should run again, the same as before. We made those changes so that we could use key presses to change some of the settings.

To do that, find the keydown listener and change it to the following:

```
document.addEventListener("keydown", function(event) {
  var code = event.keyCode;

  if (code == 67) changeCamera(); // C
  if (code == 32) changeCamera(); // space
  if (code == 80) pause = !pause; // P
  if (code == 49) speed = 1; // 1
  if (code == 50) speed = 2; // 2
  if (code == 51) speed = 10; // 3
});

function changeCamera() {
  if (camera == above_cam) camera = earth_cam;
  else camera = above_cam;
}
```

Now if you hide the code, you can change the camera by pressing either the C key or the space bar. You can pause or unpause by pressing the P key. You can even change the speed by pressing 1, 2, or 3.

Give it a try!

14.6 Understanding the Phases

The moon has four main phases: new, first quarter, full, and third quarter. New is when the moon is in between Earth and the sun. Since the sun is shining on the side of the moon that we cannot see, we do not see the moon at this time (also, it's in the same part of the sky as the sun).

First quarter means that the moon is one-quarter of the way around its orbit. It doesn't mean that it's one-quarter lit up—as you can tell, it's half full.

When the moon is two-quarters (also known as one-half) of the way around Earth, it's full. The part of the moon that we see is completely lit up.

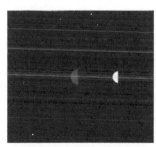

You know what third quarter is. The moon is three-quarters of the way around Earth, and again it's half lit.

In between the new moon and the quarters, the moon is a *crescent*.

In between the quarters and full moon, the moon is called *gibbous*.

When the lit side is growing, it's said to be *waxing*. When it's getting smaller, it's said to be *waning*. And now you know just about everything there is to know about the moon's phases. Better yet, you have your own simulation!

14.7 The Code So Far

In case you would like to double-check the code in this chapter, it's included in Section A1.14, *Code: Phases of the Moon*, on page 243.

And no, it doesn't include the challenge of using a frame of reference for Earth. Do it yourself!

14.8 What's Next

This ends the space simulations in the book. Congratulations—you have made it through a grand tradition in 3D programming. Hopefully you picked up a thing or two about space. More importantly for your computer skills, you've been introduced to the concept of frame of reference, which we're definitely going to use in our games.

Speaking of games, let's get started on some in the next chapter!

When you're done with this chapter, you will

- *Know how to keep score in games*
- *Understand how to keep score (or perform some other action) when objects collide*
- *Have an example of how physics are used in a game*

CHAPTER 15

Project: The Purple Fruit Monster Game

In this chapter we'll make a jumping game. The player will use the keyboard to make the purple fruit monster jump and move to capture as much rolling fruit as possible, without touching the ground. It will end up looking something like this:

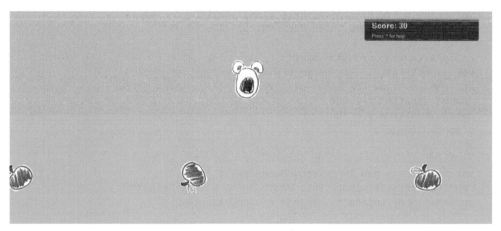

This is a fairly simple game to play, but it will give us a taste of some important gaming concepts.

15.1 Getting Started

Start a new project in ICE. Choose the 3D starter project template and name this project Purple Fruit Monster.

15.2 Let's Make Physics!

For this game, we need two new JavaScript libraries and a few configuration settings. At the very top of the file, add two new <script> tags:

```
<body></body>
<script src="http://gamingJS.com/Three.js"></script>
```
❶ `<script src="http://gamingJS.com/physi.js"></script>`
❷ `<script src="http://gamingJS.com/Scoreboard.js"></script>`
```
<script src="http://gamingJS.com/ChromeFixes.js"></script>
```

❶ We're going to use physics in this game. We use the Physijs library so we don't have to write all the physics code ourselves.

❷ This library will help keep score in the game.

Then, at the top of the code from the 3D starter project template, just below the <script> tag without an src= attribute, make these changes:

```
<script>
  // Physics settings
```
❶ `  Physijs.scripts.ammo = 'http://gamingJS.com/ammo.js';`
❷ `  Physijs.scripts.worker = 'http://gamingJS.com/physijs_worker.js';`
```

  // This is where stuff in our game will happen:
```
❸ `  var scene = new Physijs.Scene({ fixedTimeStep: 2 / 60 });`
❹ `  scene.setGravity(new THREE.Vector3( 0, -100, 0 ));`
```

  // This is what sees the stuff:
  var aspect_ratio = window.innerWidth / window.innerHeight;
  var camera = new THREE.PerspectiveCamera(75, aspect_ratio, 1, 10000);
```
❺ `  camera.position.z = 200;`
❻ `  camera.position.y = 100;`
```
  scene.add(camera);

  // This will draw what the camera sees onto the screen:
```
❼ `  var renderer = new THREE.WebGLRenderer();`
```
  renderer.setSize(window.innerWidth, window.innerHeight);
  document.body.appendChild(renderer.domElement);

  // ******** START CODING ON THE NEXT LINE ********
```

❶ A Physijs setting enables Physijs to decide when things bump into each other.

❷ A worker sits on the side and perform all of the physics calculations.

❸ Instead of a THREE.scene, we need to use a Physijs.scene.

❹ Even with physics, we will not have gravity unless we add it to the scene. In this case, we add gravity in the negative Y direction, which is down.

❺ Move the camera a little closer to the action.

❻ Move the camera up a little bit for a better view of the action.

❼ The WebGLRenderer will work better than the regular CanvasRenderer. If your browser can't do WebGL, have no fear—this chapter should still work for you (though you might not see the ground).

With that, we're ready to start coding our jumping game.

15.3 Outline the Game

Before coding, let's think about how we can organize our code. To have made it this far in the book, you've written a lot of code. At times, it must have gotten difficult to move through the code to see what you've done. You're not the first programmer to run into this problem, and you won't be the last. Thankfully, you can learn from the mistakes of programmers before you.

One of the easiest ways to organize code is to treat it a little bit like writing. When you write an essay, you might start with an outline. After you have the outline, you can fill in the details.

When organizing code, it helps to write the outline first, then add the code below it. Since we're programming, our outlines are also written in code. Type in the following, including the double slashes, below START CODING ON THE NEXT LINE.

```
//var ground = addGround();
//var avatar = addAvatar();
//var scoreboard = addScoreboard();
//animate();
//gameStep();
```

Recall from *Comments*, on page 69, that the double slashes at the beginning of each of those lines introduce a JavaScript comment. This means JavaScript will ignore those lines. This is a good thing since we have not defined those functions yet.

Programmers call this *commenting out* code so that it will not run. There are many reasons programmers do this. Here we're doing it so that JavaScript doesn't get upset when we try to call functions that we haven't defined.

As we define each of these functions, we'll go back to this code outline so that we can remove the double slashes before the function call. When programmers remove the comment symbols, we call it *uncommenting* code.

This approach makes it easier to find code. Simply by looking at the code outline, we know that the addGround() function will be defined before the addAvatar(). The faster we can find code, the faster we can fix it or add things to it. When you write a lot of code, tricks like this can really help keep things straight.

In this game we need ground, an avatar, and a scoreboard. We'll split the action into two parts: animation and game logic. All of that is listed in our code outline. Let's get started writing the code that matches this outline.

Adding Ground for the Game

The first function call in our code outline is to the addGround() function. Just below the code outline (after the commented-out //gameStep() line), define that function as follows:

```
function addGround() {
  document.body.style.backgroundColor = '#87CEEB';
  ground = new Physijs.PlaneMesh(
    new THREE.PlaneGeometry(1e6, 1e6),
    new THREE.MeshBasicMaterial({color: 0x7CFC00})
  );
  ground.rotation.x = -Math.PI/2;
  scene.add(ground);
  return ground;
}
```

The Physijs library "wraps" our 3D objects in code that makes collision detection easier. That is why the ground is a Physijs.PlaneMesh instead of our usual THREE.Mesh.

The collision detection that we did back in Chapter 10, *Project: Collisions*, on page 93, is good for only simple collisions. In this game we need to detect collisions with the ground *and* fruit. Multiple collisions are much harder, so we'll use the Physijs library to make our jobs easier.

Aside from the Physijs.PlaneMesh, everything in this function is familiar. We make a large, green plane, rotate it flat, and add it to the scene.

Once this function is defined, we uncomment the call to addGround() in our code outline. If everything is working, we should see green ground with blue sky in the background.

Build a Simple Avatar

Making the avatar is similar. We use a Physijs Box to wrap a purple cube. We do two other things to our avatar: start it moving and add event listeners for collisions.

```
function addAvatar() {
  avatar = new Physijs.BoxMesh(
    new THREE.CubeGeometry(40, 50, 1),
    new THREE.MeshBasicMaterial({color: 0x800080})
  );
```

```
avatar.position.set(-50, 50, 0);
scene.add(avatar);

avatar.setAngularFactor(new THREE.Vector3( 0, 0, 0 )); // no rotation
avatar.setLinearFactor(new THREE.Vector3( 1, 1, 0 )); // only move on X/Y axes
avatar.setLinearVelocity(new THREE.Vector3(0, 150, 0));
avatar.addEventListener('collision', function(object) {
  if (object.is_fruit) {
    scoreboard.addPoints(10);
    avatar.setLinearVelocity(new THREE.Vector3(0, 50, 0));
    scene.remove(object);
  }
  if (object == ground) {
    game_over = true;
    scoreboard.message("Game Over!");
  }
});
return avatar;
}
```

We're familiar with JavaScript event listeners from Chapter 4, *Project: Moving Avatars*, on page 35, where we used them to listen for keys being pressed on the keyboard. Here we're listening for something different: the purple fruit monster colliding with something.

If the avatar collides with fruit, we add 10 points to the score, give the avatar a little bump up, and remove the fruit from the screen (because the purple fruit monster ate the fruit). If the avatar collides with the ground, then the game is over and the purple fruit monster can eat no more.

There's a lot going on in that function. The most important is the collision event listener. This is where all the action takes place.

Several other new things in that function are worth mentioning. First is a THREE.Vector3(). If you have seen the movie *Despicable Me*, then you know that a vector is an arrow with direction and magnitude (Oh, yeah!). That means a vector includes two pieces of information: the direction in which it points and how strongly it points in that direction. You would use a vector to describe how hard you would need to jump to reach a ledge that is up and to the left.

Vectors are very important in physics, which is why they're used with Physijs things. As the comments suggest, setting the "angular factor" to a vector of all zeros prevents our avatar from rotating. Setting the "linear factor" is a way to prevent motion up, down, left, right, forward, or backward. Since we want our avatar to move only up, down, left, and right (but not into or out of the screen), we set the X and Y components of the vector to 1 (allow motion) and the Z component to 0 (don't allow motion).

Finally, the linear velocity of an object is how fast and in which direction a thing is moving. We start the avatar with a speed of 150 straight up. If the avatar collides with some fruit, we also give the avatar a little bump of 50 straight up.

Uncomment the addAvatar() call in the code outline. We still have not created the animate() function, so nothing is moving just yet. The "avatar" should be resting on the ground. For now, it's just a purple rectangle—we'll make it a little fancier later.

Add Scoring

Next we add the scoreboard:

```
function addScoreboard() {
  var scoreboard = new Scoreboard();
  scoreboard.score(0);
  scoreboard.help('Use arrow keys to move and the space bar to jump');
  return scoreboard;
}
```

This is similar to the scoreboard we used in Chapter 11, *Project: Fruit Hunt*, on page 99, so the code should look familiar. Uncomment the addScoreboard() function in the code outline, and you should see a scoreboard showing zero points.

Animate the Scene

Now we should have a scoreboard with zero points and a lovely purple box sitting on the ground. To make it do something, we move the renderer.renderer(scene, camera) at the bottom of our code into our usual animate() function—this time with a twist.

```
var game_over = false;
function animate() {
  if (game_over) return;

  requestAnimationFrame(animate);
  scene.simulate(); // run physics
  renderer.render(scene, camera);
}
```

New here is a check to see if the game is over. If it is, we return from the function, which stops the animation. Also new in here is the scene.simulate() line. As the comment suggests, that line is needed so that the physics library can move things (make them jump, fall, roll) and check for collisions. Don't forget that line!

Once the animate() function is ready, move back up to the code outline and uncomment the call to animate(). If everything is working, the avatar should jump up into the air and fall down to the ground, and the game should end.

Create Game Elements

So far, we have no fruit for the purple fruit monster to eat. We add this in the gameStep() function. We haven't seen this before, but it's very useful in 3D game programming. The animation and physics are working hard. We don't want to interrupt them every time they're doing something to decide if it's time to start rolling another piece of fruit.

So we use a separate gameStep() function, which runs every three seconds. Type in the following below the animate() function:

```
function gameStep() {
  if (game_over) return;

  launchFruit();
  setTimeout(gameStep, 3*1000);
}
```

The first time gameStep() is called, we launch some fruit at the avatar with the launchFruit() function. After a timeout of 3 seconds, this function calls itself again, which launches another piece of fruit. Telling a function to take a "time-out" until it does something else is the job of setTimeout(). The setTimeout() function is built into JavaScript to wait for some period of time, in milliseconds, before calling the function that it's given. In this case, gameStep() calls itself after 3*1000 milliseconds, or after 3 seconds.

Just like with the animate() function, we return immediately from gameStep() if the game is over.

Of course, none of this will work unless we define the function that launches the fruit:

```
function launchFruit() {
  var fruit = new Physijs.ConvexMesh(
    new THREE.CylinderGeometry(20, 20, 1, 24),
    new THREE.MeshBasicMaterial({color: 0xff0000})
  );

  fruit.is_fruit = true;
  fruit.setAngularFactor(new THREE.Vector3( 0, 0, 1 ));
  fruit.setLinearFactor(new THREE.Vector3( 1, 1, 0 ));
  fruit.position.set(300, 20, 0);
  fruit.rotation.x = Math.PI/2;
  scene.add(fruit);
```

```
  fruit.setLinearVelocity(
    new THREE.Vector3(-150, 0, 0)
  );
}
```

There's nothing new in the launchFruit() function. Its job is to create a physics-ready circle, add it to the scene, and set it rolling. Much more interesting is the gameStep() function, which we'll use again in upcoming chapters.

After completing the gameStep() and launchFruit() functions, uncomment the call to gameStep() in the code outline. If everything is working properly, you should see pieces of red fruit rolling out toward the avatar. Once the avatar hits the ground, the game should be over and the fruit should stop moving.

We have just one thing left to do in the basic game—add controls to our avatar.

Creating Avatar Controls

To control the avatar, we use the keydown event listener that we saw in earlier chapters. Add the following code below the gameStep() and launchFruit() functions:

```
document.addEventListener("keydown", function(event) {
  var code = event.keyCode;

  if (code == 37) left();  // left arrow
  if (code == 39) right(); // right arrow
  if (code == 38) up();    // up arrow
  if (code == 32) up();    // space bar
});

function left()  { move(-50, 0); }
function right() { move(50, 0); }
function up()    { move(avatar.getLinearVelocity().x, 50); }

function move(x, y) {
  avatar.setLinearVelocity(
    new THREE.Vector3(x, y, 0)
  );
}
```

With that, we should be able to move the avatar up, left, and right to eat yummy fruit! (See Figure 8, *Purple Box Monster*, on page 141.)

Congratulations! You just wrote another game from scratch. To be sure, there's still a lot that you might want to do with the game:

- Make the fruit move faster for higher scores

- Add things that the purple fruit monster doesn't like to make the score go down when he eats them

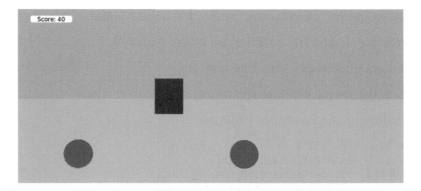

Figure 8—Purple Box Monster

- Stop the game if too much fruit gets past the purple fruit monster

- Reset if the game ends

- Incorporate graphics

Although we can add lots more to make the game even better, the core of the game is done. We can control the avatar. We can tell when the player earns points. We can tell when the game is over. We can show the score. That's a *lot* of stuff.

Adding Simple Graphics

Of course, we have graphics available for the purple fruit monster, so let's add them. First, in the addAvatar() function, make the MeshBasicMaterial invisible and add the purple fruit monster image:

```
function addAvatar() {
  avatar = new Physijs.BoxMesh(
    new THREE.CubeGeometry(40, 50, 1),
❶    new THREE.MeshBasicMaterial({visible: false})
  );
❷  var avatar_material = new THREE.MeshBasicMaterial({
    map: THREE.ImageUtils.loadTexture('/images/purple_fruit_monster.png'),
    transparent: true
  });
❸  var avatar_picture = new THREE.Mesh(
    new THREE.PlaneGeometry(40, 50), avatar_material
  );
❹  avatar.add(avatar_picture);

  // Everything else stays the same in this function, starting with this:
  avatar.position.set(-50, 50, 0);
  scene.add(avatar);
```

❶ Remove the purple color and make this box invisible.

❷ Create a new kind of material: an image material.

❸ Build a simple mesh with this material.

❹ Attach the image mesh to the avatar.

Do the same for the launchFruit() function.

```
function launchFruit() {
  var fruit = new Physijs.ConvexMesh(
    new THREE.CylinderGeometry(20, 20, 1, 24),
    new THREE.MeshBasicMaterial({visible: false})
  );
  var material = new THREE.MeshBasicMaterial({
    map: THREE.ImageUtils.loadTexture('/images/fruit.png'),
    transparent: true
  });
  var picture = new THREE.Mesh(
    new THREE.PlaneGeometry(40, 40), material
  );
  picture.rotation.x = -Math.PI/2;
  fruit.add(picture);
```

❶ Remove the red color and make this cylinder invisible.

❷ Create a new kind of material: an image material.

❸ Build a simple mesh with this material.

❹ Rotate the image mesh to align with the cylinder.

❺ Attach the image mesh to the fruit.

With that, we should have a purple fruit monster on the prowl!

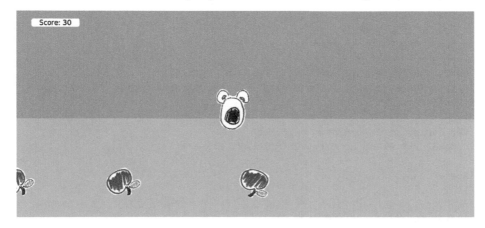

Challenge: Game Reset

Right now, the only way to restart a game is to show the code, press the Update button, and then hide the code again. Try adding a keyboard handler so that when the R key (computer code 82), is pressed, the game resets.

Some things to keep in mind:

- The avatar should go back to the starting position.
- The score should reset.
- The game is no longer over.
- Both animate() and gameStep() need to restart.

Good luck! This may prove quite a challenge—you may even want to give it a try now, and then return after a few more chapters of experience with physics.

15.4 The Code So Far

If you would like to double-check the code in this chapter, turn to Section A1.15, *Code: The Purple Fruit Monster Game*, on page 245.

15.5 What's Next

This was an impressive game to make. In the upcoming chapters we'll practice the physics skills that we developed here. We'll also build on the concept of a gameStep() function, which was fairly simple in this game.

When you're done with this chapter, you will

- *Know how to build a full 3D game*
- *Know how to build complex 3D shapes*
- *Begin to understand how interesting shapes, materials, lights, and physics work together in a game*

CHAPTER 16

Project: Tilt-a-Board

In this chapter we'll build a 3D game in which a ball lands on a game board in space. The object of the game is to use the arrow keys to tilt the board so that the ball falls through a small hole in the center of the board—*without* falling off the edge. It will end up looking something like this:

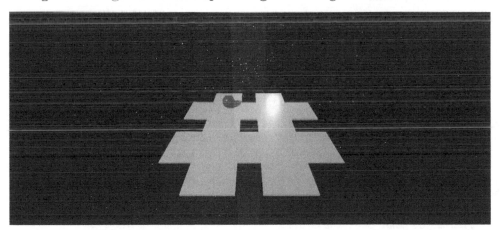

We'll make this game pretty, so we'll be using skills from Chapter 12, *Working with Lights and Materials*, on page 109. We'll need physics to make the ball fall, to make it slide back and forth on the game board, and to detect when it hits the goal, so we'll use some of the skills from Chapter 15, *Project: The Purple Fruit Monster Game*, on page 133. And we'll be adding a lot of shapes and moving them around, so we'll need the skills from the first half of the book, as well.

A word to the wise: there's a ton going on in this game, which means we'll be typing a lot of code. We won't be talking much about the code since a lot of it uses concepts from earlier chapters. If you haven't already worked through those earlier chapters, coding this game may be frustrating!

16.1 Getting Started

Start a new project in ICE. Choose the 3D starter project template and name this project Tilt-a-Board.

This Is a WebGL Game

If your browser can't do WebGL, you'll have to skip this chapter. The easiest way to tell if your computer and browser can do WebGL is to visit http://get.webgl.org/. If you see the spinning cube on that page, then you have WebGL. If not, you'll have to work on other projects.

16.2 Gravity and Other Setup

Just as we did with the Purple Fruit Monster game, we need to do a little work *before* the START CODING ON THE NEXT LINE line. Make the changes noted in the following code.

```
<body></body>
<script src="http://gamingJS.com/Three.js"></script>
① <script src="http://gamingJS.com/physi.js"></script>
<script src="http://gamingJS.com/ChromeFixes.js"></script>
<script>

    // Physics settings
②   Physijs.scripts.ammo = 'http://gamingJS.com/ammo.js';
③   Physijs.scripts.worker = 'http://gamingJS.com/physijs_worker.js';

    // This is where stuff in our game will happen:
④   var scene = new Physijs.Scene({ fixedTimeStep: 2 / 60 });
⑤   scene.setGravity(new THREE.Vector3( 0, -50, 0 ));

    // This is what sees the stuff:
    var aspect_ratio = window.innerWidth / window.innerHeight;
    var camera = new THREE.PerspectiveCamera(75, aspect_ratio, 1, 10000);
⑥   camera.position.set(0, 100, 200);
⑦   camera.rotation.x = -Math.PI/8;
    scene.add(camera);

    // This will draw what the camera sees onto the screen:
⑧   var renderer = new THREE.WebGLRenderer();
⑨   renderer.shadowMapEnabled = true;
    renderer.setSize(window.innerWidth, window.innerHeight);
    document.body.appendChild(renderer.domElement);

    // ******** START CODING ON THE NEXT LINE ********
```

❶ Load the physics library.

❷ Tell the physics library where it can find additional help to detect collisions.

❸ Set up a worker to perform all of the physics calculations.

❹ Create a physics-enabled Physijs.scene.

❺ Enable gravity.

❻ Move the camera up a little to better see the action.

❼ Tilt the camera to better see the action.

❽ Use the WebGL renderer.

❾ Enable shadows in the renderer for added realism.

The only differences between this opening and the one that we used in Chapter 15, *Project: The Purple Fruit Monster Game*, on page 133, are the camera rotation and the ability to cast shadows. Now that we're ready for physics, let's get started with the code that goes after START CODING ON THE NEXT LINE.

16.3 Outline the Game

We'll need the following in our game: a ball, a game board, a goal, lights, and a space background. As usual, we'll also need to animate the game and we'll have a separate function for game logic that doesn't need to happen as often as animation. Type in the following code outline, including the double slashes.

```
//addLights();
//var ball = addBall();
//var board = addBoard();

//addControls();
//addGoal();
//addBackground();
//animate();
//gameStep();
```

Just as we did in Chapter 15, *Project: The Purple Fruit Monster Game*, on page 133, we'll uncomment these function calls as we define the functions.

Add Lights

Before doing anything else, let's add some lights to the scene. Without lights, the rest of the stuff in our game will be hard to see.

Below the commented-out code outline, add the following function definition of addLights().

```
function addLights() {
  scene.add(new THREE.AmbientLight(0x999999));

  var back_light = new THREE.PointLight(0xffffff);
  back_light.position.set(50, 50, -100);
  scene.add(back_light);

  var spot_light = new THREE.SpotLight(0xffffff);
  spot_light.position.set(-250, 250, 250);
  spot_light.castShadow = true;
  scene.add(spot_light);
}
```

We've seen lights from our work in Chapter 12, *Working with Lights and Materials*, on page 109, and in Chapter 13, *Project: Build Your Own Solar System*, on page 117. We're using three kinds of lights here. An ambient light is a light that is everywhere—it won't cast shadows or make things shine, but will bring out colors in things. A point light is like a light bulb—we place it above and behind the center of the scene so that it can shine down on the game platform. A spot light is just what it sounds like—we use it to shine a light from the side and to cast a shadow.

Now that we've added the function definition, uncomment the call to addLights() in the code outline.

Add the Game Ball

Let's get started with the addBall() function by adding the following code below the function definition for addLights().

```
function addBall() {
  var ball = new Physijs.SphereMesh(
    new THREE.SphereGeometry(10, 25, 21),
    new THREE.MeshPhongMaterial({
      color: 0x333333,
      shininess: 100.0,
      ambient: 0xff0000,
      emissive: 0x111111,
      specular: 0xbbbbbb
    })
  );
  ball.castShadow = true;
  scene.add(ball);
  resetBall(ball);
  return ball;
}
```

From our earlier work, we're familiar with wrapping 3D shapes and materials inside a physics-aware mesh. We've also seen the various color settings. In this case, we make our ball a very shiny red (0xff0000 is red). We set its castShadow property to true so that it will have a shadow. Lastly, we add it to the scene. All very standard—except for the resetBall() function that we add now.

```
function resetBall(ball) {
  ball.__dirtyPosition = true;
  ball.position.set(-33, 50, -65);
  ball.setLinearVelocity(0,0,0);
  ball.setAngularVelocity(0,0,0);
}
```

---

dirty Starts with Two Underscores

Be sure to add two underscores before dirtyPosition. It's not _dirtyPosition. The setting is __dirtyPosition. If you use only one underscore, there will be no errors, but the movement controls won't work.

This resetBall() function starts with the very funny ball.__dirtyPosition setting. Programmers have odd senses of humor and the *dirty* position is an example of this. Programmers often use the word "dirty" to mark something that has been changed, usually in a wrong way.

In this case, we're doing something very wrong by changing the ball's position. In real life, things do not just change position. The same is true in a 3D *physics* world. Things cannot just be in a new place all of a sudden. But we need to change the ball's position at the beginning of the game and whenever the game resets.

So _dirtyPosition is our way of telling the game physics, "Look, I know this is wrong, but I know what I'm doing and I need the following position to change right away." And, since we asked so politely, the game physics will answer, "No trouble at all! Just don't forget that setting if you ever need to do it again."

Isn't That Premature Generalization?

Back in *Functions: Use and Use Again*, I said programmers should never write pretty code first. We could have added that position code directly inside addBall(). We didn't for two reasons. First, we already know we'll need to reset the game—just like we talked about with *Project: The Purple Fruit Monster Game*. Second, I didn't want you to have to change a whole bunch of code after you type it.

Still, be cautious when doing something like this.

Now that we've added the addBall() function definition to the game, we can uncomment the addBall() call in the code outline. Our code outline should now look like this:

```
addLights();
var ball = addBall();
//var board = addBoard();

//addControls();
//addGoal();
//addBackground();

//animate();
//gameStep();
```

Add the Game Board

We should now have a ball hovering in midair. Let's add the game board to give the ball something to do. Add the addBoard() function as follows (warning: there is a lot of typing for this one).

```
function addBoard() {
  var material = new THREE.MeshPhongMaterial({
    color: 0x333333,
    shininess: 40,
    ambient: 0xffd700,
    emissive: 0x111111,
    specular: 0xeeeeee
  });

  var beam = new Physijs.BoxMesh(
    new THREE.CubeGeometry(50, 2, 200),
    material,
    0
  );
  beam.position.set(-37, 0, 0);
  beam.receiveShadow = true;

  var beam2 = new Physijs.BoxMesh(
    new THREE.CubeGeometry(50, 2, 200),
    material
  );
  beam2.position.set(75, 0, 0);
  beam2.receiveShadow = true;
  beam.add(beam2);

  var beam3 = new Physijs.BoxMesh(
    new THREE.CubeGeometry(200, 2, 50),
    material
  );
```

```
    beam3.position.set(40, 0, -40);
    beam3.receiveShadow = true;
    beam.add(beam3);

    var beam4 = new Physijs.BoxMesh(
      new THREE.CubeGeometry(200, 2, 50),
      material
    );
    beam4.position.set(40, 0, 40);
    beam4.receiveShadow = true;
    beam.add(beam4);

    beam.rotation.set(0.1, 0, 0);
    scene.add(beam);
    return beam;
}
```

There's a lot of code in there, but you know most of it. We create four beams and combine them all together to make the game board. At the very end, we tilt the board a bit (to get the ball rolling) and add it to the scene. Note that we mark each of the beams as able to have shadows on them.

One thing that's new is the 0 in the first beam:

```
var beam = new Physijs.BoxMesh(
  new THREE.CubeGeometry(50, 2, 200),
  material,
  0
);
```

The 0 tells the physics library that gravity doesn't apply to this object (or anything added to it). Without the zero, our game board would fall right off the screen!

Uncomment the call to addBoard() in the code outline, and you should have the ball hovering over the game board.

Enable Animation

Before we enable the game-board controls, we need to animate the scene. At the very bottom of our code, move the renderer.render() line into an animate() function as follows:

```
function animate() {
  requestAnimationFrame(animate);
  scene.simulate(); // run physics
  renderer.render(scene, camera);
}
```

Uncomment the animate() function (it's before the final gameStep() call) from the code outline. Nothing will change, but now we can add game controls.

Add Game Controls

We have the ball and the board now, so let's add controls for the game board. Add the following function definition of addControls() above the animate() function we just added.

```
function addControls() {
  document.addEventListener("keydown", function(event) {
    var code = event.keyCode;

    if (code == 37) left();
    if (code == 39) right();
    if (code == 38) up();
    if (code == 40) down();
  });
}
```

By now we're very familiar with using JavaScript events to control gameplay. We're also starting to learn the computer numbers for the arrow keys by heart!

Notice that we need to define a few more functions to tilt the game board left, right, up, and down. Add the following five function definitions.

```
function left()  { tilt('z',  0.02); }
function right() { tilt('z', -0.02); }
function up()    { tilt('x', -0.02); }
function down()  { tilt('x',  0.02); }

function tilt(dir, amount) {
  board.__dirtyRotation = true;
  board.rotation[dir] = board.rotation[dir] + amount;
}
```

The left(), right(), up(), and down() functions are pretty easy to understand. They are so short that we can put the entire function definition on one line! What we're doing in the tilt() function called by each of those is a little trickier.

We already know what _dirtyRotation is from our work on _dirtyPosition in *Add the Game Ball* (and we know that it starts with two underscore characters). We're changing the game board's rotation. Even though the board's rotation is changing by only a tiny bit, we need to tell the physics library that we truly want to do this.

What's really sneaky in tilt() is board.rotation[dir]. When the left() function is called, it calls tilt() with the string 'z' as the value for dir. In this case, it's the same as updating board.rotation['z']. This is something new! We've seen stuff like board.rotation.z, but we've never seen square brackets and a string like that.

board.rotation['z'] is the same as board.rotation.z. JavaScript sees both as changing the z property of the rotation. Using this trick, we write just one line that can update all different directions in tilt().

```
board.rotation[dir] = board.rotation[dir] + amount;
```

Without a trick like that, we would probably have to use four different if statements. So we lazy programmers like this trick!

Uncomment the addControls() call in the code outline and give the game board a try. You should be able to tilt it left, right, up, and down.

Add the Goal

We need a goal somewhere under the game board. Even if we can't see it, we know there's a goal. When the ball falls all the way through the hole, then we've hit the goal and won the game.

Below the definition of the addControls() function, type the following.

```
function addGoal() {
  var light = new THREE.Mesh(
    new THREE.CylinderGeometry(20, 20, 1000),
    new THREE.MeshPhongMaterial({
      transparent:true,
      opacity: 0.15,
      shininess: 0,
      ambient: 0xffffff,
      emissive: 0xffffff
    })
  );
  scene.add(light);

  var score = new Physijs.ConvexMesh(
    new THREE.PlaneGeometry(20, 20),
    new THREE.MeshNormalMaterial({wireframe: true})
  );
  score.position.y = -50;
  score.rotation.x = -Math.PI/2;
  scene.add(score);

  score.addEventListener('collision', function() {
    flashGoalLight(light);
    resetBall(ball);
  });
}
```

The first part of this function adds a light to the scene, but not a real light. This is not a light that shines, but rather a fake light that shows where the goal is. You can tell that it's a fake light by the geometry and material—both of which are for regular shapes. To give it the look of a spot light shining on something important, we mark it as transparent and give it a low opacity. In other words, we make it very easy to see through.

After we add the light to the scene, we add the actual goal. This is just a small plane that we add to the scene below the game board. The important thing about this goal is the collision event listener we add. When the ball collides with the goal, we flash our goal light and reset the ball. Resetting the ball is easy, thanks to the resetBall() function.

Wireframing

You might have noticed that we set wireframe to true when we created the goal. A wireframe lets us see the geometry without a material to wrap it. It's a useful tool to explore shapes and to draw planes as we've done here.

Normally you should remove the wireframe property in finished game code (you can remove the enclosing curly braces too). In this game, it probably makes the most sense to change wireframe: true to visible: false so that the goal is invisible to the player.

To flash the light, we need to define the flashGoalLight() function as follows.

```
function flashGoalLight(light, remaining) {
  if (typeof(remaining) == 'undefined') remaining = 9;

  if (light.material.opacity == 0.4) {
    light.material.ambient.setRGB(1,1,1);
    light.material.emissive.setRGB(1,1,1);
    light.material.color.setRGB(1,1,1);
    light.material.opacity = 0.15;
  }
  else {
    light.material.ambient.setRGB(1,0,0);
    light.material.emissive.setRGB(1,0,0);
    light.material.color.setRGB(1,0,0);
    light.material.opacity = 0.4;
  }

  if (remaining > 0) {
    setTimeout(function() {flashGoalLight(light, remaining-1);}, 500);
  }
}
```

The bulk of this function is dedicated to setting the color and opacity (how easy it is to see through) of the goal light. If the opacity used to be 0.4, then we set it to 0.15 (making it easier to see through) and change the spotlight color to white.

Otherwise, we set the color to red and the opacity to 0.4. That's the bulk of the function, but not the most interesting part.

When flashGoalLight() is called, it's called with the goal light that we want to flash and the number of flashes that remain. When we called flashGoalLight() back in the collision event, we didn't tell it how many times remained to be flashed—we called it with no parameters. If a JavaScript function is called without all of its parameters, the parameters are undefined, which we first talked about back in Section 7.2, *Describing a Thing in JavaScript*, on page 67.

In this case, if remaining is undefined, then it is the first time the function has been called, and we set it to 9 more times that we flash the light.

The really interesting thing about this function happens at the end. If the number of flashes remaining is more than zero, we call the function again —from inside itself.

```
if (remaining > 0) {
  setTimeout(function() {flashGoalLight(light, remaining-1);}, 500);
}
```

This is a real-world example of recursion, which we first encountered back in *Functions: Use and Use Again*.

In this case, we call the same flashGoalLight() with the same light parameter, but we subtract one from the number of flashes remaining. So we call it with eight remaining, which then calls it with seven remaining, and so on, all the way down to zero remaining. When there are zero remaining we simply do not call flashGoalLight() again, and the recursion stops.

Also in this last bit of code is setTimeout(). This calls the function *after* waiting a little bit. In this case we're waiting 500 milliseconds, or half a second.

With that, we're done with the goal, so move back on up to the code outline and uncomment the call to addGoal().

Add a Background

Let's add our starry background from Chapter 13, *Project: Build Your Own Solar System*, on page 117, to this game. Below the addGoal() function definition, add the following:

```
function addBackground() {
  document.body.style.backgroundColor = 'black';
  var stars = new THREE.Geometry();
  while (stars.vertices.length < 1000) {
    var lat = Math.PI * Math.random() - Math.PI/2;
    var lon = 2*Math.PI * Math.random();
    stars.vertices.push(new THREE.Vector3(
      1000 * Math.cos(lon) * Math.cos(lat),
      1000 * Math.sin(lon) * Math.cos(lat),
      1000 * Math.sin(lat)
    ));
  }
  var star_stuff = new THREE.ParticleBasicMaterial({size: 5});
  var star_system = new THREE.ParticleSystem(stars, star_stuff);
  scene.add(star_system);
}
```

This is similar to the space background from the planet simulator. Once you have that, uncomment the addBackground() function in the code outline.

Game Logic

As we saw in Chapter 15, *Project: The Purple Fruit Monster Game*, on page 133, it's not a good idea to process game logic as often as we perform animation work. So in this game, we again keep the two separate. Add the following game-logic definition below the addBackground() function body.

```
function gameStep() {
  if (ball.position.y < -100) resetBall(ball);
  setTimeout(gameStep, 1000 / 60);
}
```

First our game logic tells Physijs to simulate physics in our scene. Then we check to see if the ball has fallen off the board.

We're processing game logic sixty times per second. That is, we set the timeout of that function to 1000 milliseconds divided by 60, or 16.67 milliseconds. So gameStep() is processed every 16.67 milliseconds, which may seem very frequent. In computers, though, that is not very frequent. The animation will get updated at least sixteen times, and probably a lot more, during those 1000 milliseconds.

Truth be told, it doesn't *really* matter that we have our game logic separated in this case. Processing physics in this simple game and deciding if the ball's Y position is less than -100 is not too much work for most computers. Still, this is a good habit to develop when writing games.

Now uncomment the gameStep() function from the code outline and...

That's It!

You should have a fully functioning, space-age tilt-a-game working at this point. Use the arrow keys to tilt the board and score.

16.4 The Code So Far

If you would like to double-check the code in this chapter, turn to Section A1.16, *Code: Tilt-a-Board*, on page 249.

16.5 What's Next

That was our best game yet. We combined our skills with writing 3D games with our new skills of making shadows and materials. The tilt-a-board game is really pretty to look at. It certainly took a lot of time to code, but it was worth it.

In the next chapters we'll dig a little more into JavaScript. Specifically, we'll cover *objects*, which we've been using all along but haven't talked about making. Once we have that skill, we'll build a couple more very cool games.

When you're done with this chapter, you will

- *Know what that new keyword we keep using means*
- *Be able to define your own objects*
- *Know how to copy objects*

CHAPTER 17

Project: Learning about JavaScript Objects

We've made some pretty incredible progress so far. We have an avatar that can walk around the screen and bump into obstacles. We built an animated model of the solar system and a simulation of the moon's movements. We also tried out our new skills to create a couple of pretty cool games.

We've made so much progress, in fact, that we've reached the limit of what we can do with JavaScript—at least without introducing something new. To understand why we need to learn about this new concept, consider our avatar. We can make plenty of games where our avatar could play by itself, but what if the player wanted to play with others?

If two players were to be on the screen at the same time, how would we add all those hands, feet, and bodies to the screen and not mix them up? How would we make each one move independently? How would we assign different colors and shapes to each avatar?

Things quickly get out of control if we try to accomplish all these things with what we know so far. So it's time to learn about *object*s and see what we can do with them.

This Is a Challenging Chapter

 There are a lot of new concepts in this chapter. You may find it best to skim through the first time and then come back in more depth later.

17.1 Getting Started

Create a new project in the ICE Code Editor. For this exercise, let's use the 3D starter project template and call it Objects.

We won't be creating visualizations in this chapter. Instead we'll be creating objects in ICE and looking at them in the JavaScript console. So be sure to have the JavaScript console open.

17.2 Simple Objects

Programmers refer to *things* as *objects*. Anything that we can touch or talk about in the real world can be described as an object in the computer world. Consider movies, for instance. I think we can all agree that *Star Wars* is the greatest movie of all time. Right? Well, here we describe *Star Wars* as a JavaScript object:

```
var best_movie = {
  title: 'Star Wars',
  year: 1977
};
```

Even though it's short, there's a lot going on in that example. First of all, we see that JavaScript has another use for curly braces other than just wrapping function definitions and if statements. Curly braces can also wrap JavaScript objects. Additionally, we see that JavaScript objects are just like numbers and strings—they can be assigned to a variable (best_movie in this case).

More importantly, objects let us describe something in different ways. In this case, we can describe a movie with a title, the movie's director, and the year in which the movie was made. The different pieces of information that we might use to describe things are called *attributes*.

The attributes of an object can be anything. In our *Star Wars* example, the attributes are strings and numbers. We could have used Booleans, lists, and even functions.

```
var best_movie = {
  title: 'Star Wars',
  year: 1977,
  stars: ['Mark Hamill', 'Harrison Ford', 'Carrie Fisher'],
  aboutMe: function() {
    console.log(this.title + ', starring: ' + this.stars);
  }
};
best_movie.aboutMe();
// => Star Wars, starring: Mark Hamill,Harrison Ford,Carrie Fisher
```

Calling the aboutMe() function on our best_movie objects will produce the "Star Wars, starring..." message in the JavaScript console. This is what the console.log() call does—it logs whatever we want to the JavaScript console.

When we use functions in objects like this, we call them with a different name, *method*. Methods let us change an object or, as we're doing here, return some other information about the object.

Take a look at the aboutMe() method and how we use the this keyword. The this keyword is how we refer to the current object. If we'd used title instead of this.title, we would have gotten an error message telling us that title was undefined. In this example, title was undefined because the code was looking for a variable named title somewhere else in the program. By using this.title, we are specifying that we want the title property assigned to the current object.

---

console.log() Is Your Friend

 Web programmers use console.log() all the time to double-check that variables have the value we expect them to have. It never shows up in the web page or the game, but programmers can see it—and fix things if they are broken. Just remember to remove console.log() when you're done—it is much easier to use the JavaScript console without a ton of console.log() messages!

17.3 Copying Objects

In real life, you copy a cool idea or thing by copying everything it does and changing a few things here and there to make it even better. The thing you're copying becomes the prototype for the new way of doing it. JavaScript handles copying objects in a similar way.

To describe another movie, we can copy the prototypical best_movie object by using Object.create:

```
var great_movie = Object.create(best_movie);
great_movie.aboutMe();
// => Star Wars, starring: Mark Hamill,Harrison Ford,Carrie Fisher
```

Object.create will create a new object with all the same properties and methods of the prototypical object we created earlier. So the new object, great_movie, has the same title and actors as the original best_movie. It also has the same aboutMe() method.

We don't need to make any changes to the aboutMe() method. We still want it to log the movie title and the list of the stars to the JavaScript console. Even if the title and list of stars changes, the aboutMe() method stays the same—it may log different information, but it will use the same properties to do so.

However, we do want to update the title and other information in our new object. Let's make this new object refer to a movie that's a favorite of all 3D programmers like us: *Toy Story*.

```
great_movie.title = 'Toy Story';
great_movie.year = 1995;
great_movie.stars = ['Tom Hanks', 'Tim Allen'];
great_movie.aboutMe();
// => Toy Story, starring: Tom Hanks,Tim Allen

best_movie.aboutMe();
// => Star Wars, starring: Mark Hamill,Harrison Ford,Carrie Fisher
```

In the first three lines, we change the properties of the current object. Then we tell the aboutMe() method to do its thing, which it does with the new information that we just provided. This little bit of magic happens thanks to the this keyword in aboutMe(). this.title always refers to the title property of the current object.

Note that updating properties on the new great_movie object doesn't affect the best_movie object. best_movie has all of its properties unchanged and its aboutMe() method still displays the original results.

All this talk of prototypes and prototypical objects is not just an excuse to throw fancy words around. In fact, the concept of a prototype is very important in JavaScript, and answers a question you may have had since the very first chapter in this book: what's that new keyword that we keep typing?

17.4 Constructing New Objects

We now have a good idea of what an object is in JavaScript. We also now see how an object can be a prototypical object and act as a template for creating similar objects. Creating new objects like this can be pretty tedious and mistake-prone. Consider this: if we forget to assign the year property on great_movie, then the object will think *Toy Story* was made back in 1977. Unless we tell the object differently, it copies all properties from the original (star_wars) object, including the year, 1977!

We can also use a simple function to build objects in JavaScript—yes, the simple function that we first saw all the way back in Chapter 5, *Functions: Use and Use Again*, on page 49. Surprisingly, we don't have to do anything special to a function to create new objects. Normally, as a style thing, programmers capitalize the name of a function if it creates new objects. For example, a function that will create movie objects might be called Movie.

```
function Movie(title, stars) {
  this.title = title;
  this.stars = stars;
  this.year = (new Date()).getFullYear();
}
```

This is just a normal function using the function keyword, a name Movie, and a list of parameters (such as the movie title and the list of stars in the movie). However, we do something different inside the object builder's function definition than what we would normally do for functions. Instead of performing calculations or changing values, we assign the current object's properties. In this case, we assign the current object's title in this.title, the names of the actors and actresses who starred in the movie, and even the year in the list of properties.

Aside from assigning the this values, there really is nothing special about this function. So how does it create objects? What makes it an object constructor and not a regular function?

The answer is something we saw in the very first chapter of this book: the new keyword. We don't call Movie() the way we would a regular function. It's an object constructor, so we construct new objects with it by placing new before the constructor's name.

```
var kung_fu_movie = new Movie('Kung Fu Panda', ['Jack Black', 'Angelina Jolie']);
```

The Movie() in new Movie is the constructor function we defined. It needs two parameters: the title (*Kung Fu Panda*), and a list of stars (Jack Black and Angelina Jolie).

Then, thanks to the property assignments we made in the constructor function, we can access these properties just like we did with our previous objects.

```
console.log(kung_fu_movie.title);
// => Kung Fu Panda
console.log(kung_fu_movie.stars);
// => ['Jack Black', 'Angelina Jolie']
console.log(kung_fu_movie.year);
// => 2013
```

You might notice that the year of the Kung Fu Panda movie is wrong (it came out in 2008). This is because our constructor only knows to set the year property to the current year. If you are up for a challenge, change the constructor so that it takes a third argument—the year. If the year is set, then use that instead of the current year in the constructor.

Now we know how the creators of our 3D JavaScript library write all of their code, so we can write things like this:

```
var shape = new THREE.SphereGeometry(100);
var cover = new THREE.MeshNormalMaterial();
var ball = new THREE.Mesh(shape, cover);
```

SphereGeometry, MeshNormalMaterial, and Mesh are all constructor functions in the Three.js library.

One mystery is solved, but one remains: if we're using function constructors to build objects, how can we make methods for those objects? The answer to that is why we emphasized the word "prototype" in the previous section. To create an aboutMe() method for the objects created with our Movie() constructor, we define the method on the constructor's prototype. That is, for a prototypical movie, we want the aboutMe() method to look like the following.

```
Movie.prototype.aboutMe = function() {
  console.log(this.title + ', starring: ' + this.stars);
};
```

With that method in place, we can ask the kung_fu_movie the answer to aboutMe().

```
kung_fu_movie.aboutMe();
// => Kung Fu Panda, starring: Jack Black,Angelina Jolie
```

JavaScript objects can have any number of methods, like aboutMe(), but it's good to keep the number of methods small. If you find yourself writing more than twelve or so methods, then it may be time for a second object with a new constructor.

17.5 The Code So Far

If you would like to double-check the code in this chapter, go to Section A1.17, *Code: Learning about JavaScript Objects*, on page 253.

17.6 What's Next

Object-oriented programming is a tough thing to wrap your brain around. If you understood everything in this chapter, then you're doing better than I did when I learned these concepts. If not everything made sense, don't worry. Examples we'll play with in the next few games should help clarify things.

After you've written a game or two with objects, it might help to reread this chapter. As the games you invent on your own get more and more sophisticated, you'll want to rely on objects to help organize your code.

When you're done with this chapter, you will

- *Know how to move things with a mouse*
- *Have another full-featured game to share*

CHAPTER 18

Project: Cave Puzzle

In this chapter we'll build an action-based puzzle game. In the game, the avatar can only move left or right, but to win, the avatar needs to reach the top of the screen. The person playing the game can move and rotate ramps to help the avatar reach the top of the screen and win. To make it even more challenging, the game board includes some objects that can't be moved.

A sketch of the game might look something like this:

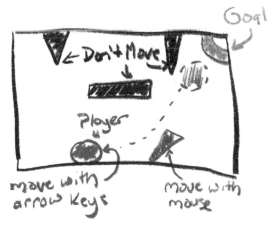

We'll be putting all our newly acquired object-oriented programming skills to good use in this chapter, so refer back to Chapter 17, *Project: Learning about JavaScript Objects*, on page 159, as needed.

18.1 Getting Started

We begin by creating a new project in the ICE Code Editor. Let's use the 3D starter project (with Physics) template (you need to change the template this time) and call it Cave Puzzle.

As you might guess, this template includes much of the physics-engine work we manually added back in Chapter 15, *Project: The Purple Fruit Monster Game*, on page 133.

We still need to make a couple of changes before the START CODING line. First, we need to include two more JavaScript libraries—one for keeping score and one for working with the mouse. Start a new line after line 4, just before the plain <script> tag, and add the following two <script> tags:

```
<script src="http://gamingJS.com/Scoreboard.js"></script>
<script src="http://gamingJS.com/Mouse.js"></script>
```

It's important that the Mouse.js <script> tag go after the physi.js <script> tag so that it can add mouse functionality to physics-ready objects.

The other thing we need to do is pick a better background color to set the game's mood. We don't want it to be completely dark, but something a little grayer and darker will make the screen feel more like the inside of a cave. So, just above the START CODING line, set the background color to the following:

```
document.body.style.backgroundColor = '#9999aa';
```

Computers Like Hexadecimal Numbers

I think we can all agree that 99 is a number. But how can aa be a number? Because computers like binary numbers (1s and 0s), they like to work with numbers in *hexadecimal*. Instead of counting to nine and then using two digits (1 and 0) to make ten, computers like to count all the way to fifteen before adding another digit. Since humans only have ten single-digit numbers (0, 1, 2, 3, 4, 5, 6, 7, 8, and 9), we use letters for hexadecimal numbers, starting with a.

The digits 0 through 9 in the *regular* number system and hexadecimal are the same. The regular number 10 is a in hexadecimal, number 11 is b in hexadecimal, and so on until we reach 15, which is f in hexadecimal. The next number, 16, is 10 in hexadecimal.

Computer colors are often two-digit hexadecimal numbers—especially on web pages. Two-digit hexadecimal numbers are given a special name in computers: one byte. With two digits of hexadecimal numbers, we can count from zero (00) to 255 (ff).

So the hexadecimal 99 tells a computer to turn on a color about 60 percent of its full brightness. The hexadecimal aa is a little brighter—around 66 percent of its full brightness. ff would turn the color up to its full brightness and 00 would turn it off completely.

The first two numbers are the amount of red we want to use, the second two numbers are the amount of green, and the last two are the amount of blue. For the cave, we're using equal amounts of red and green (99), but we'll add a little more blue by setting it to aa.

The last thing we do above the START CODING line is switch to the orthographic camera we used back in *A Quick Peek at a Weirdly Named Camera*, on page 89. This is more of a two-dimensional game, so the orthographic camera will work better for our purposes.

WebGL Only

 Make the following changes only if your computer supports WebGL as described in Section 12.3, *Realism: Shininess*, on page 111. Even if your computer does support WebGL, it's OK to skip these settings to make it easier to share this game with others.

Comment out the perspective camera and uncomment the three lines for the orthographic camera:

```
//var camera = new THREE.PerspectiveCamera(75, aspect_ratio, 1, 10000);
var camera = new THREE.OrthographicCamera(
  -width/2, width/2, height/2, -height/2, 1, 10000
),
```

And, since the orthographic camera only works in WebGL, we need to switch the renderer:

```
// This will draw what the camera sees onto the screen:
var renderer = new THREE.WebGLRenderer();
```

With that, we're ready to start coding.

18.2 Setting the Game's Boundaries

All of the action in this game will take place on the screen. So we need something to keep the avatar *in* the screen. We need boundaries—four of them. Since we need to add four of the same things, we'll do so with a make-Border() function. This function will use x and y positions to decide where to place the border. It will also define a width and height to build the correct shape. Let's add the following code to our project below the START CODING line:

```
function makeBorder(x, y, w, h) {
  var border = new Physijs.BoxMesh(
    new THREE.CubeGeometry(w, h, 100),
    Physijs.createMaterial(
      new THREE.MeshBasicMaterial({color: 0x000000}), 0.2, 1.0
    ),
```

```
    0
  );
  border.position.set(x, y, 0);
  return border;
}
```

This makes the same kinds of physics-ready meshes that we used in Chapter 15, *Project: The Purple Fruit Monster Game*, on page 133. Note that the depth of the rectangular boxes is always 100. This will ensure that the avatar cannot accidentally fall in front of or behind the borders.

The makeBorder() function builds meshes. We still need to add these meshes to the scene. Add the left, right, top, and bottom borders with the following four lines (you don't have to include all of the spaces if you don't like them):

```
scene.add(makeBorder(width/-2, 0,         50,     height));
scene.add(makeBorder(width/2,  0,         50,     height));
scene.add(makeBorder(0,        height/2,  width,  50));
scene.add(makeBorder(0,        height/-2, width,  50));
```

Adjust the Border for Perspective Cameras

If you're using the perspective camera, then the borders won't quite reach the edge of the screen. To position them correctly, we have to make the borders slightly bigger and move them a little further out.

To make the borders bigger, multiply the width and height by 1.2:

```
new THREE.CubeGeometry(1.2*w, 1.2*h, 100),
```

To move the border a little further out, multiply the x and y position by 1.2 as well:

```
border.position.set(1.2*x, 1.2*y, 0);
```

With that, we have four borders to keep our avatar on the screen. Now let's add the avatar.

Start with a Simple Avatar

We'll keep the avatar simple in this game. Feel free to use some of the techniques from Chapter 15, *Project: The Purple Fruit Monster Game*, on page 133, or Chapter 12, *Working with Lights and Materials*, on page 109, after we're done, but it's best to start simple and add complexity later. We've done most of this before, so let's go through the next code quickly.

Make the avatar's mesh a flat cylinder with a red cover:

```
var avatar = new Physijs.ConvexMesh(

  new THREE.CylinderGeometry(30, 30, 5, 16),
  Physijs.createMaterial(

    new THREE.MeshBasicMaterial({color:0xbb0000}), 0.2, 0.5
  )
);
```

Since this is a physics simulation, we make the material slippery with the 0.2 number (1.0 would be very hard to move) and somewhat bouncy with the 0.5 number (1.0 would be very bouncy).

Next we add the avatar to the scene:

```
avatar.rotation.set(Math.PI/2, 0, 0);
avatar.position.set(0.5 * width/-2, -height/2 + 25 + 30, 0);
scene.add(avatar);

avatar.setAngularFactor(new THREE.Vector3( 0, 0, 0 )); // don't rotate
avatar.setLinearFactor(new THREE.Vector3( 1, 1, 0 )); // only move on X and Y axis
```

We rotate the avatar 90 degrees (Math.PI/2) so that it's standing up rather than lying flat. We position it a bit to the left and just above the bottom boundary (25 is half the boundary's width and 30 is the size of the avatar). As in *Project: The Purple Fruit Monster Game*, we set the angular factor so that the avatar won't fall flat, and we set the linear factor so that it moves only up and down (not in and out of the screen).

Next let's decide what to do if the avatar collides with something. In most cases we won't care. It doesn't matter if the avatar bumps into a wall or ramp. It only matters if the object is a goal:

```
avatar.addEventListener('collision', function(object) {
  if (object.isGoal) gameOver();
});
```

We'll worry about the isGoal property when we add the goal a little later.

Next we need to handle interaction with the keyboard:

```
document.addEventListener("keydown", function(event) {
  var code = event.keyCode;
  if (code == 37) move(-50); // left arrow
  if (code == 39) move(50);  // right arrow
});
```

There's nothing new there. We still need to tell the avatar to increase its speed by 50 whenever the left-right arrow keys are pressed:

```
function move(x) {
  var v_y = avatar.getLinearVelocity().y,
      v_x = avatar.getLinearVelocity().x;

  if (Math.abs(v_x + x) > 200) return;
  avatar.setLinearVelocity(
    new THREE.Vector3(v_x + x, v_y, 0)
  );
}
```

This move() function is pretty intelligent. First it determines how fast the avatar is already moving. We need to know how fast the avatar is moving left or right so that we can increase or decrease the speed (depending on which arrow key is pressed). We also need to know how fast the avatar is moving up or down so that we *do not change it*. It wouldn't make sense for a falling avatar to all of a sudden stop falling.

We also do something a little sneaky in here. We set it up so that the avatar can never go faster than 200. The Math.abs() function strips negatives from numbers (maybe you've seen absolute value in your math class—that's what abs stands for here). In other words Math.abs(-200) equals 200—just like Math.abs(200). This lets us say, "if the avatar's speed is -200 (moving left) or 200 (moving right), then do not change the speed at all." The player needs to win the game with a speed no faster than 200.

That's it for the avatar. Now let's add the goal.

18.3 Building a Random, Unreachable Goal

Let's make the goal a green donut. Don't forget to wrap the normal 3D mesh inside the physics mesh for easy collisions.

```
var goal = new Physijs.ConvexMesh(
  new THREE.TorusGeometry(100, 25, 20, 30),
  Physijs.createMaterial(
    new THREE.MeshBasicMaterial({color:0x00bb00})
  ),
  0
);
goal.isGoal = true;
```

The very last line is how we tell the avatar that this is the goal. We created the avatar's collision detection so that it checked for this isGoal property. Nothing else in our game has this property set, which lets us be certain that the avatar really has reached the goal.

Next we do something a little different: we place the goal at one of three random locations. In JavaScript, a random number comes from Math.random(). It's a number between 0 and 1. So, if the random number is less than 0.33, we place the goal in the top-left corner (width/-2, height/2). If the random number is greater than 0.66, we place the goal in the top-right corner (width/2, height/2). Otherwise we place the goal in the middle of the cave ceiling (0, height/2).

```
function placeGoal() {
  var x = 0,
      rand = Math.random();
  if (rand < 0.33) x = width / -2;
  if (rand > 0.66) x = width / 2;
  goal.position.set(x, height/2, 0);
  scene.add(goal);
}
placeGoal();
```

We make this a function so that we can call it again and again. When we add multiple levels to the game in the next chapter, we'll need to call placeGoal() whenever the player completes a level. The same goes if we add a game-reset capability.

If you update the code several times, you should see the goal move to different places at the top of the screen. Of course, none of this matters yet—there's no way for the avatar to get to the top of the screen!

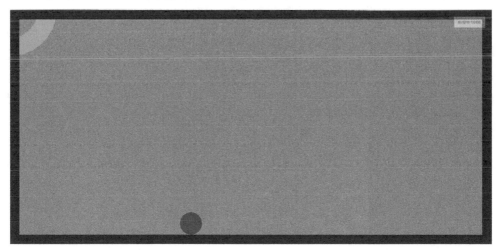

Let's add a way.

18.4 Building Draggable Ramps

It is a long way up to the top of the screen. game players are going to need at least two ramps to reach the top. To build two ramps that behave the same way but are separate, we'll need to construct some JavaScript objects as we did in Chapter 17, *Project: Learning about JavaScript Objects*, on page 159.

We start by defining our ramp constructor. Since it constructs objects, we capitalize the name of the constructor function as Ramp. In the constructor, we define one property, the ramp mesh, and call three methods:

```
function Ramp(x, y) {
  this.mesh = new Physijs.ConvexMesh(
    new THREE.CylinderGeometry(5, height * 0.05, height * 0.25),
    Physijs.createMaterial(
      new THREE.MeshBasicMaterial({color:0x0000cc}), 0.2, 1.0
    ),
    0
  );

  this.move(x, y);
  this.rotate(2*Math.PI*Math.random());
  this.listenForEvents();
}
```

We know meshes by now, so there's not much to say about this one. As in *Project: The Purple Fruit Monster Game*, we make this one a Physijs mesh so that the avatar can speed up the ramp.

The three methods we call at the end of the constructor help us to initialize a new ramp. The this.move() method moves the ramp by the amount specified in the constructor. If we make a new ramp with new Ramp(100, 100), then this.move(x, y) would move the ramp to X=100, Y=100. Next, we rotate the ramp by a random amount. Last, we tell our ramp object that it needs to listen for events. Let's look at each of those methods in turn.

The move() method expects two number parameters that tell it by how much the ramp needs to be moved:

```
Ramp.prototype.move = function(x, y) {
  this.mesh.position.x = this.mesh.position.x + x;
  this.mesh.position.y = this.mesh.position.y + y;
  this.mesh.__dirtyRotation = true;
  this.mesh.__dirtyPosition = true;
};
```

When we move a ramp, we're defying physics—one moment the ramp can be in the middle of the screen with no rotation and the next it can be at X=100, Y=100 and rotated randomly. Any time we do this, we have to tell the physics engine that we're doing something non-physics, which is why we set __dirtyPosition and __dirtyRotation. Don't forget that, as in *Add the Game Ball*, on page 148, there are two underscores before both of those "dirty" variables.

The rotate() method is very similar:

```
Ramp.prototype.rotate = function(angle) {
  this.mesh.rotation.z = this.mesh.rotation.z + angle;
  this.mesh.__dirtyRotation = true;
  this.mesh.__dirtyPosition = true;
};
```

Next is the listenForEvents() method, which is where all of the action really takes place:

```
Ramp.prototype.listenForEvents = function() {
  var me = this,
      mesh = this.mesh;
  mesh.addEventListener('drag', function(event) {
    me.move(event.x_diff, event.y_diff);
  });

  document.addEventListener('keydown', function(event) {
    if (!mesh.isActive) return;
    if (event.keyCode != 83) return; // S
    me.rotate(0.1);
  });
};
```

We start this method by assigning a new me variable to this and a new mesh variable to this.mesh. We do this mostly because JavaScript can do strange things to this—especially when dealing with events. JavaScript has very good reasons for messing with this, but we're not going to worry about them in this book.

First we listen for *drag* events, which occur when the game player clicks and drags something. In this case, the ramp is dragged by the amounts event.x_diff and event.y_diff, and we tell the ramp to move itself with the move() method that we already made.

Next, if the game player clicks a ramp (making it active) *and* presses the S key, then we rotate the ramp by a little bit.

Both the drag event and the isActive property come from the Mouse.js library that we added in Section 18.1, *Getting Started*, on page 165. Without that library, neither of those will work.

That's it! We now have a way to construct as many ramps as we like. Each ramp that we construct will have its own mesh and will move by itself. To see this in action, let's create two ramps and add their meshes to the scene:

```
var ramp1 = new Ramp(-width/4, height/4);
scene.add(ramp1.mesh);
var ramp2 = new Ramp(width/4, -height/4);
scene.add(ramp2.mesh);
```

If you click and drag the ramps with your mouse, you'll see that you can move them all over the game area. If you click and press the S key, you can make them spin. It's even possible to win the game:

We have a game with some fairly sophisticated elements. The one thing lacking is the end. So let's finish the chapter by creating the gameOver() function.

18.5 Winning the Game

At the beginning of this chapter we added two <script> tags. We've made good use of the Mouse.js library to enable our ramps to move and rotate. We haven't done anything with the Scoreboard.js library. We use that here to put a time limit on the game and to set the Game Over message.

Let's add a scoreboard that includes a timer, a countdown from 40, some help text, and something to do when the game is over:

```
var scoreboard = new Scoreboard();
scoreboard.timer();
scoreboard.countdown(40);
scoreboard.help(
  "Get the green ring. " +
  "Click and drag blue ramps. " +
  "Click blue ramps and press S to spin. " +
  "Left and right arrows to move player. " +
  "Be quick!"
);
scoreboard.onTimeExpired(function() {
  scoreboard.setMessage("Game Over!");
  gameOver();
});
```

We're doing just about everything there is to do with Scoreboard.js here. Most of these are simple directions for how the scoreboard should look: it should show the timer, the countdown timer, and some help text.

The last thing we do with the scoreboard is use a function to describe what happens when time expires—set the scoreboard message to Game Over! and call the gameOver() function.

We've already called this gameOver() function—we called it when the avatar collided with the goal. So we know that gameOver() needs to account for the case in which there's still some time remaining. That is, if the avatar reaches the goal before time runs out, the player has won the game. In this case, we set the scoreboard message to Win!:

```
var pause = false;
function gameOver() {
  if (scoreboard.getTimeRemaining() > 0) scoreboard.setMessage('Win!');
  scoreboard.stopCountdown();
  scoreboard.stopTimer();
  pause = true;
}
```

We also tell the scoreboard to stop its timers. Finally, we set a pause variable. We'll use pause to tell the animation and physics functions to stop running. In both functions, if paused == true, then we return before they have a chance to call themselves again. Update the animate() function with the line that checks pause:

```
function animate() {
  if (pause) return;
  requestAnimationFrame(animate);
  renderer.render(scene, camera);
}
animate();
```

And do the same for the gameStep() function:

```
function gameStep() {
  if (pause) return;
  scene.simulate();
  // Update physics 60 times a second so that motion is smooth
  setTimeout(gameStep, 1000/60);
}
gameStep();
```

If you have everything working correctly, and if you're very, very good, you should now be able to win the game. You might even be able to beat my high score!

18.6 The Code So Far

In case you would like to double-check the code in this chapter, it's included in Section A1.18, *Code: Cave Puzzle*, on page 255.

18.7 What's Next

That was quite a lot of coding, but it was worth it, don't you think? We got our first taste of real object-oriented programming. *And* we were rewarded with a pretty cool game for our efforts.

There's still more we can do with this game. In the next chapter we'll change this into a multilevel affair. And in each of the levels, the game is going to get even harder!

When you're done with this chapter, you will

- *Have a strategy for building multilevel games*
- *Understand how to reset countdown timers*
- *See an example of coding progressively harder games*

CHAPTER 19

Project: Multilevel Game

Once you get the hang of playing the cave-puzzle game we coded in Chapter 18, *Project: Cave Puzzle*, on page 165, it's pretty easy to win. As a game player, it quickly grows boring and you want to move on to more exciting things. As game designers, it's our job to build games that make players want to keep playing. Games should start off easy and keep getting harder (but never impossible—it's not fun to play impossible games). With that in mind, let's revisit the sketch of our game from the last chapter.

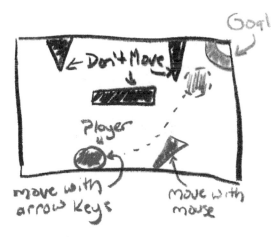

We never got around to adding those immovable obstacles last time, did we? Let's do that now—but only after the player has reached the goal for the first time.

19.1 Getting Started

Before starting this game, you need to work through the game in the previous chapter. If you've already finished the entire program, let's make a copy of it by clicking the three-line menu button and selecting Make a Copy from the menu:

We make a copy because we have a good, working game that took us a while to write. We can always delete it later if this game turns out great, but it never hurts to make a copy.

Never Throw Away Working Code

If you have working code, *always* make sure you have a copy somewhere. You might think your next changes are small and couldn't possibly break things. It is supereasy to break things badly when programming, though. When that happens, a backup is like gold. You can refer to your backup or delete your new code and start again.

After clicking Make a Copy, you'll get the usual save dialog. Name this game Multi-Level Cave Puzzle and click Save.

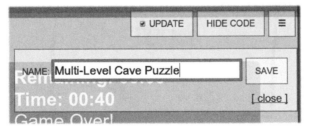

We're now ready to code—all of the physics and camera work were already done in the last chapter.

19.2 Building Levels

There are lots of ways for programmers to move players between levels. One way is to remove everything from the screen—even the scene itself—before rebuilding a new scene from scratch on the next level. For this to work, the game has to store information like the number of points the player currently has, items the player may have picked up, and levels already completed. This approach works well on consoles like the Wii or Xbox.

Another way to handle moving between levels is to remove and create specific game elements—like platforms and obstacles—while the rest of the scene stays the same. As games get more complicated, this becomes a very hard way to do it. But in this game we only have a few obstacles, so this approach will work just fine.

Let's build a Levels object to hold this information. This is a slightly different reason to use objects than we saw in the previous chapter. There we used a Ramp object to help us easily create multiple ramps. This time we build a Levels object because it will be easier to think of it as a single *thing*.

Add the Levels code below the scoreboard code, but before the animate() function. Create the Levels function constructor as follows so that it sets four properties:

```
function Levels(scoreboard, scene) {
  this.scoreboard = scoreboard;
  this.scene = scene;
  this.levels = [];
  this.current_level = 0;
}
```

The Levels object will need to know about each of these things to do what it needs to do. It needs access to the scoreboard to reset the counter between levels. It needs access to the scene to draw and remove obstacles. It needs to have a list of things on the different levels. Finally, it needs to know what the current level is.

Objects Should Work on Only Their Own Properties

We don't *really* need to pass the scoreboard and scene objects into our constructor. Since all of our code is in the same place, it's possible for our Levels object to do something directly to the scoreboard variable.

 Never do that.

There are two reasons. First, if we split all of this code into separate JavaScript libraries, then scoreboard and scene won't always be defined in the library. Second, your code will be *cleaner*. Object-oriented programming is not easy. Use whatever rules you can to keep it from getting messy. This is a good rule.

With the constructor out of the way, let's define the methods for the Levels object. First, we need a way to add a new level:

```
Levels.prototype.addLevel = function(things_on_this_level) {
  this.levels.push(things_on_this_level);
};
```

This method will take a list of things that belong to a new level. That list will include everything that needs to be shown when the player reaches the level. It's also everything that needs to be removed when the player completes the level. We push this onto the list of all levels. If push seems like a strange name to you, you're not alone. Sometimes we programmers have to remember strange names.

Next we need a quick way to get the objects defined for the current level:

```
Levels.prototype.thingsOnCurrentLevel = function() {
  return this.levels[this.current_level];
};
```

Remember that computers like counting from zero. If the current level is zero, then this method will return this.levels[0], which is another way of looking up the first item in a list.

Next, we need to be able to draw the current level on the scene:

```
Levels.prototype.draw = function() {
  var scene = this.scene;
  this.thingsOnCurrentLevel().forEach(function(thing) {
    scene.add(thing);
  });
};
```

We use the thingsOnCurrentLevel() method that we just created to get a list of the things we need to draw. Then we say that, for each of those, we want to run a function that adds the thing to the scene.

Functions Can Do the Unexpected to this

JavaScript functions can do strange things to this, which is why we make a copy of the scene variable. In *Project: Learning about Java-Script Objects*, we saw that this normally refers to the current object. That is true, except inside functions. Inside a function, like the one we use to add things to the scene, this refers to the function itself. To deal with this JavaScript quirk, programmers normally make a copy of this (or one of its properties) before a function call.

If we have a way to draw objects, then we need a way to erase them:

```
Levels.prototype.erase = function() {
  var scene = this.scene;
  this.thingsOnCurrentLevel().forEach(function(obstacle) {
    scene.remove(obstacle);
  });
};
```

Now comes the interesting work that Levels does. It needs to be able to *level up* when the player clears a level. As long as there are more levels, leveling up should erase the current level, increase the current level number, then draw the next level. Last, we need to tell the countdown timer to reset, but with a bit less time.

```
Levels.prototype.levelUp = function() {
  if (!this.hasMoreLevels()) return;
  this.erase();
  this.current_level++;
  this.draw();
  this.scoreboard.resetCountdown(50 - this.current_level * 5);
};
```

That's a nice little method that does exactly what we want it to do. It is tricky to write code that reads like simple instructions (and sometimes it's not possible). But code like that this is something to strive for.

We're not quite done with the Levels object. The first thing the levelUp() method does is ask if it has more levels. We need to add that method as follows:

```
Levels.prototype.hasMoreLevels = function() {
  var last_level = this.levels.length-1;
  return this.current_level < last_level;
};
```

If there are two levels in the game, then hasMoreLevels() should be true when we're on the first level and false when we're on the second level. Since JavaScript likes to start counting from zero, this.current_level will be zero on the first level and one on the second level. In other words, the last level in a two-level game would be when this.current_level is one.

Counting from Zero Can Be Difficult

Doing math when you start counting at zero instead of one can be confusing. It usually helps to plug in real numbers—especially numbers just before and after the end of a list.

That does it for defining our Levels object. Before we try using it, add the following buildObstacle() method:

```
function buildObstacle(shape_name, x, y) {
  var shape;
  if (shape_name == 'platform') {
    shape = new THREE.CubeGeometry(height/2, height/10, 10);
  } else {
    shape = new THREE.CylinderGeometry(50, 2, height);
```

```
  }
  var material = Physijs.createMaterial(
    new THREE.MeshBasicMaterial({color:0x333333}), 0.2, 1.0
  );

  var obstacle = new Physijs.ConvexMesh(shape, material, 0);
  obstacle.position.set(x, y, 0);
  return obstacle;
}
```

This builds two different kinds of obstacles—platforms and stalactites.[1]

Now we're ready to build levels. Create a new Levels object and add the first
two levels:

```
var levels = new Levels(scoreboard, scene);
levels.addLevel([]);
levels.addLevel([
  buildObstacle('platform', 0, 0.5 * height/2 * Math.random())
]);
```

The first level has nothing in it and the second has a platform from the
buildObstacle() function.

The last thing we need to do is call that levelUp() method when the player
reaches a goal on the current level. To do that, find the code that adds the
collision event listener to the avatar. It should look something like this:

```
avatar.addEventListener('collision', function(object) {
  if (object.isGoal) gameOver();
});
```

Delete this code.

Now back down below our levels code, add the following:

```
avatar.addEventListener('collision', function(object) {
  if (!object.isGoal) return;
  if (!levels.hasMoreLevels()) return gameOver();
  moveGoal();
  levels.levelUp();
});
```

This changes the collision code slightly. We still do nothing if the avatar collides with something that's not a goal (like the walls, ramps, and obstacles).
We also add a check to see if there are any more levels. If there are no more

---

1. Stalactites are on the ceiling. Stalagmites are on the ground. Stalactites hang on tight
   to the ceiling. Stalagmites start on the ground and might reach the ceiling.

levels, then we return the results of the gameOver() function. If levels remain, then we move the goal and level up.

The following will move the goal (after a 2-second delay):

```
function moveGoal() {
  scene.remove(goal);
  setTimeout(placeGoal, 2*1000);
}
```

That should do it. Now if you reach the goal on the first level, you should be greeted not with a Win! message on the scoreboard, but with a new level that has a single obstacle in the way. If you're very skilled, you can win after the second level:

19.3 Adding Finishing Touches to the Game

This is already a pretty cool game, but we've positioned ourselves nicely for adding touches that can make it more unique and fun. The most obvious thing to do is add new levels. You can try the following (and possibly add a few of your own) after the first level and before the avatar.addEventListener():

```
levels.addLevel([
  buildObstacle('platform', 0, 0.5 * height/2 * Math.random()),
  buildObstacle('platform', 0, -0.5 * height/2 * Math.random())
]);
levels.addLevel([
  buildObstacle('platform', 0, 0.5 * height/2 * Math.random()),
  buildObstacle('platform', 0, -0.5 * height/2 * Math.random()),
  buildObstacle('stalactite', -0.33 * width, height/2),
  buildObstacle('stalactite', 0.33 * width, height/2)
]);
```

We can also add some of the sounds from Chapter 11, *Project: Fruit Hunt*, on page 99. We can make the avatar click when it hits something that is not the goal, and play the guitar when we reach the goal. Add the following just below your avatar.addEventListener() and before moveGoal():

```
avatar.addEventListener('collision', function(object) {
  if (object.isGoal) Sounds.guitar.play();
  else Sounds.click.play();
});
```

Don't forget to add the Sounds.js library at the top if you want sound:

```
<script src="http://gamingJS.com/Sounds.js"></script>
```

There are all sorts of things that *you* can do to make this game as special as possible for players. Get creative!

19.4 The Code So Far

If you would like to double-check the code in this chapter, compare yours with the code in Section A1.19, *Code: Multilevel Game*, on page 259.

19.5 What's Next

Most of the action in this game took place in two dimensions. To be sure, we used some impressive programming skills (and even a little 3D programming) to make this game. Still, let's get back to 3D programming in our next game. We'll use all of our skills in the next chapter, so let's go!

When you're done with this chapter, you will

- *Have made a full 3D game*
- *Be able to add scoring to games*
- *Understand how to warp shapes into something new*

CHAPTER 20

Project: River Rafting

For our final project, let's build a river-rafting game in which the player needs to navigate the raft along a river, dodging obstacles and picking up bonus points where possible. The game will look something like this sketch:

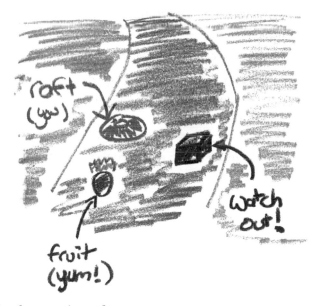

We'll also add a few goodies of our own.

20.1 Getting Started

We start by creating a new project in the ICE Code Editor. We use the 3D starter project (with Physics) template and call it River Rafting.

We'll want a scoreboard for the game, so let's insert a new line after line 4, just before the plain <script> tag, and add the following:

```
<script src="http://gamingJS.com/Scoreboard.js"></script>
```

After the <script> tag, let's change the gravity from -100 to -20:

```
scene.setGravity(new THREE.Vector3( 0, -20, 0 ));
```

You can experiment with this number after you complete the project, but this will give it a more realistic feel than the -100 with which it starts.

Let's change the camera position as well. While we build the game, it will help to have a bird's-eye view. We need to remove the line that sets the camera's position—but don't remove the next line that adds the camera to the scene! Replace it with the following two lines:

```
camera.position.set(250, 250, 250);
camera.lookAt(new THREE.Vector3(0, 0, 0));
```

This moves the camera to the right, up, and forward by 250. After moving the camera, we need to tell it to look at the center of the screen, which is what the second line does.

Lastly, this is a WebGL game, so we have to change the CanvasRenderer to a WebGLRenderer:

```
var renderer = new THREE.WebGLRenderer();
```

That is all we need to do above the START CODING line for now. Let's move down into the rest of the code and start making stuff!

20.2 Organizing Code

A code outline for our rafting game might look something like this:

```
// DON'T TYPE THIS !!!!
addSunlight();
addScoreboard();
addRiver();
addRaft();
```

Do not type that in just yet—our game is going to wind up looking a little different. But you get the idea.

We'll use a code outline like we did in Chapter 15, *Project: The Purple Fruit Monster Game*, on page 133, and Chapter 16, *Project: Tilt-a-Board*, on page 145, but we'll work a little differently. Instead of writing the outline first, we'll build the code outline at the same time that we build the functions themselves.

There is no right or wrong way to start a project—just choose what works best for you. Once you've built this project, you'll have tried several different approaches in this book, and you can choose which you like best for your next project.

Adding Sunlight

Our raft is going to be making jumps and bumping into things. This will be more fun if there are shadows. For shadows, we need light. Let's start our code outline just below the START CODING line with an addSunlight() call:

```
addSunlight(scene);
```

Adding sunlight to a game is something of an art. Now that you're a programmer, I'll let you in on a secret: when programmers say that something is more art than science, we really mean we're just guessing. In other words, we try some numbers and play with them until we think they look right. The following should end up looking right for us (but feel free to play with the numbers yourself!):

```
function addSunlight(scene) {
  var sunlight = new THREE.DirectionalLight();
  sunlight.intensity = 0.5;
  sunlight.castShadow = true;
  sunlight.position.set(250, 250, 250);
  sunlight.shadowCameraNear = 250;
  sunlight.shadowCameraFar = 600;
  sunlight.shadowCameraLeft = -200;
  sunlight.shadowCameraRight = 200;
  sunlight.shadowCameraTop = 200;
  sunlight.shadowCameraBottom = -200;
  sunlight.shadowMapWidth = 4096;
  sunlight.shadowMapHeight = 4096;

  scene.add(sunlight);
}
```

That looks like a lot of code for what might seem like simple light. Most of it has to do with the art of 3D programming. In fact, only the first two lines are *really* needed. They tell the light to be not too bright (intensity = 0.5) and to cast shadows (castShadows = true).

So what are the rest of the lines for? Well, the remaining numbers help make nice-looking shadows without forcing the computer to work too hard. You can skip to the next section if you don't need the details.

Adding a directional light to a scene is like adding the sun to the sky. The position that we give a directional light in a scene describes the location of the sun in the sky. Here it's 250 to the right, 250 to the front, and 250 above the center of the scene. So, when this directional light shines down, shadows will be to the left, toward the back, and fall on the ground.

We could have used 1 for each of the numbers and the effect would be the same. The sun would still be shining down from the same direction in the sky (to the right, the front, and up). We used 250 not so that the "sun" will be far away, but rather because moving the position of the light far away moves the light's *shadow box*.

In addition to describing the location of the directional light in the sky, the position of a directional light provides a starting point for the shadow box. It would be too much work for a computer to try to draw shadows everywhere in a scene. The shadow box is the area within a scene where shadows are drawn. The box starts from the directional light's position.

The remaining properties in the addSunlight() function describe the shadow box for this game. The shadowCameraNear property specifies how far away from the light we want shadows to appear. In this case, we don't need shadows until the light is 200 away from the camera. By setting shadowCameraFar to 600, we're telling the camera that it can stop drawing shadows after a distance of 600. The thickness of the box is then 400, which helps the computer do less work making shadows so that it can spend more time on more-important tasks.

The shadowCameraLeft, shadowCameraRight, shadowCameraTop, and shadowCameraBottom properties describe how wide and long the shadow box should be. All of these were chosen by experimentation. Feel free to come back to play with them yourself after you've finished coding the game.

The last two numbers, shadowMapWidth and shadowMapHeight, describe how much detail we want in the shadows. Larger numbers mean more details (and more work for the computer, so don't make them too big). The normal value of 512, which would have been used if we didn't set these properties at all, is too low for our purposes. The shadows would have been too hard to see. The values of 4096 were found through art, or just random experimentation.

With light added to our river-rafting game, let's add another important thing: the scoreboard to track our scores.

Keeping Score

We'll use a similar scoreboard to those in *Project: The Purple Fruit Monster Game* and *Project: Cave Puzzle*. We start by adding a second line to the code outline:

```
addSunlight(scene);
var scoreboard = addScoreboard();
```

Then add the following function definition below the addSunlight() function:

```
function addScoreboard() {
  var scoreboard = new Scoreboard();
  scoreboard.score(0);
  scoreboard.timer();
  scoreboard.help(
    'left / right arrow keys to turn. ' +
    'space bar to move forward.'
  );

  return scoreboard;
}
```

We've seen this Scoreboard code before. We construct a new scoreboard object with a timer, include some help text, and start the score at zero.

We should keep our code outline in mind as we do this. We now have an outline with addSunlight() followed by addScoreboard(). Below the code outline, we added the addSunlight() function, followed by the addScoreboard() function. We'll keep adding to the outline and the function definitions like this so things stay easy to find.

With these two functions out of the way, we're ready to jump into some seriously cool 3D-programming coding next.

20.3 Warping Shapes to Make Unique Things

So far in this book we've managed to build interesting games by combining basic shapes. Often that's enough to make unique and challenging games. But sometimes we need to push 3D programming just a bit further to build truly interesting shapes and landscapes. We'll do that for the river in this game.

We'll build our river out of just two pieces: land and water. Our land will be a flat plane. Our water will also be a flat plane that lies just a little bit beneath land. To make the river, we'll pull pieces of land below the water. This is a very powerful technique in 3D animation made even more powerful thanks to the laws of physics. Let's get started.

Add the addRiver() function to the bottom of our code outline so that the outline now looks like this:

```
addSunlight(scene);
var scoreboard = addScoreboard();
var river = addRiver(scene);
```

Inside the addRiver() function (that we're coding below the addScoreboard() function), we'll add another code outline. This code outline will describe how to build the river:

```
function addRiver(scene) {
  var ground = makeGround(500);
  addWater(ground, 500);
  addLid(ground, 500);
  scene.add(ground);

  return ground;
}
```

Our code is now calling three functions that don't exist because we haven't written them yet. This will generate errors in the JavaScript console and, even more important, break our code in such a way that nothing shows up on the ICE Code Editor screen. To prevent this, add the following *skeleton* functions:

```
function makeGround(size) {
}
function addWater(ground, size) {
}
function addLid(ground, size) {
}
```

These functions won't do anything when they're called, but since they're defined there are no more errors and our code will run again.

Each of these functions will add flat planes to our game world. The only complicated one will be the ground since we need to pull parts of it down to expose the river water. The *lid* drawn with the last function will be an invisible barrier over the ground so that our raft won't jump out of the river.

Let's get started with the makeGround() function:

```
function makeGround(size) {
  var faces = 100;
  var shape = new THREE.PlaneGeometry(size, size, faces, faces);
  var cover = Physijs.createMaterial(
    new THREE.MeshPhongMaterial({
      emissive: new THREE.Color(0x339933), // a little green
      specular: new THREE.Color(0x333333)  // dark gray / not shiny
    }),
    1,   // high friction (hard to move across)
    0.1 // not very bouncy
  );
  var ground = new Physijs.HeightfieldMesh(
    shape, cover, 0
  );
  ground.rotation.set(-Math.PI/2, 0.2, Math.PI/2);
  ground.receiveShadow = true;
  ground.castShadow = true;
  return ground;
}
```

This will produce a flat, green plane. (As always, you don't need to type in the comments that are in the code, though later they may help you figure out what's going on.)

```
function makeGround(size) {
  var faces = 100;
  var shape = new THREE.PlaneGeometry(size, size, faces, faces);

  var cover = Physijs.createMaterial(
    new THREE.MeshPhongMaterial({
      emissive: new THREE.Color(0x339933), // a little green
      specular: new THREE.Color(0x333333)  // dark grey / not shiny
    }),
    1,  // high friction (hard to move across)
    0.1 // not very bouncy
  );

  var ground = new Physijs.HeightfieldMesh(
    shape, cover, 0
  );
  ground.rotation.set(-Math.PI/2, 0.2, Math.PI/2);
  ground.receiveShadow = true;
  ground.castShadow = true;

  return ground;
}
```

At first glance, this looks a lot like the meshes that we've been building since Chapter 1, *Project: Creating Simple Shapes*, on page 1. After looking a little closer, however, you'll notice some differences.

First off, we built a flat plane with 100 *faces* (squares). We want a lot of faces so that pulling down a corner of one of the faces doesn't pull down the entire plane—just a tiny part of it. Most of the other code in the function is stuff we've seen already—creating a physical material with Physijs.createMaterial() and telling the mesh that it can both cast and receive shadows.

New in this code block is something called a *height field mesh*. This lets the physics engine work with shapes that are *warped* (we'll get to that in a second). Also different in here is that we have to rotate this mesh in three directions. Actually, the two 90° (Math.PI/2) turns are not very surprising—they make the ground lay flat instead of standing up. The slight turn by 0.2 is a clever trick to make it seem like the river is pushing the raft. Just like a ball will roll down a hill, so will our raft. The game players don't need to know that it's a hill making our raft move—they can believe that it's the river.

Of course, we still don't have a river, let alone a raft to float down it. Let's fix that now. We need to add two lines to makeGround() to *dig* the river. The first line calls a function to do the actual digging, and the other adds to the ground mesh the list of points in the river. We now add the following line just below the line that makes the ground shape:

```
var river_points = digRiver(shape, faces + 1);
```

Then we add the following points after the ground's shadow properties:

```
ground.river_points = river_points;
```

The entire makeGround() function should now look like this:

```
function makeGround(size) {
  var faces = 100;
  var shape = new THREE.PlaneGeometry(size, size, faces, faces);
  var river_points = digRiver(shape, faces + 1);

  var cover = Physijs.createMaterial(
    new THREE.MeshPhongMaterial({
      emissive: new THREE.Color(0x339933), // a little green
      specular: new THREE.Color(0x333333)  // dark gray / not shiny
    }),
    1,  // high friction (hard to move across)
    0.1 // not very bouncy
  );

  var ground = new Physijs.HeightfieldMesh(
    shape, cover, 0
  );
  ground.rotation.set(-Math.PI/2, 0.2, -Math.PI/2);
  ground.receiveShadow = true;
  ground.castShadow = true;
  ground.river_points = river_points;

  return ground;
}
```

Can you see what the problem is? That's right—this will break our code because we haven't defined the digRiver() function. We'll do that next.

Pulling Corners

We dig our river by typing in the following code after the makeGround() function:

```
function digRiver(shape, size) {
  var center_points = [];
  for (var row=0; row<size; row++) {
    var center = Math.sin(4*Math.PI*row/size);
    center = center * 0.1 * size;
    center = Math.floor(center + size/2);
    center = row*size + center;

    for (var distance=0; distance<12; distance++) {
      shape.vertices[center + distance].z = -5 * (12 - distance);
      shape.vertices[center - distance].z = -5 * (12 - distance);
    }

    center_points.push(shape.vertices[center]);
```

```
    }
    shape.computeFaceNormals();
    shape.computeVertexNormals();
    return center_points;
}
```

The main purpose of this function is to find the center of the river so that it, and surrounding points, can be *pulled down*. We pull down a shape's vertices by setting the z property to a negative number.

In the preceding function we worked through the entire plane, one row at a time. The first for loop sets the row variable to zero, then figures out where the center of the river should be for that row. From Chapter 6, *Project: Moving Hands and Feet*, on page 59, we already know that Math.sin() makes a nice winding path, so we use it again here.

The four lines that compute and then recompute the center determine how many curves there should be, how far the bends are from the center, where this point is in the current row, and where that point falls in the entire list of vertices. You should experiment with 4 in the first center line and 0.1 in the second line. If you've already taken trigonometry in school, you know these numbers represent the *frequency* and *amplitude* of the *sine wave*. Mostly, it's just fun to play with them.

We dig a trench in each row and then combine them to form the river. We start from the center point for each and work our way out to ten vertices on either side (plus and minus the distance). Last, we store the center vertex in case we want to use it later as a way to put stuff on the river.

Once all of the rows have had some portion of them dug out, we have to recompute *normals*. 3D renderers work hard to keep track of the direction in which faces and their corners are pointing. This direction is called a normal and it helps with lighting, shading, and shadows. We don't have to worry much about how normals work, but we do need to tell the renderer that we've changed them by telling the shape to computeFaceNormals() and computeVertexNormals().

With that, we have a trench for the river to flow through (see Figure 9, *The River Trench*, on page 194).

Next we add the actual river.

Tricking the Eye

Adding the river water and the lid to keep the raft inside the river is pretty easy for us. We need two planes—one for the water, which will be blue, and

```
function digRiver(shape, size) {
  var center_points = [];
  for (var row=0; row<size; row++) {
    var center = Math.sin(4*Math.PI*row/size);
    center = center * 0.1 * size;
    center = Math.floor(center + size/2);
    center = row*size + center;

    for (var distance=0; distance<10; distance++) {
      shape.vertices[center + distance].z = -5 * (10 - distance);
      shape.vertices[center - distance].z = -5 * (10 - distance);
    }

    center_points.push(shape.vertices[center]);
  }
  shape.computeFaceNormals();
  shape.computeVertexNormals();
  return center_points;
}

function addWater(ground, size) {
```

Figure 9—The River Trench

one for the lid, which will be invisible. We already have empty addWater() and addLid() functions that just need to be defined. We add the following lines to draw the water:

```
function addWater(ground, size) {
  var water = new Physijs.ConvexMesh(
    new THREE.CubeGeometry(1.4*size, 1.4*size, 10),
    Physijs.createMaterial(
      new THREE.MeshBasicMaterial({color: 0x0000bb}),
      0,   // No friction (slippery as ice)
      0.01 // Not very bouncy at all
    ),
    0 // Never move
  );
  water.position.z = -20;
  water.receiveShadow = true;
  ground.add(water);
}
```

We're familiar with everything in there, though a couple of things are worth mentioning. We use a cube rather than a plane to make it hard to accidentally fall through the water. Physics engines are cool, but they are not perfect. Giving the water a little thickness makes it less likely that kind of mistake will happen.

The water is 1.4 times bigger than the ground so that the raft won't fall off the world when it reaches the finish line. The last thing to note is that we're changing the Z position instead of the usual Y to move up and down. We do this because the ground was rotated when we added it to the scene.

With that, we have a cool-looking river winding its way through the land:

```
function addWater(ground, size) {
  var water = new Physijs.ConvexMesh(
    new THREE.CubeGeometry(1.4*size, 1.4*size, 10),
    Physijs.createMaterial(
      new THREE.MeshBasicMaterial({color: 0x0000bb}),
      0,   // No friction (slipery as ice)
      0.01 // Not very bouncy at all
    ),
    0 // Never move
  );
  water.position.z = -20;
  water.receiveShadow = true;
  ground.add(water);
}

function addLid(ground, size) {
  var lid = new Physijs.ConvexMesh(
    new THREE.CubeGeometry(size, size, 10),
    new THREE.MeshBasicMaterial({visible:false})
  );
  lid.position.z = 6;
  ground.add(lid);
}
```

Finally, we define the lid function as the following:

```
function addLid(ground, size) {
  var lid = new Physijs.ConvexMesh(
    new THREE.CubeGeometry(size, size, 1),
    new THREE.MeshBasicMaterial({visible:false})
  );
  ground.add(lid);
}
```

This invisible lid is an easy addition to keep our raft from jumping the river banks. Speaking of the raft, we'll add that next.

20.4 Build a Raft for Racing

A donut shape will work very nicely as a river raft. Add the addRaft() call to the code outline at the top:

```
addSunlight(scene);
var scoreboard = addScoreboard();
var river = addRiver(scene);
var raft = addRaft(scene);
```

Now, after the last of the river code, which should be addLid(), we start addRaft() like this:

```
function addRaft(scene) {
  var mesh = new Physijs.ConvexMesh(
    new THREE.TorusGeometry(2, 0.5, 8, 20),
    Physijs.createMaterial(
      new THREE.MeshPhongMaterial({
        emissive: 0xcc2222,
        specular: 0xeeeeee
```

```
    }),
    0.1,
    0.01
  )
);
mesh.rotation.x = -Math.PI/2;
mesh.castShadow = true;

scene.add(mesh);
mesh.setAngularFactor(new THREE.Vector3(0, 0, 0));

var rudder = new THREE.Mesh(
  new THREE.SphereGeometry(0.5),
  new THREE.MeshBasicMaterial({color: 0x000099})
);
rudder.position.set(3, 0, 0);
mesh.add(rudder);

  return mesh;
}
```

We know this code by now. We build the raft using two shapes: a torus and a sphere. The sphere is a tiny dot that we add to the front of the raft so we know which direction the raft is pointing.

The raft has been added to the scene at this point, but is not at the start of the river. We'll change that in the next part of our code.

Resetting the Game

So far in our code outline, we have three variables that hold the scoreboard, the river, and the raft. All three have already been added to the scene, so there's not much left to do with them—except make each one ready for the beginning of the game.

Starting a game is not always exactly the same as resetting a game, but in this case it is. So let's add another function, startGame(), to the code outline:

```
addSunlight(scene);
var scoreboard = addScoreboard();
var river = addRiver(scene);
var raft = addRaft(scene);
startGame(raft, river, scoreboard);
```

Below addRaft(), let's add the following:

```
function startGame(raft, river, scoreboard) {
  var start = river.river_points[100];
  raft.__dirtyPosition = true;
```

```
    raft.position.set(start.y, start.z + 100, 0);
    raft.setLinearVelocity(new THREE.Vector3());
    scoreboard.resetTimer();
    scoreboard.score(0);
    updateCamera();
    camera.lookAt(new THREE.Vector3(start.y, 0, 0));
}
```

Don't forget that _dirtyPosition starts with two underscore characters!

The code in this function has to work for both starting the game and restarting the game. The setLinearVelocity() call sets the speed of the raft to zero every time it's called. Without that, a player restarting the game midway through a race would restart at the starting line already at full speed.

Aside from placing the raft at the starting line and resetting the scoreboard, this code repositions the camera by first moving it, then telling it to look at the starting line. updateCamera() moves the camera; it's a new function that we need to add to our code just below the startGame() function:

```
function updateCamera() {
  camera.position.set(
    raft.position.x + 75,
    raft.position.y + 40,
    raft.position.z
  );
}
```

We make updateCamera() a separate function so that animate() can call it every time the scene gets updated. We add a call to updateCamera() just above the line with renderer.render() in animate(), as shown here:

```
function animate() {
  requestAnimationFrame(animate);

  updateCamera();
  renderer.render(scene, camera);
}
animate();
```

This ensures the camera will be in front of the raft every time the scene is rendered.

At this point you should have a raft moving down the river, with the camera watching it the whole way. Of course, this is pretty useless without controls.

The following keyboard listener and two functions give the game some basic controls. Add them at the very bottom of your code (before the final </script> tag).

```
document.addEventListener("keydown", function(event) {
  var code = event.keyCode;
  if (code == 32) pushRaft();      // space
  if (code == 37) rotateRaft(-1); // left
  if (code == 39) rotateRaft(1);  // right
  if (code == 82) startGame(raft, river, scoreboard); // R
});

function pushRaft() {
  var angle = raft.rotation.z;

  raft.applyCentralForce(
    new THREE.Vector3(
      500 * Math.cos(angle),
      0,
      -500 * Math.sin(angle)
    )
  );
}

function rotateRaft(direction) {
  raft.__dirtyRotation = true;
  raft.rotation.z = raft.rotation.z + direction * Math.PI/10;
}
```

We've seen keyboard listeners a lot by this point, so document.addEventListener() should already be familiar. The pushRaft() function uses a new method for physics objects: applyCentralForce(). This is just a fancy way of saying "push a thing from the middle and not the edge." Lastly, the rotation, including _dirtyRotation, should be familiar—we last saw it in Chapter 18, *Project: Cave Puzzle*, on page 165.

With that, we have the basic pieces of a pretty cool game! The left and right arrow keys will turn the raft and the `space bar` will push the raft forward in the direction it's facing.

We can do a *lot* more with this game. We'll add simple scoring and an obstacle or two in the river.

20.5 Setting the Finish Line

Eventually the raft reaches the finish line. And then it keeps right on going. And going. Instead, let's pause the game so that players can take a moment to admire their score before trying again. We need to make changes in four places: in our code outline and in startGame(), animate(), and gameStep().

Let's start with the code outline. Before the call to the startGame() function, we need to add a line for the paused variable:

```
var paused;
startGame(raft, river, scoreboard);
```

Other functions will use that variable to decide if they need to animate or update the game. JavaScript is pretty uptight about when variables are declared. The rule of thumb is that variables need to be declared before they're used. The paused variable will be used when startGame(), animate(), and gameStep() are called, so we declare it before any of them are called.

We set paused for the first time in the startGame() function. Whenever the game is started, which is what startGame() does, the game shouldn't be paused. So we set paused to false at the bottom of startGame():

```
function startGame(raft, river, scoreboard) {
  var start = river.river_points[100];
  raft.__dirtyPosition = true;
  raft.position.set(start.y, start.z + 100, 0);
  raft.setLinearVelocity(new THREE.Vector3());

  scoreboard.resetTimer();
  scoreboard.score(0);
  scoreboard.message('');

  updateCamera();
  camera.lookAt(new THREE.Vector3(start.y, 0, 0));
  paused = false;
}
```

Next we tell the animate() function that it doesn't have to render the scene when the game is paused. That is, if paused is set to true, then we exit the animate() function before updating the camera or rendering the scene:

```
function animate() {
  requestAnimationFrame(animate);
  if (paused) return;

  updateCamera();
  renderer.render(scene, camera);
}
```

We check for paused *after* calling requestAnimationFrame() so the animation function will continue to work—even though it's not doing anything. This way when the game is reset and paused is set to true, the animation is still running and the computer can update the camera without any extra work.

We do something similar in the gameStep() function. If the game is paused, then we exit immediately from the function without completing any of the usual steps:

```
function gameStep() {
  // Update physics 60 times a second so that motion is smooth
  setTimeout(gameStep, 1000/60);

  if (paused) return;
  checkForGameOver();
  scene.simulate();
}
```

Note that we've changed the order of the function calls in gameStep() to work with pausing. The scene.simulate() and checkForGameOver() calls both come after the if (paused) statement—there's no sense in simulating physics or checking if the game is over when the game is paused.

The checkForGameOver() function is new. It can go right after the gameStep() function and should look like this:

```
function checkForGameOver() {
  if (raft.position.x < 250) return;
  paused = true;
  scoreboard.stopTimer();
  scoreboard.message("You made it!");
}
```

If the raft's X position has not reached the finish line, or when X is 250, then this function does nothing—it returns immediately and nothing else happens. If the raft has reached the finish line, then we set paused to true so that all the other functions can stop working. We also stop the scoreboard timer and add a message to display.

The game should pause at the end of the river and display the time it took the player to complete the race, and a message of "You made it!" You might even be able to make it pretty fast:

Scoring Points by Distance

In some games, a player receives points simply for making it further away from the starting point. Keeping score is something that belongs in the gameStep() method because it's game logic, rather than animation, which would belong in the animate() function.

If you want to increase the score as the raft makes its way along the river, we can add a call to the updateScore() function in gameStep():

```
function gameStep() {
  // Update physics 60 times a second so that motion is smooth
  setTimeout(gameStep, 1000/60);

  if (paused) return;

  updateScore();
  checkForGameOver();
  scene.simulate();
}
```

Due to the way we have the river scene rotated, the raft's X position changes as it moves down the river. To increase the score as the raft reaches the next 25 units of distance, we can use the following (the code goes below the gameStep() function):

```
var next_x;
function updateScore() {
  if (!next_x) next_x = raft.position.x + 25;
  if (raft.position.x > next_x) {
    scoreboard.addPoints(10);
    next_x = next_x + 25;
  }
}
```

Each time the raft reaches the next X scoring point, this function adds ten points to the score and recalculates the next X scoring area to be 25 units further away.

Another distance-based scoring feature we can add is a time bonus for finishing the rafting course within a certain amount of time. We do this by adding the last three lines shown here to the checkForGameOver() function:

```
function checkForGameOver() {
  if (raft.position.x < 250) return;

  paused = true;
  scoreboard.stopTimer();
  scoreboard.message("You made it!");
  if (scoreboard.getTime() < 30) scoreboard.addPoints(100);
  if (scoreboard.getTime() < 25) scoreboard.addPoints(200);
  if (scoreboard.getTime() < 20) scoreboard.addPoints(500);
}
```

If the player finishes in less than 30 seconds, an additional 100 points are awarded. If the player finishes in less than 25 seconds, then both the 100 points and 200 more are awarded. If the player finishes in less than 20 seconds, then the 100 and the 200 points are awarded, along with an additional 500 points, for a possible total of 800 extra points to be won. Can you do it?

Power-Up Points

Many games reward a player for capturing bonus items. If we want to do that in our raft game, we have to do two things: add those items to the river and add to the player's score when the raft bumps into those objects.

We'll want to add items to the game whenever it gets reset, so much of our work needs to take place in and after the startGame() function. But first, we need to declare a variable to hold the list of items in the game. Add it before the paused variable and the first call to startGame() in the code outline:

```
var game_items = [];
var paused;
startGame(raft, river, scoreboard);
```

Then, in the definition of startGame(), add a call to resetItems():

```
function startGame(raft, river, scoreboard) {
  var start = river.river_points[100];
  raft.__dirtyPosition = true;
  raft.position.set(start.y, start.z + 100, 0);
  raft.setLinearVelocity(new THREE.Vector3());
  scoreboard.resetTimer();
  scoreboard.score(0);
  scoreboard.clearMessage();
  updateCamera();
  camera.lookAt(new THREE.Vector3(start.y, 0, 0));
  resetItems(river, scoreboard);
  paused = false;
}
```

Since the call to resetItems() comes after the camera changes, the definition of the resetItems() function should come after camera functions like updateCamera(). The definition of this function is simple enough. It calls two other functions—one to remove all existing items from the screen and the other to add new items to the screen:

```
function resetItems(ground, scoreboard) {
  removeItems();
  addItems(ground, scoreboard);
}
```

Removing items from the game is a simple matter of removing each one from the scene. Once each item has been removed from the scene, we can set the list of game items to an empty list:

```
function removeItems() {
  game_items.forEach(function(item) {
    scene.remove(item);
  });
  game_items = [];
}
```

Adding items to the river is where things start to get interesting. The ground still has the river_points property. We'll use that list of points to randomly place *power-up fruit* at a couple of places along the river. Randomly placing the fruit will make each new game a different challenge for players.

Only we don't want to be quite random about it. If it were completely random, we might end up with two pieces of fruit in the same place or one right at the start.

Recall that there are 100 faces in the ground and 100 points in the ground that we are using to describe the middle of the river. Lets randomly place a power-up fruit around river point 20 and another around point 70. The following will do what we need:

```
function addItems(ground, scoreboard) {
  var points = ground.river_points;

  var random20 = Math.floor(20 + 10*Math.random()),
      fruit20 = addFruitPowerUp(points[random20], ground, scoreboard);
  game_items.push(fruit20);

  var random70 = Math.floor(70 + 10*Math.random()),
      fruit70 = addFruitPowerUp(points[random70], ground, scoreboard);
  game_items.push(fruit70);
}
```

The main purpose of this code block is to call the addFruitPowerUp() function that we'll build shortly. The fruit20 and fruit70 items are then pushed onto the list of all game items (so that they can later be removed as needed).

The random20 and random70 numbers might look a little complicated at first, but if you look closely, they ought to make some sense. Let's look at just random20 to better understand. The Math.random() function generates a number between 0 and 1.

- If Math.random() is 0, then 10*Math.random() is 0, making 20 + 10*Math.random() end up as 20.

- If Math.random() is 0.5, then 10*Math.random() is 5, making 20 + 10*Math.random() end up as 25.

- If Math.random() is 1, then 10*Math.random() is 10, making 20 + 10*Math.random() end up as 30.

In other words, since Math.random() is guaranteed to be between 0 and 1, we're guaranteed of getting a number between 20 and 30.

The random numbers are wrapped in a Math.floor() function call. Math.floor() removes everything after the decimal point. If Math.random() returns 0.01, then 10*Math.random() would wind up as 0.1. Math.floor() removes the decimal point and everything after it, leaving us with 0.

The random number fetches a point from the river_points property to send to addFruitPowerUp(). That function mostly does stuff that we've seen before—it builds a physical mesh, assigns a collision event listener, and adds the yellow fruit to the scene:

```
function addFruitPowerUp(location, ground, scoreboard) {
  var mesh = new Physijs.ConvexMesh(
    new THREE.SphereGeometry(10, 25),
    new THREE.MeshPhongMaterial({emissive: 0xbbcc00}),
    0
  );
  mesh.receiveShadow = true;
  mesh.castShadow = true;

  mesh.addEventListener('collision', function() {
    var list_index = game_items.indexOf(mesh);
    game_items.splice(list_index, 1);
    scene.remove(mesh);
    scoreboard.addPoints(200);
    scoreboard.message('Yum!');
    setTimeout(function() {scoreboard.clearMessage();}, 2.5* 1000);
  });

  ground.updateMatrixWorld();
  var p = new THREE.Vector3(location.x, location.y, -20);
  ground.localToWorld(p);
  mesh.position.copy(p);
  scene.add(mesh);
  return mesh;
}
```

The first thing we do in the collision-handling function is remove the fruit from the list of game items. JavaScript doesn't make this easy—we get the *index* (the location in the list) of the item to be removed, then remove it by *splicing* from that index to the one following it. There is a famous JavaScript book named *JavaScript: The Good Parts*—removing things from lists is *definitely* not in that book (which you should read).

Also new to us is converting from local coordinates to world coordinates with the localToWorld() method. For most of this book we have found it very useful to work in a frame of reference—it's an invaluable trick for 3D programmers. Every now and then we have to put things back in the regular scene coordinates. This is one of those times. The localToWorld() method gives us the scene coordinates for the random river points so that when the fruit is added to the scene, it looks as though it was added to the river.

Before a localToWorld() call, it's a good idea to call updateMatrixWorld() on the thing whose world coordinates we need. A matrix is a mathematical way to describe position, direction, and other values in 3D. The updateMatrixWorld() call ensures that these values are all up-to-date and accurate.

With that, we have two pieces of fruit that can help you score points like crazy while playing the game. You might even be able to beat my high score:

20.6 The Code So Far

If you would like to double-check the code in this chapter, turn to Section A1.20, *Code: River Rafting*, on page 265.

20.7 What's Next

That was a lot of code. But it was worth it. We put many of our skills to use with physics, lights, and materials. We also saw glimpses of what else is possible in 3D programming by pulling vertices of shapes and converting local coordinates to "world" coordinates.

Like our other games, do not consider this one final. There's still plenty that you can add. Maybe you can incorporate obstacles that take away points? Add some jumps? Make this a multilevel game as we did in Chapter 19, *Project: Multilevel Game*, on page 177? Make the course longer? You might try adding camera controls so you can see from the viewpoint of a raft passenger instead of viewing everything from above. Or maybe you already have ideas for how to improve this game that I can't even begin to think of.

In our final chapter we'll switch gears to putting our projects out on the Web.

When you're done with this chapter, you will

- *Have a better idea of the parts that make up a website*
- *Understand what we need to build our own websites*
- *Know how to put a project on a site like Tumblr*

CHAPTER 21

Getting Code on the Web

Since we're programming a web language, it's worth a quick look at how the Web works. We're not going into too much detail here—just enough for us to understand why we do some of the things that we do in this book.

An Abstraction Is Worth a Thousand Words

You may have heard the phrase "a picture is worth a thousand words." Programmers like you and me do a lot of work in our brains. When we're thinking about a problem or trying to come up with a cool new way of doing something, we use mental pictures of the problem. These pictures in our brains are called *abstractions*.

Abstractions don't always have a ton of detail. They usually have just enough to help us understand the problem. An abstraction for a cloud might be that it's made up of a whole bunch of cotton balls. That's enough of a mental picture to understand the shape and appearance of a cloud, and sometimes that is all we need.

But abstractions don't always suffice. If we try to understand why a cloud produces rain, the idea that clouds are made of cotton balls won't help at all.

Keep this in mind as we talk about the Web. We're using abstractions, and they will help most of the time. But sometimes they will be wet cotton balls.

21.1 The Mighty, Mighty Browser

Behold the mighty browser:

A web browser is an extraordinarily complex piece of technology that we use every day. Amazingly, it's also pretty dumb about some things.

When we tell a browser that we want a website or a page on a website, it sends a request through the Internet to a publicly available machine:

As you can see, when you ask your browser to show a site, your browser makes a request through the Internet. This request asks one particular *web server* for information that it has. That information might be an HTML web page, it might be an image, it might be a movie, and it might be JavaScript.

To reach the right server, our browser has to look up the public Internet address of the web server. Google's Internet address for www.google.com is 173.194.73.147. The numbers in the address are enough for the Internet to get the browser's request to the web server.

Web Servers Must Be Publicly Available on the Internet

Remember that the machine holding a website must be publicly available on the Internet. The machines that you use at home are almost never publicly available. Even if someone else on the Internet knows your machine's network address, they would still not be able to reach it because it's not publicly available.

Unfortunately, this means you usually need to pay a little money to get your cool web games available on the Internet. You need to pay a web hosting company to host your games.

When the browser's request reaches the web server, the server checks to see if it has the requested item. Web servers can have all sorts of information stored on them:

Usually the first request that a browser sends to a server is for an HTML web page:

If the server has the web page the user is looking for, then it sends it back to the browser:

This is the kind of dumb part. The web page is usually pretty small and uninteresting. Web pages often look pretty and do lots of amazing things, but by themselves they don't look pretty. A web page by itself can't do lots of amazing things. For anything fun to happen, the web page needs to tell the browser to make lots and lots of other requests.

We saw HTML web pages in Chapter 9, *What's All That Other Code?*, on page 85. They have funny angle brackets that are the markup important to browsers:

```
<body>
  <h1>Hello!</h1>
  <p>
    You can make <b>bold</b> words,
    <i>italic</i> words,
    even <u>underlined</u> words.
  </p>
  <p>
    You can link to
    <a href="http://gamingJS.com">other pages</a>.
    You can also add images from web servers:
    <img src="/images/purple_fruit_monster.png">
  </p>
</body>
```

Some markup has things like JavaScript files or images or styles that make cool stuff happen. And so, as soon as the browser gets the web page that it asked for, it has to ask for tons and tons more things:

And here is the really dumb part about all of this: the browser usually has to wait until most or all of these things come back before it does anything important.

There are two ways to wait for things to be ready before doing important work. The first is what we've been doing—putting the most important stuff last in the HTML document:

```
<body></body>
<script>
  // This is where we have been coding - after the <body> tags
</script>
```

In this case, we have the <script> tag at the very bottom of the document, meaning that browser will display the web-page stuff (text, images, style information, etc.) before it runs our code. Hopefully everything else will be ready by the time the browser runs that code.

The other way to deal with this situation is to use a browser trick known as *on-dom-ready*. DOM stands for Document Object Model. When browsers think about web pages, they use the DOM. Browsers also let web programmers use the DOM to make changes to web pages (change colors, show pop-up boxes). When the browser has read a web page and converted it into the DOM, the DOM is said to be "ready." With on-dom-ready, we listen to the document:

```
// Wait until the web page is fully loaded
document.addEventListener("DOMContentLoaded", function() {
  document.body.appendChild(renderer.domElement);
});
```

This trick goes in the JavaScript, not the web page, and takes advantage of an important aspect of web pages: they like to shout about things that happen. A lot of the time, no one and nothing is listening when the browser shouts. But knowing that a browser does this gives us power.

In this case, we have the power to listen to one particular browser event: DOMContentLoaded. When the browser loads all of the content a page needs, the browser shouts to anybody who is interested. Here we tell that browser that yes, we're interested, and that when such an event happens, we should add our 3D renderer to the page.

21.2 Free Websites

Earlier we noted that only publicly available web servers can serve up web pages, images, JavaScript, and so on. Normally this will cost you some money. But there are ways to get your web pages and JavaScript games publicly available for free:

- Tumblr[1]
- Blogger[2]
- WordPress[3]

When You Might Need to Pay

We just talked about ways to get a public site without paying. Why would you ever need to pay?

The answer is that you need to pay when your website needs to store new information. If a website needs to keep track of users, then you need to pay to have space to save that information. If a website needs to remember players' scores, then you'll need to pay for a place to keep that information.

---

1. http://tumblr.com
2. http://blogger.com
3. http://www.wordpress.com

Most free websites have their own way to create web pages, script files and images. To get an idea of how to copy some of our projects into a real website, we'll take a look at putting one of our 3D animations on Tumblr.

21.3 Putting Your Code on Another Site

This section assumes that you already have a Tumblr account (or an account on a similar service). The instructions should work for most sites, but all posting services have their own quirks that you may have to debug on your own. Also note that the Tumblr controls may change over time and may not look or work exactly as shown here.

Posting our code to Tumblr is pretty easy. Start a post like normal, but be sure to click the <html> button in the post's toolbar:

The <html> button should be blue when enabled (but it might be a different color, depending on your Tumblr theme).

Next add some HTML and a place for your simulation to go. The following creates a short paragraph, followed by a spot for your 3D game, followed by another short paragraph:

```
<p>I made this!</p>
<div id="ice-code-2013-06-06">
<p>It's in the first chapter of
<a href="http://gamingjs.com">3D Game Programming for Kids</a>.
</p>
```

It's important that the id= attribute for the <div> be unique—that there are no other tags with the same id= anywhere on the page. A good tagging scheme to use is a combination of the purpose (ice-editor) and today's date (2013-06-06, for example). You can change the words inside the <p> tags to be whatever you like.

Next, copy your code from ICE and paste it into the Tumblr post. When copying code from ICE, *be sure to skip the first line* that contains <body> </body>. Only copy from the first <script> tag to the end.

Paste this into the Tumblr post below the HTML that we added earlier. (See Figure 10, *The Tumblr Post*, on page 214.)

We're not quite done. The code we've been writing in this book takes up the entire browser window. In these posts, we want to take up only a small portion of the post. We also want to attach our animations to the <div> that we added earlier.

Figure 10—The Tumblr Post

To get the size correct, adjust the aspect_ratio and renderer size. To make the renderer 400 wide and 300 tall, you would use this:

```
// This will draw what the camera sees onto the screen:
var renderer = new THREE.CanvasRenderer();
renderer.setSize(400, 300);
```

The aspect ratio would then be as follows:

```
// This is what sees the stuff:
var aspect_ratio = 400/300;
var camera = new THREE.PerspectiveCamera(75, aspect_ratio, 1, 10000);
```

You math whizzes will know that you could also write 4/3 for the aspect ratio there. You do not have to use these numbers—experiment and use what works best on the page.

Last, attach the animation to the <div> tag. Find the line that adds the renderer.domElement (it should look like document.body.appendChild(renderer.domElement)). Change it so that the renderer's domElement is added to the <div> tag:

```
document.getElementById('ice-code-2013-06-06').appendChild(renderer.domElement);
```

Be sure to change the value in the getElementById() method call to whatever you used for the id= of the <div> tag earlier.

With that, you should be able to publish your post and see your handiwork:

Amazing 3D Animation

I made this!

It's in the first chapter of 3D Game Programming for Kids.

Be sure to share your work on the book forums: http://pragprog.com/book/csjava/3d-game-programming-for-kids?tab=tab-forums!

21.4 What's Next

You're on your own now! I've taught you all I can, which means it's time for you to let your creativity loose. None of the games in this book are meant to be finished products. Each and every game can be made better, but only if you add code and enhance gameplay. You've learned a ton just by making it to the end of the book. And now is when things get interesting—when you find out what you can do by yourself. That's the most exciting adventure I can imagine for you.

Good luck! And if you need some help, don't forget to ask in the book forums! I look forward to hearing what you're working on.

Project Code

This appendix contains completed versions of all of the projects created in this book. Your code may not be exactly the same as the code that follows —that's OK. The code is included in case you run into problems and want to be able to compare your code to a working version

A1.1 Code: Creating Simple Shapes

This is the final version of the shapes code from Chapter 1, *Project: Creating Simple Shapes*, on page 1.

```
<body></body>
<script src="http://gamingJS.com/Three.js"></script>
<script src="http://gamingJS.com/ChromeFixes.js"></script>
<script>
  // This is where stuff in our game will happen:
  var scene = new THREE.Scene();

  // This is what sees the stuff:
  var aspect_ratio = window.innerWidth / window.innerHeight;
  var camera = new THREE.PerspectiveCamera(75, aspect_ratio, 1, 10000);
  camera.position.z = 400;
  scene.add(camera);

  // This will draw what the camera sees onto the screen:
  var renderer = new THREE.CanvasRenderer();
  renderer.setSize(window.innerWidth, window.innerHeight);
  document.body.appendChild(renderer.domElement);

  // ******** START CODING ON THE NEXT LINE ********
  var shape = new THREE.SphereGeometry(100);
  var cover = new THREE.MeshNormalMaterial();
  var ball = new THREE.Mesh(shape, cover);
  scene.add(ball);
  ball.position.set(-250,250,-250);
```

```
var shape = new THREE.CubeGeometry(300, 100, 20);
var cover = new THREE.MeshNormalMaterial();
var box = new THREE.Mesh(shape, cover);
scene.add(box);
box.position.set(250, 250, -250);

var shape = new THREE.CylinderGeometry(110, 100, 100);
var cover = new THREE.MeshNormalMaterial();
var tube = new THREE.Mesh(shape, cover);
scene.add(tube);
tube.position.set(250, -250, -250);

var shape = new THREE.PlaneGeometry(300, 100);
var cover = new THREE.MeshNormalMaterial();
var ground = new THREE.Mesh(shape, cover);
scene.add(ground);
ground.position.set(-250, -250, -250);

var shape = new THREE.TorusGeometry(100, 25, 8, 25);
var cover = new THREE.MeshNormalMaterial();
var donut = new THREE.Mesh(shape, cover);
scene.add(donut);

var clock = new THREE.Clock();

function animate() {
  requestAnimationFrame(animate);
  var t = clock.getElapsedTime();

  ball.rotation.set(t, 2*t, 0);
  box.rotation.set(t, 2*t, 0);
  tube.rotation.set(t, 2*t, 0);
  ground.rotation.set(t, 2*t, 0);
  donut.rotation.set(t, 2*t, 0);

  renderer.render(scene, camera);
}

animate();

// Now, show what the camera sees on the screen:
renderer.render(scene, camera);
</script>
```

A1.2 Code: Playing with the Console and Finding What's Broken

There was no working code from Chapter 2, *Playing with the Console and Finding What's Broken*, on page 17. We wrote some broken code in ICE and explored the JavaScript console.

A1.3 Code: Making an Avatar

This is the final version of the avatar code from Chapter 3, *Project: Making an Avatar*, on page 25.

```
<body></body>
<script src="http://gamingJS.com/Three.js"></script>
<script src="http://gamingJS.com/ChromeFixes.js"></script>
<script>
  // This is where stuff in our game will happen:
  var scene = new THREE.Scene();

  // This is what sees the stuff:
  var aspect_ratio = window.innerWidth / window.innerHeight;
  var camera = new THREE.PerspectiveCamera(75, aspect_ratio, 1, 10000);
  camera.position.z = 500;
  scene.add(camera);

  // This will draw what the camera sees onto the screen:
  var renderer = new THREE.CanvasRenderer();
  renderer.setSize(window.innerWidth, window.innerHeight);
  document.body.appendChild(renderer.domElement);

  // ******** START CODING ON THE NEXT LINE ********

  var cover = new THREE.MeshNormalMaterial();
  var body = new THREE.SphereGeometry(100);
  var avatar = new THREE.Mesh(body, cover);
  scene.add(avatar);

  var hand = new THREE.SphereGeometry(50);

  var right_hand = new THREE.Mesh(hand, cover);
  right_hand.position.set(-150, 0, 0);
  avatar.add(right_hand);

  var left_hand = new THREE.Mesh(hand, cover);
  left_hand.position.set(150, 0, 0);
  avatar.add(left_hand);

  var foot = new THREE.SphereGeometry(50);

  var right_foot = new THREE.Mesh(foot, cover);
  right_foot.position.set(-75, -125, 0);
  avatar.add(right_foot);

  var left_foot = new THREE.Mesh(foot, cover);
  left_foot.position.set(75, -125, 0);
  avatar.add(left_foot);
```

```
  // Now, animate what the camera sees on the screen:
  var is_cartwheeling = false;
  var is_flipping = true;
  function animate() {
    requestAnimationFrame(animate);
    if (is_cartwheeling) {
      avatar.rotation.z = avatar.rotation.z + 0.05;
    }
    if (is_flipping) {
      avatar.rotation.x = avatar.rotation.x + 0.05;
    }
    renderer.render(scene, camera);
  }
  animate();
</script>
```

A1.4 Code: Moving Avatars

This is the moving-avatar code from Chapter 4, *Project: Moving Avatars*, on page 35.

```
<body></body>
<script src="http://gamingJS.com/Three.js"></script>
<script src="http://gamingJS.com/ChromeFixes.js"></script>
<script>
  // This is where stuff in our game will happen:
  var scene = new THREE.Scene();

  // This is what sees the stuff:
  var aspect_ratio = window.innerWidth / window.innerHeight;
  var camera = new THREE.PerspectiveCamera(75, aspect_ratio, 1, 10000);
  camera.position.z = 500;
  //scene.add(camera);

  // This will draw what the camera sees onto the screen:
  var renderer = new THREE.CanvasRenderer();
  renderer.setSize(window.innerWidth, window.innerHeight);
  document.body.appendChild(renderer.domElement);

  // ******** START CODING ON THE NEXT LINE ********
  var marker = new THREE.Object3D();
  scene.add(marker);

  var cover = new THREE.MeshNormalMaterial();
  var body = new THREE.SphereGeometry(100);
  var avatar = new THREE.Mesh(body, cover);
  marker.add(avatar);

  var hand = new THREE.SphereGeometry(50);

  var right_hand = new THREE.Mesh(hand, cover);
```

```
right_hand.position.set(-150, 0, 0);
avatar.add(right_hand);

var left_hand = new THREE.Mesh(hand, cover);
left_hand.position.set(150, 0, 0);
avatar.add(left_hand);

var foot = new THREE.SphereGeometry(50);

var right_foot = new THREE.Mesh(foot, cover);
right_foot.position.set(-75, -125, 0);
avatar.add(right_foot);

var left_foot = new THREE.Mesh(foot, cover);
left_foot.position.set(75, -125, 0);
avatar.add(left_foot);

marker.add(camera);

// Trees
makeTreeAt( 500,   0);
makeTreeAt(-500,   0);
makeTreeAt( 750, -1000);
makeTreeAt(-750, -1000);

function makeTreeAt(x, z) {
  var trunk = new THREE.Mesh(
    new THREE.CylinderGeometry(50, 50, 200),
    new THREE.MeshBasicMaterial({color: 0xA0522D})
  );

  var top = new THREE.Mesh(
    new THREE.SphereGeometry(150),
    new THREE.MeshBasicMaterial({color: 0x228B22})
  );
  top.position.y = 175;
  trunk.add(top);

  trunk.position.set(x, -75, z);
  scene.add(trunk);
}

// Now, animate what the camera sees on the screen:
var is_cartwheeling = false;
var is_flipping = false;
function animate() {
  requestAnimationFrame(animate);
  if (is_cartwheeling) {
    avatar.rotation.z = avatar.rotation.z + 0.05;
  }
```

```
    if (is_flipping) {
      avatar.rotation.x = avatar.rotation.x + 0.05;
    }
    renderer.render(scene, camera);
  }
  animate();

  document.addEventListener('keydown', function(event) {
    var code = event.keyCode;
    if (code == 37) marker.position.x = marker.position.x-5; // left
    if (code == 38) marker.position.z = marker.position.z-5; // up
    if (code == 39) marker.position.x = marker.position.x+5; // right
    if (code == 40) marker.position.z = marker.position.z+5; // down

    if (code == 67) is_cartwheeling = !is_cartwheeling;      // C
    if (code == 70) is_flipping = !is_flipping;              // F
  });
</script>
```

A1.5 Code: Functions: Use and Use Again

We intentionally broke a lot of things as we explored functions in Chapter 5, *Functions: Use and Use Again*, on page 49. A copy of the code that works follows (note that it doesn't include the recursion example).

```
<body></body>
<script src="http://gamingJS.com/Three.js"></script>
<script src="http://gamingJS.com/ChromeFixes.js"></script>
<script>
var log = makeLog();
logMessage(hello("President Obama"), log);
logMessage(hello("Mom"), log);
logMessage(hello("Purple Fruit Monster"), log);
logMessage(hello("Chris"), log);

/*
// Missing a curly brace - this won't work!
function hello(name) {
  return 'Hello, ' + name + '! You look very pretty today :)';

*/

function hello(name) {
  return 'Hello, ' + name + '! You look very pretty today :)';
}

function makeLog() {
  var holder = document.createElement('div');
  holder.style.height = '75px';
  holder.style.width = '450px';
```

```
    holder.style.overflow = 'auto';
    holder.style.border = '1px solid #666';
    holder.style.backgroundColor = '#ccc';
    holder.style.padding = '8px';
    holder.style.position = 'absolute';
    holder.style.bottom = '10px';
    holder.style.right = '20px';
    document.body.appendChild(holder);

    return holder;
}

function logMessage(message, log) {
    var holder = document.createElement('div');
    holder.textContent = message;
    log.appendChild(holder);
}
</script>
```

A1.6 Code: Moving Hands and Feet

This is the code from Chapter 6, *Project: Moving Hands and Feet*, on page 59.

```
<body></body>
<script src="http://gamingJS.com/Three.js"></script>
<script src="http://gamingJS.com/ChromeFixes.js"></script>
<script>
  // This is where stuff in our game will happen:
  var scene = new THREE.Scene();

  // This is what sees the stuff:
  var aspect_ratio = window.innerWidth / window.innerHeight;
  var camera = new THREE.PerspectiveCamera(75, aspect_ratio, 1, 10000);
  camera.position.z = 500;
  //scene.add(camera);

  // This will draw what the camera sees onto the screen:
  var renderer = new THREE.CanvasRenderer();
  renderer.setSize(window.innerWidth, window.innerHeight);
  document.body.appendChild(renderer.domElement);

  // ******** START CODING ON THE NEXT LINE ********
  var marker = new THREE.Object3D();
  scene.add(marker);

  var cover = new THREE.MeshNormalMaterial();
  var body = new THREE.SphereGeometry(100);
  var avatar = new THREE.Mesh(body, cover);
  marker.add(avatar);

  var hand = new THREE.SphereGeometry(50);
```

```
var right_hand = new THREE.Mesh(hand, cover);
right_hand.position.set(-150, 0, 0);
avatar.add(right_hand);

var left_hand = new THREE.Mesh(hand, cover);
left_hand.position.set(150, 0, 0);
avatar.add(left_hand);

var foot = new THREE.SphereGeometry(50);

var right_foot = new THREE.Mesh(foot, cover);
right_foot.position.set(-75, -125, 0);
avatar.add(right_foot);

var left_foot = new THREE.Mesh(foot, cover);
left_foot.position.set(75, -125, 0);
avatar.add(left_foot);

marker.add(camera);

// Trees
makeTreeAt( 500,    0);
makeTreeAt(-500,    0);
makeTreeAt( 750, -1000);
makeTreeAt(-750, -1000);

function makeTreeAt(x, z) {
  var trunk = new THREE.Mesh(
    new THREE.CylinderGeometry(50, 50, 200),
    new THREE.MeshBasicMaterial({color: 0xA0522D})
  );

  var top = new THREE.Mesh(
    new THREE.SphereGeometry(150),
    new THREE.MeshBasicMaterial({color: 0x228B22})
  );
  top.position.y = 175;
  trunk.add(top);

  trunk.position.set(x, -75, z);
  scene.add(trunk);
}

// Now, animate what the camera sees on the screen:
var clock = new THREE.Clock(true);
function animate() {
  requestAnimationFrame(animate);
  walk();
  acrobatics();
```

```
    renderer.render(scene, camera);
}
animate();

function walk() {
  if (!isWalking()) return;
  var position = Math.sin(clock.getElapsedTime()*5) * 50;
  right_hand.position.z = position;
  left_hand.position.z = -position;
  right_foot.position.z = -position;
  left_foot.position.z = position;
}

var is_cartwheeling = false;
var is_flipping = false;
function acrobatics() {
  if (is_cartwheeling) {
    avatar.rotation.z = avatar.rotation.z + 0.05;
  }
  if (is_flipping) {
    avatar.rotation.x = avatar.rotation.x + 0.05;
  }
}

var is_moving_right, is_moving_left, is_moving_forward, is_moving_back;
function isWalking() {
  if (is_moving_right) return true;
  if (is_moving_left) return true;
  if (is_moving_forward) return true;
  if (is_moving_back) return true;
  return false;
}

document.addEventListener('keydown', function(event) {
  var code = event.keyCode;

  if (code == 37) {                              // left
    marker.position.x = marker.position.x-5;
    is_moving_left = true;
  }
  if (code == 38) {                              // up
    marker.position.z = marker.position.z-5;
    is_moving_forward = true;
  }
  if (code == 39) {                              // right
    marker.position.x = marker.position.x+5;
    is_moving_right = true;
  }
  if (code == 40) {                              // down
    marker.position.z = marker.position.z+5;
```

```
    is_moving_back = true;
  }
  if (code == 67) is_cartwheeling = !is_cartwheeling; // C
  if (code == 70) is_flipping = !is_flipping;         // F
});

document.addEventListener('keyup', function(event) {
  var code = event.keyCode;

  if (code == 37) is_moving_left = false;
  if (code == 38) is_moving_forward = false;
  if (code == 39) is_moving_right = false;
  if (code == 40) is_moving_back = false;
});
</script>
```

A1.7 Code: A Closer Look at JavaScript Fundamentals

There was no project code in Chapter 7, *A Closer Look at JavaScript Fundamentals*, on page 67.

A1.8 Code: Turning Our Avatar

This is the code from Chapter 8, *Project: Turning Our Avatar*, on page 79.

```
<body></body>
<script src="http://gamingJS.com/Three.js"></script>
<script src="http://gamingJS.com/Tween.js"></script>
<script src="http://gamingJS.com/ChromeFixes.js"></script>
<body></body><script>
  // This is where stuff in our game will happen:
  var scene = new THREE.Scene();

  // This is what sees the stuff:
  var aspect_ratio = window.innerWidth / window.innerHeight;
  var camera = new THREE.PerspectiveCamera(75, aspect_ratio, 1, 10000);
  camera.position.z = 500;
  //scene.add(camera);

  // This will draw what the camera sees onto the screen:
  var renderer = new THREE.CanvasRenderer();
  renderer.setSize(window.innerWidth, window.innerHeight);
  document.body.appendChild(renderer.domElement);

  // ******** START CODING ON THE NEXT LINE ********
  var marker = new THREE.Object3D();
  scene.add(marker);

  var cover = new THREE.MeshNormalMaterial();
  var body = new THREE.SphereGeometry(100);
  var avatar = new THREE.Mesh(body, cover);
```

```javascript
marker.add(avatar);

var hand = new THREE.SphereGeometry(50);

var right_hand = new THREE.Mesh(hand, cover);
right_hand.position.set(-150, 0, 0);
avatar.add(right_hand);

var left_hand = new THREE.Mesh(hand, cover);
left_hand.position.set(150, 0, 0);
avatar.add(left_hand);

var foot = new THREE.SphereGeometry(50);

var right_foot = new THREE.Mesh(foot, cover);
right_foot.position.set(-75, -125, 0);
avatar.add(right_foot);

var left_foot = new THREE.Mesh(foot, cover);
left_foot.position.set(75, -125, 0);
avatar.add(left_foot);

marker.add(camera);

// Trees
makeTreeAt( 500,  0);
makeTreeAt(-500,  0);
makeTreeAt( 750, -1000);
makeTreeAt(-750, -1000);

function makeTreeAt(x, z) {
  var trunk = new THREE.Mesh(
    new THREE.CylinderGeometry(50, 50, 200),
    new THREE.MeshBasicMaterial({color: 0xA0522D})
  );

  var top = new THREE.Mesh(
    new THREE.SphereGeometry(150),
    new THREE.MeshBasicMaterial({color: 0x228B22})
  );
  top.position.y = 175;
  trunk.add(top);

  trunk.position.set(x, -75, z);
  scene.add(trunk);
}

// Now, animate what the camera sees on the screen:
var clock = new THREE.Clock(true);
function animate() {
```

```
  requestAnimationFrame(animate);
  TWEEN.update();
  walk();
  turn();
  acrobatics();
  renderer.render(scene, camera);
}
animate();

function walk() {
  if (!isWalking()) return;
  var position = Math.sin(clock.getElapsedTime()*5) * 50;
  right_hand.position.z = position;
  left_hand.position.z = -position;
  right_foot.position.z = -position;
  left_foot.position.z = position;
}

function turn() {
  var direction = 0;
  if (is_moving_forward) direction = Math.PI;
  if (is_moving_back) direction = 0;
  if (is_moving_right) direction = Math.PI/2;
  if (is_moving_left) direction =  -Math.PI/2;

  spinAvatar(direction);
}

function spinAvatar(direction) {
  new TWEEN.
    Tween({y: avatar.rotation.y}).
    to({y: direction}, 100).
    onUpdate(function () {
      avatar.rotation.y = this.y;
    }).
    start();
}

var is_cartwheeling = false;
var is_flipping = false;
function acrobatics() {
  if (is_cartwheeling) {
    avatar.rotation.z = avatar.rotation.z + 0.05;
  }
  if (is_flipping) {
    avatar.rotation.x = avatar.rotation.x + 0.05;
  }
}

var is_moving_left, is_moving_right, is_moving_forward, is_moving_back;
```

```
  function isWalking() {
    if (is_moving_right) return true;
    if (is_moving_left) return true;
    if (is_moving_forward) return true;
    if (is_moving_back) return true;
    return false;
  }

  document.addEventListener('keydown', function(event) {
    var code = event.keyCode;

    if (code == 37) {                               // left
      marker.position.x = marker.position.x-5;
      is_moving_left = true;
    }
    if (code == 38) {                               // up
      marker.position.z = marker.position.z-5;
      is_moving_forward = true;
    }
    if (code == 39) {                               // right
      marker.position.x = marker.position.x+5;
      is_moving_right = true;
    }
    if (code == 40) {                               // down
      marker.position.z = marker.position.z+5;
      is_moving_back = true;
    }
    if (code == 67) is_cartwheeling = !is_cartwheeling; // C
    if (code == 70) is_flipping = !is_flipping;        // F
  });

  document.addEventListener('keyup', function(event) {
    var code = event.keyCode;

    if (code == 37) {
      console.log("not left anymore");
      is_moving_left = false;
    }
    if (code == 38) is_moving_forward = false;
    if (code == 39) is_moving_right = false;
    if (code == 40) is_moving_back = false;
  });
</script>
```

A1.9 Code: What's All That Other Code?

There was no new code in Chapter 9, *What's All That Other Code?*, on page 85. We only explored the code that is automatically created when we start new projects.

A1.10 Code: Collisions

This is the avatar code after we added collisions in Chapter 10, *Project: Collisions*, on page 93.

```
<body></body>
<script src="http://gamingJS.com/Three.js"></script>
<script src="http://gamingJS.com/Tween.js"></script>
<script src="http://gamingJS.com/ChromeFixes.js"></script>
<script>
  // This is where stuff in our game will happen:
  var scene = new THREE.Scene();

  // This is what sees the stuff:
  var aspect_ratio = window.innerWidth / window.innerHeight;
  var camera = new THREE.PerspectiveCamera(75, aspect_ratio, 1, 10000);
  camera.position.z = 500;
  //scene.add(camera);

  // This will draw what the camera sees onto the screen:
  var renderer = new THREE.CanvasRenderer();
  renderer.setSize(window.innerWidth, window.innerHeight);
  document.body.appendChild(renderer.domElement);

  // ******** START CODING ON THE NEXT LINE ********
  var not_allowed = [];

  var marker = new THREE.Object3D();
  scene.add(marker);

  var cover = new THREE.MeshNormalMaterial();
  var body = new THREE.SphereGeometry(100);
  var avatar = new THREE.Mesh(body, cover);
  marker.add(avatar);

  var hand = new THREE.SphereGeometry(50);

  var right_hand = new THREE.Mesh(hand, cover);
  right_hand.position.set(-150, 0, 0);
  avatar.add(right_hand);

  var left_hand = new THREE.Mesh(hand, cover);
  left_hand.position.set(150, 0, 0);
  avatar.add(left_hand);

  var foot = new THREE.SphereGeometry(50);

  var right_foot = new THREE.Mesh(foot, cover);
  right_foot.position.set(-75, -125, 0);
  avatar.add(right_foot);
```

```
  var left_foot = new THREE.Mesh(foot, cover);
  left_foot.position.set(75, -125, 0);
  avatar.add(left_foot);

  marker.add(camera);

  // Trees
  makeTreeAt( 500,   0);
  makeTreeAt(-500,   0);
  makeTreeAt( 750, -1000);
  makeTreeAt(-750, -1000);

  function makeTreeAt(x, z) {
    var trunk = new THREE.Mesh(
      new THREE.CylinderGeometry(50, 50, 200),
      new THREE.MeshBasicMaterial({color: 0xA0522D})
    );

    var top = new THREE.Mesh(
      new THREE.SphereGeometry(150),
      new THREE.MeshBasicMaterial({color: 0x228B22})
    );
    top.position.y = 175;
    trunk.add(top);

    var boundary = new THREE.Mesh(
      new THREE.CircleGeometry(300),
      new THREE.MeshNormalMaterial()
    );
    boundary.position.y = -100;
    boundary.rotation.x = -Math.PI/2;
    trunk.add(boundary);

    not_allowed.push(boundary);

    trunk.position.set(x, -75, z);
    scene.add(trunk);
  }

  // Now, animate what the camera sees on the screen:
  var clock = new THREE.Clock(true);
  function animate() {
    requestAnimationFrame(animate);
    TWEEN.update();
    walk();
    turn();
    acrobatics();
    renderer.render(scene, camera);
  }
```

```javascript
animate();

function walk() {
  if (!isWalking()) return;
  var position = Math.sin(clock.getElapsedTime()*5) * 50;
  right_hand.position.z = position;
  left_hand.position.z = -position;
  right_foot.position.z = -position;
  left_foot.position.z = position;
}

function turn() {
  var direction = 0;
  if (is_moving_forward) direction = Math.PI;
  if (is_moving_back) direction = 0;
  if (is_moving_right) direction = Math.PI/2;
  if (is_moving_left) direction =  -Math.PI/2;

  spinAvatar(direction);
}

function spinAvatar(direction) {
  new TWEEN
    .Tween({y: avatar.rotation.y})
    .to({y: direction}, 100)
    .onUpdate(function () {
      avatar.rotation.y = this.y;
    })
    .start();
}

var is_cartwheeling = false;
var is_flipping = false;
function acrobatics() {
  if (is_cartwheeling) {
    avatar.rotation.z = avatar.rotation.z + 0.05;
  }
  if (is_flipping) {
    avatar.rotation.x = avatar.rotation.x + 0.05;
  }
}

var is_moving_left, is_moving_right, is_moving_forward, is_moving_back;
function isWalking() {
  if (is_moving_right) return true;
  if (is_moving_left) return true;
  if (is_moving_forward) return true;
  if (is_moving_back) return true;
  return false;
}
```

```
document.addEventListener('keydown', function(event) {
  var code = event.keyCode;

  if (code == 37) {                                    // left
    marker.position.x = marker.position.x-5;
    is_moving_left = true;
  }
  if (code == 38) {                                    // up
    marker.position.z = marker.position.z-5;
    is_moving_forward = true;
  }
  if (code == 39) {                                    // right
    marker.position.x = marker.position.x+5;
    is_moving_right = true;
  }
  if (code == 40) {                                    // down
    marker.position.z = marker.position.z+5;
    is_moving_back = true;
  }
  if (code == 67) is_cartwheeling = !is_cartwheeling; // C
  if (code == 70) is_flipping = !is_flipping;          // F

  if (detectCollisions()) {
    if (is_moving_left) marker.position.x = marker.position.x+5;
    if (is_moving_right) marker.position.x = marker.position.x-5;
    if (is_moving_forward) marker.position.z = marker.position.z+5;
    if (is_moving_back) marker.position.z = marker.position.z-5;
  }
});

document.addEventListener('keyup', function(event) {
  var code = event.keyCode;

  if (code == 37) is_moving_left = false;
  if (code == 38) is_moving_forward = false;
  if (code == 39) is_moving_right = false;
  if (code == 40) is_moving_back = false;
});

function detectCollisions() {
  var vector = new THREE.Vector3(0, -1, 0);
  var ray = new THREE.Ray(marker.position, vector);
  var intersects = ray.intersectObjects(not_allowed);
  if (intersects.length > 0) return true;
  return false;
}
</script>
```

A1.11 Code: Fruit Hunt

This is the avatar code after we added it to the fruit-hunt game in Chapter 11, *Project: Fruit Hunt*, on page 99. This code uses WebGLRenderer to make the trees a little prettier, but the CanvasRenderer should work nearly as well.

```
<body></body>
<script src="http://gamingJS.com/Three.js"></script>
<script src="http://gamingJS.com/Tween.js"></script>
<script src="http://gamingJS.com/ChromeFixes.js"></script>
<script src="http://gamingJS.com/Scoreboard.js"></script>
<script src="http://gamingJS.com/Sounds.js"></script>
<script>
  // This is where stuff in our game will happen:
  var scene = new THREE.Scene();

  // This is what sees the stuff:
  var aspect_ratio = window.innerWidth / window.innerHeight;
  var camera = new THREE.PerspectiveCamera(75, aspect_ratio, 1, 10000);
  camera.position.z = 500;
  //scene.add(camera);

  // This will draw what the camera sees onto the screen:
  var renderer = new THREE.WebGLRenderer();
  renderer.setSize(window.innerWidth, window.innerHeight);
  document.body.appendChild(renderer.domElement);

  // ******** START CODING ON THE NEXT LINE ********
  var not_allowed = [];

  var scoreboard = new Scoreboard();
  scoreboard.countdown(45);
  scoreboard.score();
  scoreboard.help(
    'Arrow keys to move; ' +
    'Space bar to jump for fruit; ' +
    'Watch for shaking trees with fruit.' +
    'Get near the tree and jump before the fruit is gone!'
  );
  var game_over = false;
  scoreboard.onTimeExpired(function() {
    scoreboard.message("Game Over!");
    game_over = true;
  });

  var marker = new THREE.Object3D();
  scene.add(marker);

  var cover = new THREE.MeshNormalMaterial();
  var body = new THREE.SphereGeometry(100);
```

```javascript
var avatar = new THREE.Mesh(body, cover);
marker.add(avatar);

var hand = new THREE.SphereGeometry(50);

var right_hand = new THREE.Mesh(hand, cover);
right_hand.position.set(-150, 0, 0);
avatar.add(right_hand);

var left_hand = new THREE.Mesh(hand, cover);
left_hand.position.set(150, 0, 0);
avatar.add(left_hand);

var foot = new THREE.SphereGeometry(50);

var right_foot = new THREE.Mesh(foot, cover);
right_foot.position.set(-75, -125, 0);
avatar.add(right_foot);

var left_foot = new THREE.Mesh(foot, cover);
left_foot.position.set(75, -125, 0);
avatar.add(left_foot);

marker.add(camera);

var tree_with_treasure;
var trees = [];
trees.push(makeTreeAt( 500,    0));
trees.push(makeTreeAt(-500,    0));
trees.push(makeTreeAt( 750, -1000));
trees.push(makeTreeAt(-750, -1000));

function makeTreeAt(x, z) {
  // Don't change any code at the start...
  var trunk = new THREE.Mesh(
    new THREE.CylinderGeometry(50, 50, 200),
    new THREE.MeshBasicMaterial({color: 0xA0522D})
  );

  var top = new THREE.Mesh(
    new THREE.SphereGeometry(150),
    new THREE.MeshBasicMaterial({color: 0x228B22})
  );
  top.position.y = 175;
  trunk.add(top);

  var boundary = new THREE.Mesh(
    new THREE.CircleGeometry(300),
    new THREE.MeshNormalMaterial()
  );
```

```
    boundary.position.y = -100;
    boundary.rotation.x = -Math.PI/2;
    trunk.add(boundary);

    not_allowed.push(boundary);

    trunk.position.set(x, -75, z);
    scene.add(trunk);
    // ... but add the following line to the end:
    return top;
}

function shakeTree() {
    tree_with_treasure = Math.floor(Math.random() * trees.length);

    new TWEEN
        .Tween({x: 0})
        .to({x: 2*Math.PI}, 200)
        .repeat(20)
        .onUpdate(function () {
            trees[tree_with_treasure].position.x = 75 * Math.sin(this.x);
        })
        .start();

    setTimeout(shakeTree, 12*1000);
}
shakeTree();

// Now, animate what the camera sees on the screen:
var clock = new THREE.Clock(true);
function animate() {
    requestAnimationFrame(animate);
    TWEEN.update();
    walk();
    turn();
    acrobatics();
    renderer.render(scene, camera);
}
animate();

function walk() {
    if (!isWalking()) return;
    var position = Math.sin(clock.getElapsedTime()*5) * 50;
    right_hand.position.z = position;
    left_hand.position.z = -position;
    right_foot.position.z = -position;
    left_foot.position.z = position;
}

function turn() {
```

```javascript
  var direction = 0;
  if (is_moving_forward) direction = Math.PI;
  if (is_moving_back) direction = 0;
  if (is_moving_right) direction = Math.PI/2;
  if (is_moving_left) direction =  -Math.PI/2;

  spinAvatar(direction);
}

function spinAvatar(direction) {
  new TWEEN
    .Tween({y: avatar.rotation.y})
    .to({y: direction}, 100)
    .onUpdate(function () {
      avatar.rotation.y = this.y;
    })
    .start();
}

var is_cartwheeling = false;
var is_flipping = false;
function acrobatics() {
  if (is_cartwheeling) {
    avatar.rotation.z = avatar.rotation.z + 0.05;
  }
  if (is_flipping) {
    avatar.rotation.x = avatar.rotation.x + 0.05;
  }
}

var is_moving_left, is_moving_right, is_moving_forward, is_moving_back;
function isWalking() {
  if (is_moving_right) return true;
  if (is_moving_left) return true;
  if (is_moving_forward) return true;
  if (is_moving_back) return true;
  return false;
}

document.addEventListener('keydown', function(event) {
  var code = event.keyCode;
  if (code == 32) jump();                         // space

  if (code == 37) {                               // left
    marker.position.x = marker.position.x-5;
    is_moving_left = true;
  }
  if (code == 38) {                               // up
    marker.position.z = marker.position.z-5;
    is_moving_forward = true;
```

```
  }
  if (code == 39) {                                    // right
    marker.position.x = marker.position.x+5;
    is_moving_right = true;
  }
  if (code == 40) {                                    // down
    marker.position.z = marker.position.z+5;
    is_moving_back = true;
  }
  if (code == 67) is_cartwheeling = !is_cartwheeling; // C
  if (code == 70) is_flipping = !is_flipping;         // F

  if (detectCollisions()) {
    if (is_moving_left) marker.position.x = marker.position.x+5;
    if (is_moving_right) marker.position.x = marker.position.x-5;
    if (is_moving_forward) marker.position.z = marker.position.z+5;
    if (is_moving_back) marker.position.z = marker.position.z-5;
  }
});

document.addEventListener('keyup', function(event) {
  var code = event.keyCode;

  if (code == 37) is_moving_left = false;
  if (code == 38) is_moving_forward = false;
  if (code == 39) is_moving_right = false;
  if (code == 40) is_moving_back = false;
});

function detectCollisions() {
  var vector = new THREE.Vector3(0, -1, 0);
  var ray = new THREE.Ray(marker.position, vector);
  var intersects = ray.intersectObjects(not_allowed);
  if (intersects.length > 0) return true;
  return false;
}

function jump() {
  checkForTreasure();
  animateJump();
}

function checkForTreasure() {
  if (tree_with_treasure == undefined) return;

  var treasure_tree = trees[tree_with_treasure],
      p1 = treasure_tree.parent.position,
      p2 = marker.position;

  var distance = Math.sqrt(
```

```
      (p1.x - p2.x)*(p1.x - p2.x) +
      (p1.z - p2.z)*(p1.z - p2.z)
    );

    if (distance < 500) {
      scorePoints();
    }
  }

function scorePoints() {
  if (scoreboard.getTimeRemaining() === 0) return;
  scoreboard.addPoints(10);
  Sounds.bubble.play();
  animateFruit();
}

var fruit;
function animateFruit() {
  if (fruit) return;

  fruit = new THREE.Mesh(
    new THREE.CylinderGeometry(25, 25, 5, 25),
    new THREE.MeshBasicMaterial({color: 0xFFD700})
  );
  fruit.rotation.x = Math.PI/2;

  marker.add(fruit);

  new TWEEN.
    Tween({
      height: 150,
      spin: 0
    }).
    to({
      height: 250,
      spin: 4
    }, 500).
    onUpdate(function () {
      fruit.position.y = this.height;
      fruit.rotation.z = this.spin;
    }).
    onComplete(function() {
      marker.remove(fruit);
      fruit = undefined;
    }).
    start();
}

function animateJump() {
  new TWEEN
```

```
        .Tween({jump: 0})
        .to({jump: Math.PI}, 500)
        .onUpdate(function () {
          marker.position.y = 200* Math.sin(this.jump);
        })
        .start();
  }
</script>
```

A1.12 Code: Working with Lights and Materials

This is the final version of the code that we used to explore lights and materials in Chapter 12, *Working with Lights and Materials*, on page 109.

```
<body></body>
<script src="http://gamingJS.com/Three.js"></script>
<script src="http://gamingJS.com/ChromeFixes.js"></script>
<script>
  // This is where stuff in our game will happen:
  var scene = new THREE.Scene();

  // This is what sees the stuff:
  var aspect_ratio = window.innerWidth / window.innerHeight;
  var camera = new THREE.PerspectiveCamera(75, aspect_ratio, 1, 10000);
  camera.position.z = 500;
  scene.add(camera);

  // This will draw what the camera sees onto the screen:
  var renderer = new THREE.WebGLRenderer();
  renderer.shadowMapEnabled = true;
  //var renderer = new THREE.CanvasRenderer();
  renderer.setSize(window.innerWidth, window.innerHeight);
  document.body.appendChild(renderer.domElement);

  // ******** START CODING ON THE NEXT LINE ********

  var shape = new THREE.SphereGeometry(100);
  var cover = new THREE.MeshBasicMaterial();
  cover.color.setRGB(1, 0, 0);
  var ball = new THREE.Mesh(shape, cover);
  scene.add(ball);
  ball.position.set(500, 0, 0);

  var shape = new THREE.TorusGeometry(100, 50, 8, 20);
  var cover = new THREE.MeshPhongMaterial();
  cover.emissive.setRGB(0.8, 0.1, 0.1);
  cover.specular.setRGB(0.9, 0.9, 0.9);
  var donut = new THREE.Mesh(shape, cover);
  scene.add(donut);
  donut.castShadow = true;
```

```
var sunlight = new THREE.DirectionalLight();
sunlight.intensity = 0.5;
sunlight.position.set(100, 100, 100);
scene.add(sunlight);
sunlight.castShadow = true;

var shape = new THREE.PlaneGeometry(1000, 1000);
var cover = new THREE.MeshBasicMaterial();
var ground = new THREE.Mesh(shape, cover);
scene.add(ground);
ground.position.set(0, -200, 0);
ground.rotation.set(-Math.PI/2, 0, 0);
ground.receiveShadow = true;

var clock = new THREE.Clock();
function animate() {
  requestAnimationFrame(animate);

  var time = clock.getElapsedTime();
  donut.rotation.set(time, 2*time, 0);

  renderer.render(scene, camera);
}
animate();
</script>
```

A1.13 Code: Build Your Own Solar System

This is the final version of the solar-system code from Chapter 13, *Project: Build Your Own Solar System*, on page 117.

```
<body></body>
<script src="http://gamingJS.com/Three.js"></script>
<script src="http://gamingJS.com/ChromeFixes.js"></script>
<script>
  // This is where stuff in our game will happen:
  var scene = new THREE.Scene();

  // This is what sees the stuff:
  var aspect_ratio = window.innerWidth / window.innerHeight;
  var above_cam = new THREE.PerspectiveCamera(75, aspect_ratio, 1, 1e6);
  above_cam.position.z = 1000;
  scene.add(above_cam);

  var earth_cam = new THREE.PerspectiveCamera(75, aspect_ratio, 1, 1e6);
  scene.add(earth_cam);

  var camera = above_cam;

  // This will draw what the camera sees onto the screen:
  var renderer = new THREE.WebGLRenderer();
```

```
renderer.setSize(window.innerWidth, window.innerHeight);
document.body.appendChild(renderer.domElement);

// ******** START CODING ON THE NEXT LINE ********
document.body.style.backgroundColor = 'black';

var surface = new THREE.MeshPhongMaterial({ambient: 0xFFD700});
var star = new THREE.SphereGeometry(50, 28, 21);
var sun = new THREE.Mesh(star, surface);
scene.add(sun);

var ambient = new THREE.AmbientLight(0xffffff);
scene.add(ambient);

var sunlight = new THREE.PointLight(0xffffff, 5, 1000);
sun.add(sunlight);

var surface = new THREE.MeshPhongMaterial({ambient: 0x1a1a1a, color: 0x0000cd});
var planet = new THREE.SphereGeometry(20, 20, 15);
var earth = new THREE.Mesh(planet, surface);
earth.position.set(250, 0, 0);
scene.add(earth);

var surface = new THREE.MeshPhongMaterial({ambient: 0x1a1a1a, color: 0xb22222});
var planet = new THREE.SphereGeometry(20, 20, 15);
var mars = new THREE.Mesh(planet, surface);
mars.position.set(500, 0, 0);
scene.add(mars);

clock = new THREE.Clock();

function animate() {
  requestAnimationFrame(animate);

  var time = clock.getElapsedTime();

  var e_angle = time * 0.8;
  earth.position.set(250* Math.cos(e_angle), 250* Math.sin(e_angle), 0);

  var m_angle = time * 0.3;
  mars.position.set(500* Math.cos(m_angle), 500* Math.sin(m_angle), 0);

  var y_diff = mars.position.y - earth.position.y,
      x_diff = mars.position.x - earth.position.x,
      angle = Math.atan2(x_diff, y_diff);

  earth_cam.rotation.set(Math.PI/2, -angle, 0);
  earth_cam.position.set(earth.position.x, earth.position.y, 22);

  // Now, show what the camera sees on the screen:
```

```
  renderer.render(scene, camera);
}

animate();

var stars = new THREE.Geometry();
while (stars.vertices.length < 1e4) {
  var lat = Math.PI * Math.random() - Math.PI/2;
  var lon = 2*Math.PI * Math.random();

  stars.vertices.push(new THREE.Vector3(
    1e5 * Math.cos(lon) * Math.cos(lat),
    1e5 * Math.sin(lon) * Math.cos(lat),
    1e5 * Math.sin(lat)
  ));
}
var star_stuff = new THREE.ParticleBasicMaterial({size: 500});
var star_system = new THREE.ParticleSystem(stars, star_stuff);
scene.add(star_system);

document.addEventListener("keydown", function(event) {
  var code = event.keyCode;

  if (code == 65) { // A
    camera = above_cam;
  }
  if (code == 69) { // E
    camera = earth_cam;
  }
});

</script>
```

A1.14 Code: Phases of the Moon

This is the final version of the moon-phases code from Chapter 14, *Project: Phases of the Moon*, on page 125.

```
<body></body>
<script src="http://gamingJS.com/Three.js"></script>
<script src="http://gamingJS.com/ChromeFixes.js"></script>
<script>
  // This is where stuff in our game will happen:
  var scene = new THREE.Scene();

  // This is what sees the stuff:
  var aspect_ratio = window.innerWidth / window.innerHeight;
  var above_cam = new THREE.PerspectiveCamera(75, aspect_ratio, 1, 1e6);
  above_cam.position.z = 1000;
  scene.add(above_cam);
```

```javascript
    var earth_cam = new THREE.PerspectiveCamera(75, aspect_ratio, 1, 1e6);

    var camera = above_cam;

    // This will draw what the camera sees onto the screen:
    var renderer = new THREE.WebGLRenderer();
    renderer.setSize(window.innerWidth, window.innerHeight);
    document.body.appendChild(renderer.domElement);

    // ******** START CODING ON THE NEXT LINE ********
    document.body.style.backgroundColor = 'black';

    var surface = new THREE.MeshPhongMaterial({ambient: 0xFFD700});
    var star = new THREE.SphereGeometry(50, 28, 21);
    var sun = new THREE.Mesh(star, surface);
    scene.add(sun);

    var ambient = new THREE.AmbientLight(0xffffff);
    scene.add(ambient);

    var sunlight = new THREE.PointLight(0xffffff, 5, 1000);
    sun.add(sunlight);

    var surface = new THREE.MeshPhongMaterial({ambient: 0x1a1a1a, color: 0x0000cd});
    var planet = new THREE.SphereGeometry(20, 20, 15);
    var earth = new THREE.Mesh(planet, surface);
    earth.position.set(250, 0, 0);
    scene.add(earth);

    var surface = new THREE.MeshPhongMaterial({ambient: 0x1a1a1a, color: 0xffffff});
    var planet = new THREE.SphereGeometry(15, 30, 25);
    var moon = new THREE.Mesh(planet, surface);

    var moon_orbit = new THREE.Object3D();
    earth.add(moon_orbit);
    moon_orbit.add(moon);
    moon.position.set(0, 100, 0);
    moon_orbit.add(earth_cam);
    earth_cam.rotation.set(Math.PI/2, 0, 0);

    var time = 0,
        speed = 1,
        pause = false;

    function animate() {
      requestAnimationFrame(animate);
      renderer.render(scene, camera);

      if (pause) return;
      time = time + speed;
```

```
      var e_angle = time * 0.001;
      earth.position.set(250* Math.cos(e_angle), 250* Math.sin(e_angle), 0);
      var m_angle = time * 0.02;
      moon_orbit.rotation.set(0, 0, m_angle);
    }
    animate();

    var stars = new THREE.Geometry();
    while (stars.vertices.length < 1e4) {
      var lat = Math.PI * Math.random() - Math.PI/2;
      var lon = 2*Math.PI * Math.random();

      stars.vertices.push(new THREE.Vector3(
        1e5 * Math.cos(lon) * Math.cos(lat),
        1e5 * Math.sin(lon) * Math.cos(lat),
        1e5 * Math.sin(lat)
      ));
    }
    var star_stuff = new THREE.ParticleBasicMaterial({size: 500});
    var star_system = new THREE.ParticleSystem(stars, star_stuff);
    scene.add(star_system);

    document.addEventListener("keydown", function(event) {
      var code = event.keyCode;

      if (code == 67) changeCamera(); // C
      if (code == 32) changeCamera(); // space
      if (code == 80) pause = !pause; // P
      if (code == 49) speed = 1; // 1
      if (code == 50) speed = 2; // 2
      if (code == 51) speed = 10; // 3
    });

    function changeCamera() {
      if (camera == above_cam) camera = earth_cam;
      else camera = above_cam;
    }
</script>
```

A1.15 Code: The Purple Fruit Monster Game

This is the final version of the game code from Chapter 15, *Project: The Purple Fruit Monster Game*, on page 133.

```
<body></body>
<script src="http://gamingJS.com/Three.js"></script>
<script src="http://gamingJS.com/physi.js"></script>
<script src="http://gamingJS.com/Scoreboard.js"></script>
<script src="http://gamingJS.com/ChromeFixes.js"></script>
<script>
  // This is where stuff in our game will happen:
```

```
Physijs.scripts.ammo = 'http://gamingJS.com/ammo.js';
Physijs.scripts.worker = 'http://gamingJS.com/physijs_worker.js';

var scene = new Physijs.Scene({ fixedTimeStep: 2 / 60 });
scene.setGravity(new THREE.Vector3( 0, -100, 0 ));

// This is what sees the stuff:
var aspect_ratio = window.innerWidth / window.innerHeight;
var camera = new THREE.PerspectiveCamera(75, aspect_ratio, 1, 10000);
camera.position.z = 200;
camera.position.y = 100;
scene.add(camera);

// This will draw what the camera sees onto the screen:
var renderer = new THREE.WebGLRenderer();
renderer.setSize(window.innerWidth, window.innerHeight);
document.body.appendChild(renderer.domElement);

// ******** START CODING ON THE NEXT LINE ********
var ground = addGround();
var avatar = addAvatar();
var scoreboard = addScoreboard();
animate();
gameStep();

function addGround() {
  document.body.style.backgroundColor = '#87CEEB';
  ground = new Physijs.PlaneMesh(
    new THREE.PlaneGeometry(1e6, 1e6),
    new THREE.MeshBasicMaterial({color: 0x7CFC00})
  );
  ground.rotation.x = -Math.PI/2;
  scene.add(ground);
  return ground;
}

function addAvatar() {
  avatar = new Physijs.BoxMesh(
    new THREE.CubeGeometry(40, 50, 1),
    new THREE.MeshBasicMaterial({visible: false})
  );
  var avatar_material = new THREE.MeshBasicMaterial({
    map: THREE.ImageUtils.loadTexture('/images/purple_fruit_monster.png'),
    transparent: true
  });
  var avatar_picture = new THREE.Mesh(
    new THREE.PlaneGeometry(40, 50), avatar_material
  );
  avatar.add(avatar_picture);
```

```
  avatar.position.set(-50, 50, 0);
  scene.add(avatar);

  avatar.setAngularFactor(new THREE.Vector3( 0, 0, 0 )); // no rotation
  avatar.setLinearFactor(new THREE.Vector3( 1, 1, 0 )); // only move on X/Y axes
  avatar.setLinearVelocity(new THREE.Vector3(0, 150, 0));

  avatar.addEventListener('collision', function(object) {
    if (object.is_fruit) {
      scoreboard.addPoints(10);
      avatar.setLinearVelocity(new THREE.Vector3(0, 50, 0));
      scene.remove(object);
    }
    if (object == ground) {
      game_over = true;
      scoreboard.message("Game Over!");
    }
  });
  return avatar;
}

function addScoreboard() {
  var scoreboard = new Scoreboard();
  scoreboard.score(0);
  scoreboard.help('Use arrow keys to move and the space bar to jump');
  return scoreboard;
}

var game_over = false;
function animate() {
  if (game_over) return;

  requestAnimationFrame(animate);
  scene.simulate(); // run physics
  renderer.render(scene, camera);
}

function gameStep() {
  if (game_over) return;

  launchFruit();
  setTimeout(gameStep, 3*1000);
}

function launchFruit() {
  var fruit = new Physijs.ConvexMesh(
    new THREE.CylinderGeometry(20, 20, 1, 24),
    new THREE.MeshBasicMaterial({visible: false})
  );
  var material = new THREE.MeshBasicMaterial({
```

```
    map: THREE.ImageUtils.loadTexture('/images/fruit.png'),
    transparent: true
  });
  var picture = new THREE.Mesh(new THREE.PlaneGeometry(40, 40), material);
  picture.rotation.x = -Math.PI/2;
  fruit.add(picture);

  fruit.is_fruit = true;
  fruit.setAngularFactor(new THREE.Vector3( 0, 0, 1 ));
  fruit.setLinearFactor(new THREE.Vector3( 1, 1, 0 ));
  fruit.position.set(300, 20, 0);
  fruit.rotation.x = Math.PI/2;
  scene.add(fruit);
  fruit.setLinearVelocity(
    new THREE.Vector3(-150, 0, 0)
  );
}

document.addEventListener("keydown", function(event) {
  var code = event.keyCode;

  if (code == 37) left();  // left arrow
  if (code == 39) right(); // right arrow
  if (code == 38) up();    // up arrow
  if (code == 32) up();    // space bar
  if (code == 82) reset(); // R
});

function left()  { move(-50, 0); }
function right() { move(50, 0); }
function up()    { move(avatar.getLinearVelocity().x, 50); }

function move(x, y) {
  avatar.setLinearVelocity(
    new THREE.Vector3(x, y, 0)
  );
}

function reset() {
  avatar.__dirtyPosition = true;
  avatar.position.set(-50, 50, 0);
  avatar.setLinearVelocity(new THREE.Vector3(0, 150, 0));

  for (var i in scene._objects) {
    if (scene._objects[i].is_fruit) {
     scene.remove(scene._objects[i]);
    }
  }

  scoreboard.score(0);
```

```
    if (game_over) {
      game_over = false;
      animate();
      gameStep();
    }
  }
</script>
```

A1.16 Code: Tilt-a-Board

This is the final version of the game code from Chapter 16, *Project: Tilt-a-Board*, on page 145.

```
<body></body>
<script src="http://gamingJS.com/Three.js"></script>
<script src="http://gamingJS.com/phys1.js"></script>
<script src="http://gamingJS.com/ChromeFixes.js"></script>
<script>
  // Physics settings
  Physijs.scripts.ammo = 'http://gamingJS.com/ammo.js';
  Physijs.scripts.worker = 'http://gamingJS.com/physijs_worker.js';

  // This is where stuff in our game will happen:
  var scene = new Physijs.Scene({ fixedTimeStep: 2 / 60 });
  scene.setGravity(new THREE.Vector3( 0, -50, 0 ));

  // This is what sees the stuff:
  var aspect_ratio = window.innerWidth / window.innerHeight;
  var camera = new THREE.PerspectiveCamera(75, aspect_ratio, 1, 10000);
  camera.position.set(0, 100, 200);
  camera.rotation.x = -Math.PI/8;
  scene.add(camera);

  // This will draw what the camera sees onto the screen:
  var renderer = new THREE.WebGLRenderer();
  renderer.shadowMapEnabled = true;
  renderer.setSize(window.innerWidth, window.innerHeight);
  document.body.appendChild(renderer.domElement);

  // ******** START CODING ON THE NEXT LINE ********
  addLights();

  var ball = addBall();
  var board = addBoard();

  addControls();
  addGoal();
  addBackground();

  animate();
```

```
gameStep();

function addLights() {
  scene.add(new THREE.AmbientLight(0x999999));

  var back_light = new THREE.PointLight(0xffffff);
  back_light.position.set(50, 50, -100);
  scene.add(back_light);

  var spot_light = new THREE.SpotLight(0xffffff);
  spot_light.position.set(-250, 250, 250);
  spot_light.castShadow = true;
  scene.add(spot_light);
}

function addBall() {
  var ball = new Physijs.SphereMesh(
    new THREE.SphereGeometry(10, 25, 21),
    new THREE.MeshPhongMaterial({
      color: 0x333333,
      shininess: 100.0,
      ambient: 0xff0000,
      emissive: 0x111111,
      specular: 0xbbbbbb
    })
  );
  ball.castShadow = true;
  scene.add(ball);
  resetBall(ball);
  return ball;
}

function resetBall(ball) {
  ball.__dirtyPosition = true;
  ball.position.set(-33, 50, -65);
  ball.setLinearVelocity(0,0,0);
  ball.setAngularVelocity(0,0,0);
}

function addBoard() {
  var material = new THREE.MeshPhongMaterial({
    color: 0x333333,
    shininess: 40,
    ambient: 0xffd700,
    emissive: 0x111111,
    specular: 0xeeeeee
  });

  var beam = new Physijs.BoxMesh(
    new THREE.CubeGeometry(50, 2, 200),
```

```
    material,
      0
  );
  beam.position.set(-37, 0, 0);
  beam.receiveShadow = true;

  var beam2 = new Physijs.BoxMesh(
    new THREE.CubeGeometry(50, 2, 200),
    material
  );
  beam2.position.set(75, 0, 0);
  beam2.receiveShadow = true;
  beam.add(beam2);

  var beam3 = new Physijs.BoxMesh(
    new THREE.CubeGeometry(200, 2, 50),
    material
  );
  beam3.position.set(40, 0, -40);
  beam3.receiveShadow = true;
  beam.add(beam3);

  var beam4 = new Physijs.BoxMesh(
    new THREE.CubeGeometry(200, 2, 50),
    material
  );
  beam4.position.set(40, 0, 40);
  beam4.receiveShadow = true;
  beam.add(beam4);

  beam.rotation.set(0.1, 0, 0);
  scene.add(beam);
  return beam;
}

function addControls() {
  document.addEventListener("keydown", function(event) {
    var code = event.keyCode;

    if (code == 37) left();
    if (code == 39) right();
    if (code == 38) up();
    if (code == 40) down();
  });
}

function left()  { tilt('z',  0.02); }
function right() { tilt('z', -0.02); }
function up()    { tilt('x', -0.02); }
function down()  { tilt('x',  0.02); }
```

```javascript
function tilt(dir, amount) {
  board.__dirtyRotation = true;
  board.rotation[dir] = board.rotation[dir] + amount;
}

function addGoal() {
  var light = new THREE.Mesh(
    new THREE.CylinderGeometry(20, 20, 1000),
    new THREE.MeshPhongMaterial({
      transparent:true,
      opacity: 0.15,
      shininess: 0,
      ambient: 0xffffff,
      emissive: 0xffffff
    })
  );
  scene.add(light);

  var score = new Physijs.ConvexMesh(
    new THREE.PlaneGeometry(20, 20),
    new THREE.MeshNormalMaterial({wireframe: true})
  );
  score.position.y = -50;
  score.rotation.x = -Math.PI/2;
  scene.add(score);

  score.addEventListener('collision', function() {
    flashGoalLight(light);
    resetBall(ball);
  });
}

function addBackground() {
  document.body.style.backgroundColor = 'black';
  var stars = new THREE.Geometry();
  while (stars.vertices.length < 1000) {
    var lat = Math.PI * Math.random() - Math.PI/2;
    var lon = 2*Math.PI * Math.random();
    stars.vertices.push(new THREE.Vector3(
      1000 * Math.cos(lon) * Math.cos(lat),
      1000 * Math.sin(lon) * Math.cos(lat),
      1000 * Math.sin(lat)
    ));
  }
  var star_stuff = new THREE.ParticleBasicMaterial({size: 5});
  var star_system = new THREE.ParticleSystem(stars, star_stuff);
  scene.add(star_system);
}
```

```javascript
function animate() {
  requestAnimationFrame(animate);
  scene.simulate(); // run physics
  renderer.render(scene, camera);
}

function gameStep() {
  if (ball.position.y < -100) resetBall(ball);
  setTimeout(gameStep, 1000 / 60);
}

function flashGoalLight(light, remaining) {
  if (typeof(remaining) == 'undefined') remaining = 9;

  if (light.material.opacity == 0.4) {
    light.material.ambient.setRGB(1,1,1);
    light.material.emissive.setRGB(1,1,1);
    light.material.color.setRGB(1,1,1);
    light.material.opacity = 0.15;
  }
  else {
    light.material.ambient.setRGB(1,0,0);
    light.material.emissive.setRGB(1,0,0);
    light.material.color.setRGB(1,0,0);
    light.material.opacity = 0.4;
  }

  if (remaining > 0) {
    setTimeout(function() {flashGoalLight(light, remaining-1);}, 500);
  }
}
</script>
```

A1.17 Code: Learning about JavaScript Objects

The code from Chapter 17, *Project: Learning about JavaScript Objects*, on page 159, should look something like the following.

```html
<body></body>
<script src="http://gamingJS.com/Three.js"></script>
<script src="http://gamingJS.com/ChromeFixes.js"></script>
<script>
  // This is where stuff in our game will happen:
  var scene = new THREE.Scene();

  // This is what sees the stuff:
  var aspect_ratio = window.innerWidth / window.innerHeight;
  var camera = new THREE.PerspectiveCamera(75, aspect_ratio, 1, 10000);
  camera.position.z = 500;
  scene.add(camera);
```

```javascript
// This will draw what the camera sees onto the screen:
var renderer = new THREE.CanvasRenderer();
renderer.setSize(window.innerWidth, window.innerHeight);
document.body.appendChild(renderer.domElement);

// ******** START CODING ON THE NEXT LINE ********

var best_movie = {
  title: 'Star Wars',
  year: 1977
};

var best_movie = {
  title: 'Star Wars',
  year: 1977,
  stars: ['Mark Hamill', 'Harrison Ford', 'Carrie Fisher'],
  aboutMe: function() {
    console.log(this.title + ', starring: ' + this.stars);
  }
};
best_movie.aboutMe();
// => Star Wars, starring: Mark Hamill,Harrison Ford,Carrie Fisher

var great_movie = Object.create(best_movie);
great_movie.aboutMe();
// => Star Wars, starring: Mark Hamill,Harrison Ford,Carrie Fisher

great_movie.title = 'Toy Story';
great_movie.year = 1995;
great_movie.stars = ['Tom Hanks', 'Tim Allen'];
great_movie.aboutMe();
// => Toy Story, starring: Tom Hanks,Tim Allen

best_movie.aboutMe();
// => Star Wars, starring: Mark Hamill,Harrison Ford,Carrie Fisher

function Movie(title, stars) {
  this.title = title;
  this.stars = stars;
  this.year = (new Date()).getFullYear();
}
var kung_fu_movie = new Movie('Kung Fu Panda', ['Jack Black', 'Angelina Jolie']);
console.log(kung_fu_movie.title);
// => Kung Fu Panda
console.log(kung_fu_movie.stars);
// => ['Jack Black', 'Angelina Jolie']
console.log(kung_fu_movie.year);
// => 2013

Movie.prototype.aboutMe = function() {
```

```
    console.log(this.title + ', starring: ' + this.stars);
  };
  kung_fu_movie.aboutMe();
  // => Kung Fu Panda, starring: Jack Black,Angelina Jolie


  var donut = {
    mesh: new THREE.Mesh(
      new THREE.TorusGeometry(100, 50, 8, 20),
      new THREE.MeshBasicMaterial({color: 0x33cc33})
    ),
    speed: 1,
    spin: function() {
      var mesh = this.mesh;
      scene.add(mesh);


    }
  };




  // Now, show what the camera sees on the screen:
  renderer.render(scene, camera);
</script>
```

A1.18 Code: Cave Puzzle

This is the final version of the game code from Chapter 18, *Project: Cave Puzzle*, on page 165.

```
<body></body>
<script src="http://gamingJS.com/Three.js"></script>
<script src="http://gamingJS.com/physi.js"></script>
<script src="http://gamingJS.com/ChromeFixes.js"></script>
<script src="http://gamingJS.com/Scoreboard.js"></script>
<script src="http://gamingJS.com/Mouse.js"></script>
<script>
  // Physics settings
  Physijs.scripts.ammo = 'http://gamingJS.com/ammo.js';
  Physijs.scripts.worker = 'http://gamingJS.com/physijs_worker.js';

  // This is where stuff in our game will happen:
  var scene = new Physijs.Scene({ fixedTimeStep: 2 / 60 });
  scene.setGravity(new THREE.Vector3( 0, -100, 0 ));

  // This is what sees the stuff:
  var width = window.innerWidth,
      height = window.innerHeight,
      aspect_ratio = width / height;
  //var camera = new THREE.PerspectiveCamera(75, aspect_ratio, 1, 10000);
  var camera = new THREE.OrthographicCamera(
```

```
    -width/2, width/2, height/2, -height/2, 1, 10000
);

camera.position.z = 500;
scene.add(camera);

// This will draw what the camera sees onto the screen:
var renderer = new THREE.WebGLRenderer();
renderer.setSize(window.innerWidth, window.innerHeight);
document.body.appendChild(renderer.domElement);
document.body.style.backgroundColor = '#9999aa';

// ******** START CODING ON THE NEXT LINE ********

/*
// Perspective camera border
function makeBorder(x, y, w, h)  {
  var border = new Physijs.BoxMesh(
    new THREE.CubeGeometry(1.2*w, 1.2*h, 100),
    Physijs.createMaterial(
      new THREE.MeshBasicMaterial({color: 0x000000}), 0.2, 1.0
    ),
    0
  );
  border.position.set(1.2*x, 1.2*y, 0);
  return border;
}
*/
function makeBorder(x, y, w, h)  {
  var border = new Physijs.BoxMesh(
    new THREE.CubeGeometry(w, h, 100),
    Physijs.createMaterial(
      new THREE.MeshBasicMaterial({color: 0x000000}), 0.2, 1.0
    ),
    0
  );
  border.position.set(x, y, 0);
  return border;
}
scene.add(makeBorder(width/-2, 0,         50,     height));
scene.add(makeBorder(width/2,  0,         50,     height));
scene.add(makeBorder(0,        height/2,  width,  50));
scene.add(makeBorder(0,        height/-2, width,  50));

var avatar = new Physijs.ConvexMesh(

  new THREE.CylinderGeometry(30, 30, 5, 16),
  Physijs.createMaterial(

    new THREE.MeshBasicMaterial({color:0xbb0000}), 0.2, 0.5
```

```
    )
);
avatar.rotation.set(Math.PI/2, 0, 0);
avatar.position.set(0.5 * width/-2, -height/2 + 25 + 30, 0);
scene.add(avatar);

avatar.setAngularFactor(new THREE.Vector3( 0, 0, 0 )); // don't rotate
avatar.setLinearFactor(new THREE.Vector3( 1, 1, 0 )); // only move on X and Y axis

avatar.addEventListener('collision', function(object) {
  if (object.isGoal) gameOver();
});

document.addEventListener("keydown", function(event) {
  var code = event.keyCode;
  if (code == 37) move(-50); // left arrow
  if (code == 39) move(50);  // right arrow
});

function move(x) {
  var v_y = avatar.getLinearVelocity().y,
      v_x = avatar.getLinearVelocity().x;

  if (Math.abs(v_x + x) > 200) return;
  avatar.setLinearVelocity(
    new THREE.Vector3(v_x + x, v_y, 0)
  );
}

var goal = new Physijs.ConvexMesh(
  new THREE.TorusGeometry(100, 25, 20, 30),
  Physijs.createMaterial(
    new THREE.MeshBasicMaterial({color:0x00bb00})
  ),
  0
);
goal.isGoal = true;

function placeGoal() {
  var x = 0,
      rand = Math.random();
  if (rand < 0.33) x = width / -2;
  if (rand > 0.66) x = width / 2;
  goal.position.set(x, height/2, 0);
  scene.add(goal);
}
placeGoal();

function Ramp(x, y) {
  this.mesh = new Physijs.ConvexMesh(
```

```
      new THREE.CylinderGeometry(5, height * 0.05, height * 0.25),
      Physijs.createMaterial(
        new THREE.MeshBasicMaterial({color:0x0000cc}), 0.2, 1.0
      ),
      0
    );

  this.move(x, y);
  this.rotate(2*Math.PI*Math.random());
  this.listenForEvents();
}

Ramp.prototype.move = function(x, y) {
  this.mesh.position.x = this.mesh.position.x + x;
  this.mesh.position.y = this.mesh.position.y + y;
  this.mesh.__dirtyRotation = true;
  this.mesh.__dirtyPosition = true;
};

Ramp.prototype.rotate = function(angle) {
  this.mesh.rotation.z = this.mesh.rotation.z + angle;
  this.mesh.__dirtyRotation = true;
  this.mesh.__dirtyPosition = true;
};

Ramp.prototype.listenForEvents = function() {
  var me = this,
      mesh = this.mesh;
  mesh.addEventListener('drag', function(event) {
    me.move(event.x_diff, event.y_diff);
  });

  document.addEventListener('keydown', function(event) {
    if (!mesh.isActive) return;
    if (event.keyCode != 83) return; // S
    me.rotate(0.1);
  });
};

var ramp1 = new Ramp(-width/4, height/4);
scene.add(ramp1.mesh);
var ramp2 = new Ramp(width/4, -height/4);
scene.add(ramp2.mesh);

var scoreboard = new Scoreboard();
scoreboard.timer();
scoreboard.countdown(40);
scoreboard.help(
  "Get the green ring. " +
  "Click and drag blue ramps. " +
```

```
      "Click blue ramps and press S to spin. " +
      "Left and right arrows to move player. " +
      "Be quick!"
    );
    scoreboard.onTimeExpired(function() {
      scoreboard.setMessage("Game Over!");
      gameOver();
    });

    var pause = false;
    function gameOver() {
      if (scoreboard.getTimeRemaining() > 0) scoreboard.setMessage('Win!');
      scoreboard.stopCountdown();
      scoreboard.stopTimer();
      pause = true;
    }

    // Animate motion in the game
    function animate() {
      if (pause) return;
      requestAnimationFrame(animate);
      renderer.render(scene, camera);
    }
    animate();

    // Run physics
    function gameStep() {
      if (pause) return;
      scene.simulate();
      // Update physics 60 times a second so that motion is smooth
      setTimeout(gameStep, 1000/60);
    }
    gameStep();
</script>
```

A1.19 Code: Multilevel Game

This is the final version of the game code from Chapter 19, *Project: Multilevel Game*, on page 177.

```
<body></body>
<script src="http://gamingJS.com/Three.js"></script>
<script src="http://gamingJS.com/physi.js"></script>
<script src="http://gamingJS.com/ChromeFixes.js"></script>
<script src="http://gamingJS.com/Scoreboard.js"></script>
<script src="http://gamingJS.com/Mouse.js"></script>
<script src="http://gamingJS.com/Sounds.js"></script>
<script>
  // Physics settings
  Physijs.scripts.ammo = 'http://gamingJS.com/ammo.js';
  Physijs.scripts.worker = 'http://gamingJS.com/physijs_worker.js';
```

```javascript
// This is where stuff in our game will happen:
var scene = new Physijs.Scene({ fixedTimeStep: 2 / 60 });
scene.setGravity(new THREE.Vector3( 0, -100, 0 ));

// This is what sees the stuff:
var width = window.innerWidth,
    height = window.innerHeight,
    aspect_ratio = width / height;
//var camera = new THREE.PerspectiveCamera(75, aspect_ratio, 1, 10000);
var camera = new THREE.OrthographicCamera(
  -width/2, width/2, height/2, -height/2, 1, 10000
);

camera.position.z = 500;
scene.add(camera);

// This will draw what the camera sees onto the screen:
var renderer = new THREE.WebGLRenderer();
renderer.setSize(window.innerWidth, window.innerHeight);
document.body.appendChild(renderer.domElement);
document.body.style.backgroundColor = '#9999aa';

// ******** START CODING ON THE NEXT LINE ********

/*
// Perspective camera border
function makeBorder(x, y, w, h)  {
  var border = new Physijs.BoxMesh(
    new THREE.CubeGeometry(1.2*w, 1.2*h, 100),
    Physijs.createMaterial(
      new THREE.MeshBasicMaterial({color: 0x000000}), 0.2, 1.0
    ),
    0
  );
  border.position.set(1.2*x, 1.2*y, 0);
  return border;
}
*/
function makeBorder(x, y, w, h)  {
  var border = new Physijs.BoxMesh(
    new THREE.CubeGeometry(w, h, 100),
    Physijs.createMaterial(
      new THREE.MeshBasicMaterial({color: 0x000000}), 0.2, 1.0
    ),
    0
  );
  border.position.set(x, y, 0);
  return border;
}
```

```
scene.add(makeBorder(width/-2, 0,          50,     height));
scene.add(makeBorder(width/2,  0,          50,     height));
scene.add(makeBorder(0,        height/2,   width,  50));
scene.add(makeBorder(0,        height/-2,  width,  50));

var avatar = new Physijs.ConvexMesh(
  new THREE.CylinderGeometry(30, 30, 5, 16),
  Physijs.createMaterial(
    new THREE.MeshBasicMaterial({color:0xbb0000}), 0.2, 0.5
  )
);
avatar.rotation.set(Math.PI/2, 0, 0);
avatar.position.set(0.5 * width/-2, -height/2 + 25 + 30, 0);
scene.add(avatar);

avatar.setAngularFactor(new THREE.Vector3( 0, 0, 0 )); // don't rotate
avatar.setLinearFactor(new THREE.Vector3( 1, 1, 0 )); // only move on X and Y axis

document.addEventListener("keydown", function(event) {
  var code = event.keyCode;
  if (code == 37) move(-50); // left arrow
  if (code == 39) move(50);  // right arrow
});

function move(x) {
  var v_y = avatar.getLinearVelocity().y,
      v_x = avatar.getLinearVelocity().x;

  if (Math.abs(v_x + x) > 200) return;
  avatar.setLinearVelocity(
    new THREE.Vector3(v_x + x, v_y, 0)
  );
}

var goal = new Physijs.ConvexMesh(
  new THREE.TorusGeometry(100, 25, 20, 30),
  Physijs.createMaterial(
    new THREE.MeshBasicMaterial({color:0x00bb00})
  ),
  0
);
goal.isGoal = true;

function placeGoal() {
  var x = 0,
      rand = Math.random();
  if (rand < 0.33) x = width / -2;
  if (rand > 0.66) x = width / 2;
  goal.position.set(x, height/2, 0);
  scene.add(goal);
```

```
}
placeGoal();

function Ramp(x, y) {
  this.mesh = new Physijs.ConvexMesh(
    new THREE.CylinderGeometry(5, height * 0.05, height * 0.25),
    Physijs.createMaterial(
      new THREE.MeshBasicMaterial({color:0x0000cc}), 0.2, 1.0
    ),
    0
  );

  this.move(x, y);
  this.rotate(2*Math.PI*Math.random());
  this.listenForEvents();
}

Ramp.prototype.move = function(x, y) {
  this.mesh.position.x = this.mesh.position.x + x;
  this.mesh.position.y = this.mesh.position.y + y;
  this.mesh.__dirtyRotation = true;
  this.mesh.__dirtyPosition = true;
};

Ramp.prototype.rotate = function(angle) {
  this.mesh.rotation.z = this.mesh.rotation.z + angle;
  this.mesh.__dirtyRotation = true;
  this.mesh.__dirtyPosition = true;
};

Ramp.prototype.listenForEvents = function() {
  var me = this,
      mesh = this.mesh;
  mesh.addEventListener('drag', function(event) {
    me.move(event.x_diff, event.y_diff);
  });

  document.addEventListener('keydown', function(event) {
    if (!mesh.isActive) return;
    if (event.keyCode != 83) return; // S
    me.rotate(0.1);
  });
};

var ramp1 = new Ramp(-width/4, height/4);
scene.add(ramp1.mesh);

var ramp2 = new Ramp(width/4, -height/4);
scene.add(ramp2.mesh);
```

```
var scoreboard = new Scoreboard();
scoreboard.timer();
scoreboard.countdown(40);
scoreboard.help(
  "Get the green ring. " +
  "Click and drag blue ramps. " +
  "Click blue ramps and press S to spin. " +
  "Left and right arrows to move player. " +
  "Be quick!"
);
scoreboard.onTimeExpired(function() {
  scoreboard.setMessage("Game Over!");
  gameOver();
});

var pause = false;
function gameOver() {
  if (scoreboard.getTimeRemaining() > 0) scoreboard.setMessage('Win!');
  scoreboard.stopCountdown();
  scoreboard.stopTimer();
  pause = true;
}

function Levels(scoreboard, scene) {
  this.scoreboard = scoreboard;
  this.scene = scene;
  this.levels = [];
  this.current_level = 0;
}

Levels.prototype.addLevel = function(things_on_this_level) {
  this.levels.push(things_on_this_level);
};

Levels.prototype.thingsOnCurrentLevel = function() {
  return this.levels[this.current_level];
};

Levels.prototype.draw = function() {
  var scene = this.scene;
  this.thingsOnCurrentLevel().forEach(function(thing) {
    scene.add(thing);
  });
};

Levels.prototype.erase = function() {
  var scene = this.scene;
  this.thingsOnCurrentLevel().forEach(function(obstacle) {
    scene.remove(obstacle);
  });
```

```
};

Levels.prototype.levelUp = function() {
  if (!this.hasMoreLevels()) return;
  this.erase();
  this.current_level++;
  this.draw();
  this.scoreboard.resetCountdown(50 - this.current_level * 5);
};

Levels.prototype.hasMoreLevels = function() {
  var last_level = this.levels.length-1;
  return this.current_level < last_level;
};

function buildObstacle(shape_name, x, y) {
  var shape;
  if (shape_name == 'platform') {
    shape = new THREE.CubeGeometry(height/2, height/10, 10);
  } else {
    shape = new THREE.CylinderGeometry(50, 2, height);
  }
  var material = Physijs.createMaterial(
    new THREE.MeshBasicMaterial({color:0x333333}), 0.2, 1.0
  );

  var obstacle = new Physijs.ConvexMesh(shape, material, 0);
  obstacle.position.set(x, y, 0);
  return obstacle;
}

var levels = new Levels(scoreboard, scene);
levels.addLevel([]);
levels.addLevel([
  buildObstacle('platform', 0, 0.5 * height/2 * Math.random())
]);
levels.addLevel([
  buildObstacle('platform', 0, 0.5 * height/2 * Math.random()),
  buildObstacle('platform', 0, -0.5 * height/2 * Math.random())
]);
levels.addLevel([
  buildObstacle('platform', 0, 0.5 * height/2 * Math.random()),
  buildObstacle('platform', 0, -0.5 * height/2 * Math.random()),
  buildObstacle('stalactite', -0.33 * width, height/2),
  buildObstacle('stalactite', 0.33 * width, height/2)
]);

avatar.addEventListener('collision', function(object) {
  if (!object.isGoal) return;
  if (!levels.hasMoreLevels()) return gameOver();
```

```
    moveGoal();
    levels.levelUp();
  });

  avatar.addEventListener('collision', function(object) {
    if (object.isGoal) Sounds.guitar.play();
    else Sounds.click.play();
  });

  function moveGoal() {
    scene.remove(goal);
    setTimeout(placeGoal, 2*1000);
  }

  // Animate motion in the game
  function animate() {
    if (pause) return;
    requestAnimationFrame(animate);
    renderer.render(scene, camera);
  }
  animate();

  // Run physics
  function gameStep() {
    if (pause) return;
    scene.simulate();
    // Update physics 60 times a second so that motion is smooth
    setTimeout(gameStep, 1000/60);
  }
  gameStep();
</script>
```

A1.20 Code: River Rafting

This is the final version of the game code from Chapter 20, *Project: River Rafting*, on page 185. It is very long. There are a few extras to play around with, as well.

```
<body></body>
<script src="http://gamingJS.com/Three.js"></script>
<script src="http://gamingJS.com/physi.js"></script>
<script src="http://gamingJS.com/ChromeFixes.js"></script>
<script src="http://gamingJS.com/Scoreboard.js"></script>

<script>
  // Physics settings
  Physijs.scripts.ammo = 'http://gamingJS.com/ammo.js';
  Physijs.scripts.worker = 'http://gamingJS.com/physijs_worker.js';

  // This is where stuff in our game will happen:
```

```
var scene = new Physijs.Scene({ fixedTimeStep: 2 / 60 });
scene.setGravity(new THREE.Vector3( 0, -20, 0 ));

// This is what sees the stuff:
var width = window.innerWidth,
    height = window.innerHeight,
    aspect_ratio = width / height;
var camera = new THREE.PerspectiveCamera(75, aspect_ratio, 1, 1e6);
// var camera = new THREE.OrthographicCamera(
//    -width/2, width/2, height/2, -height/2, 1, 10000
// );

camera.position.set(250, 250, 250);
camera.lookAt(new THREE.Vector3(0, 0, 0));
scene.add(camera);

// This will draw what the camera sees onto the screen:
var renderer = new THREE.WebGLRenderer();
renderer.shadowMapEnabled = true;
renderer.setSize(window.innerWidth, window.innerHeight);
document.body.appendChild(renderer.domElement);
document.body.style.backgroundColor = '#ffffff';

// ******** START CODING ON THE NEXT LINE ********

addSunlight(scene);
var scoreboard = addScoreboard();
var river = addRiver(scene);
var raft = addRaft(scene);
var game_items = [];
var paused;
startGame(raft, river, scoreboard);

function addSunlight(scene) {
  var sunlight = new THREE.DirectionalLight();
  sunlight.intensity = 0.5;
  sunlight.castShadow = true;
  sunlight.position.set(250, 250, 250);
  sunlight.shadowCameraNear = 250;
  sunlight.shadowCameraFar = 600;
  sunlight.shadowCameraLeft = -200;
  sunlight.shadowCameraRight = 200;
  sunlight.shadowCameraTop = 200;
  sunlight.shadowCameraBottom = -200;
  sunlight.shadowMapWidth = 4096;
  sunlight.shadowMapHeight = 4096;

  scene.add(sunlight);
}
```

```
function addScoreboard() {
  var scoreboard = new Scoreboard();
  scoreboard.score(0);
  scoreboard.timer();
  scoreboard.help(
    'left / right arrow keys to turn. ' +
    'space bar to move forward.'
  );

  return scoreboard;
}

function addRiver(scene) {
  var ground = makeGround(500);
  addWater(ground, 500);
  addLid(ground, 500);

  scene.add(ground);

  return ground;
}

function makeGround(size) {
  var faces = 100;
  var shape = new THREE.PlaneGeometry(size, size, faces, faces);
  var river_points = digRiver(shape, faces + 1);

  var cover = Physijs.createMaterial(
    new THREE.MeshPhongMaterial({
      emissive: new THREE.Color(0x339933), // a little green
      specular: new THREE.Color(0x333333)  // dark gray / not shiny
    }),
    1,  // high friction (hard to move across)
    0.1 // not very bouncy
  );

  var ground = new Physijs.HeightfieldMesh(
    shape, cover, 0
  );
  ground.rotation.set(-Math.PI/2, 0.2, -Math.PI/2);
  ground.receiveShadow = true;
  ground.castShadow = true;
  ground.river_points = river_points;

  return ground;
}

function digRiver(shape, size) {
  var center_points = [];
  for (var row=0; row<size; row++) {
```

```
    var center = Math.sin(4*Math.PI*row/size);
    center = center * 0.1 * size;
    center = Math.floor(center + size/2);
    center = row*size + center;

    for (var distance=0; distance<12; distance++) {
      shape.vertices[center + distance].z = -5 * (12 - distance);
      shape.vertices[center - distance].z = -5 * (12 - distance);
    }

    center_points.push(shape.vertices[center]);
  }
  shape.computeFaceNormals();
  shape.computeVertexNormals();
  return center_points;
}

function addWater(ground, size) {
  var water = new Physijs.ConvexMesh(
    new THREE.CubeGeometry(1.4*size, 1.4*size, 10),
    Physijs.createMaterial(
      new THREE.MeshBasicMaterial({color: 0x0000bb}),
      0,   // No friction (slippery as ice)
      0.01 // Not very bouncy at all
    ),
    0 // Never move
  );
  water.position.z = -20;
  water.receiveShadow = true;
  ground.add(water);
}

function addLid(ground, size) {
  var lid = new Physijs.ConvexMesh(
    new THREE.CubeGeometry(size, size, 1),
    new THREE.MeshBasicMaterial({visible:false})
  );
  ground.add(lid);
}

function addSharkJump(pos, ground) {
  var ramp = new Physijs.ConvexMesh(
    new THREE.CubeGeometry(10, 8, 3),
    new THREE.MeshPhongMaterial({emissive: 0xbb0000})
  );
  ramp.receiveShadow = true;
  ramp.rotation.x = -Math.PI/10;
  ramp.position.copy(pos);
  ramp.position.z = pos.z + 10;
  ground.add(ramp);
```

```
  var shark = new Physijs.ConvexMesh(
    new THREE.CylinderGeometry(0.1, 2, 3),
    new THREE.MeshPhongMaterial({emissive: 0x999999})
  );
  shark.receiveShadow = true;
  shark.position.copy(pos);
  shark.rotation.x = Math.PI/2;
  shark.rotation.z = Math.PI/8;
  shark.position.z = pos.z + 12;
  shark.position.y = pos.y - 15;
  ground.add(shark);
}

function addRaft(scene) {
  var mesh = new Physijs.ConvexMesh(
    new THREE.TorusGeometry(2, 0.5, 8, 20),
    Physijs.createMaterial(
      new THREE.MeshPhongMaterial({
        emissive: 0xcc2222,
        specular: 0xeeeeee
      }),
      0.1,
      0.01
    )
  );
  mesh.rotation.x = -Math.PI/2;
  mesh.castShadow = true;

  scene.add(mesh);
  mesh.setAngularFactor(new THREE.Vector3(0, 0, 0));

  var rudder = new THREE.Mesh(
    new THREE.SphereGeometry(0.5),
    new THREE.MeshBasicMaterial({color: 0x000099})
  );
  rudder.position.set(3, 0, 0);
  mesh.add(rudder);

  return mesh;
}
//raft.setLinearVelocity(
//  new THREE.Vector3(50, 0, -10)
//);

function startGame(raft, river, scoreboard) {
  var start = river.river_points[100];
  raft.__dirtyPosition = true;
  raft.position.set(start.y, start.z + 100, 0);
  raft.setLinearVelocity(new THREE.Vector3());
```

```
      scoreboard.resetTimer();
      scoreboard.score(0);
      scoreboard.clearMessage();
      updateCamera();
      camera.lookAt(new THREE.Vector3(start.y, 0, 0));
      resetItems(river, scoreboard);
      paused = false;
    }

    function updateCamera() {
      camera.position.set(
        raft.position.x + 75,
        raft.position.y + 40,
        raft.position.z
      );
    }

    function resetItems(ground, scoreboard) {
      removeItems();
      addItems(ground, scoreboard);
    }

    function removeItems() {
      game_items.forEach(function(item) {
        scene.remove(item);
      });
      game_items = [];
    }


    function addItems(ground, scoreboard) {
      var points = ground.river_points;

      var random20 = Math.floor(20 + 10*Math.random()),
          fruit20 = addFruitPowerUp(points[random20], ground, scoreboard);
      game_items.push(fruit20);

      var random70 = Math.floor(70 + 10*Math.random()),
          fruit70 = addFruitPowerUp(points[random70], ground, scoreboard);
      game_items.push(fruit70);
    }
    function addFruitPowerUp(location, ground, scoreboard) {
      var mesh = new Physijs.ConvexMesh(
        new THREE.SphereGeometry(10, 25),
        new THREE.MeshPhongMaterial({emissive: 0xbbcc00}),
        0
      );
      mesh.receiveShadow = true;
      mesh.castShadow = true;
```

```
  mesh.addEventListener('collision', function() {
    var list_index = game_items.indexOf(mesh);
    game_items.splice(list_index, 1);
    scene.remove(mesh);
    scoreboard.addPoints(200);
    scoreboard.message('Yum!');
    setTimeout(function() {scoreboard.clearMessage();}, 2.5* 1000);
  });

  ground.updateMatrixWorld();
  var p = new THREE.Vector3(location.x, location.y, -20);
  ground.localToWorld(p);
  mesh.position.copy(p);
  scene.add(mesh);
  return mesh;
}


// Animate motion in the game
function animate() {
  requestAnimationFrame(animate);
  if (paused) return;

  updateCamera();
  renderer.render(scene, camera);
}
animate();

// Run physics
function gameStep() {
  // Update physics 60 times a second so that motion is smooth
  setTimeout(gameStep, 1000/60);

  if (paused) return;

  updateScore();
  checkForGameOver();
  scene.simulate();
}
gameStep();

var next_x;
function updateScore() {
  if (!next_x) next_x = raft.position.x + 25;
  if (raft.position.x > next_x) {
    scoreboard.addPoints(10);
    next_x = next_x + 25;
  }
}
```

```
  function checkForGameOver() {
    if (raft.position.x < 250) return;

    paused = true;
    scoreboard.stopTimer();
    scoreboard.message("You made it!");
    if (scoreboard.getTime() < 30) scoreboard.addPoints(100);
    if (scoreboard.getTime() < 25) scoreboard.addPoints(200);
    if (scoreboard.getTime() < 20) scoreboard.addPoints(500);
  }
  var mass, velocity;
  document.addEventListener("keydown", function(event) {
    var code = event.keyCode;
    if (code == 32) pushRaft();       // space
    if (code == 38) pushRaft();       // up
    if (code == 40) pushRaft();       // down
    if (code == 37) rotateRaft(-1); // left
    if (code == 39) rotateRaft(1);   // right
    if (code == 82) startGame(raft, river, scoreboard); // r
    if (code == 80)  { // p
      paused = !paused;
      if (paused) {
        mass = raft.mass;
        velocity = raft.getLinearVelocity();
        raft.mass=0;
      }
      else {
        raft.mass = mass;
        raft.setLinearVelocity(velocity);
      }
    }
  });

  function pushRaft() {
    var angle = raft.rotation.z;

    raft.applyCentralForce(
      new THREE.Vector3(
        500 * Math.cos(angle),
        0,
        -500 * Math.sin(angle)
      )
    );
  }
  function rotateRaft(direction) {
    raft.__dirtyRotation = true;
    raft.rotation.z = raft.rotation.z + direction * Math.PI/10;
  }
</script>
```

JavaScript Libraries Used in This Book

This appendix contains a list of the JavaScript libraries used in this book, and details on how you can find more information about each.

A2.1 Three.js

The Three.js JavaScript library is the main library used throughout this book. The home page for the project is http://threejs.org/. The home page includes lots of cool animations and samples, many of which you can try in the ICE Code Editor.

We're using version 52 of Three.js. Detailed documentation for properties and methods not discussed in this book can be found at http://gamingjs.com/docs/threejs/.

A2.2 Physijs

The physics engine that is used in this book is Physijs. The home page for the library is http://chandlerprall.github.io/Physijs/. That page includes brief samples and some introductory articles.

The Physijs project doesn't have as much documentation as the Three.js project, but there is some on the project wiki: https://github.com/chandlerprall/Physijs/wiki. We're using the version of Physijs that is compatible with Three.js 52. Since Physijs continues to grow, the wiki may refer to newer features than those supported by the version we're using.

A2.3 Tween.js

When we want to change values (location, rotation, speed) over the course of time in this book, we use the Tween library. The project home page is http://github.com/sole/tween.js.

Building a Tween involves several parts. A Tween needs the starting value or values, the ending values, the time that it takes to move from the start to the end values, and a function that's called as the Tween is running. A Tween also needs to be started and updated to work.

The Tween from Chapter 11, *Project: Fruit Hunt*, on page 99, contains a good example.

```
new TWEEN.
  Tween({
    height: 150,
    spin: 0
  }).
  to({
    height: 250,
    spin: 4
  }, 500).
  onUpdate(function () {
    fruit.position.y = this.height;
    fruit.rotation.z = this.spin;
  }).
  start();
```

This moves between two values: the height and the spin. Over the course of half a second (500 milliseconds), the height moves from 150 to 250. The spin moves from 0 to 4. Each time the Tween is updated, we change the position and rotation of the fruit being animated. The current values being Tweened are made available as a property of the special this object.

The last thing we do in the preceding example is to start the Tween.

Tweens also need something to tell them to update. In 3D programming, we normally do this in the animate() function with a TWEEN.update() call.

```
function animate() {
  requestAnimationFrame(animate);
  TWEEN.update();
  renderer.render(scene, camera);
}
```

In addition to onUpdate(), there are onStart() and onComplete() methods that call a function when the Tween starts and finishes.

A2.4 Scoreboard.js

The Scoreboard.js library is a *simple* JavaScript library that provides the basics of scoring in games. It supports very little configuration, but aims to be easy to use for programmers.

The project home page is https://github.com/eee-c/scoreboard.js.

The Scoreboard.js library supports messages, help text, scoring, an elapsed timer, and a countdown timer.

Scoreboard Messages

Use messages to provide in-game messages to the game player. If you create a scoreboard with var scoreboard = new Scoreboard(), the following methods are available:

- scoreboard.message('your message here')—sets the current scoreboard message. This will replace any existing messages. If the message section of the scoreboard is not shown already, this will show it.

- scoreboard.addMessage('your message here')—adds more messages to the current scoreboard message.

- scoreboard.addMessage('your message here')—adds more messages to the current scoreboard message.

- scoreboard.showMessage()—shows the message section of the scoreboard.

- scoreboard.hideMessage()—hides the message section of the scoreboard.

- scoreboard.clearMessage()—erases the message section of the scoreboard.

Help

Scoreboard help provides a way to give instructions to the player without cluttering up the message section of the scoreboard. Players need to type a question mark to see the help on the scoreboard.

If you create a scoreboard with var scoreboard = new Scoreboard(), the following methods are available:

- scoreboard.help('your help instructions here')—sets the scoreboard help. This will replace any existing help. If the help section of the scoreboard is not shown already, this will show it.

- scoreboard.showHelp()—shows the help section of the scoreboard.

- scoreboard.hideHelp()—hides the help section of the scoreboard.

Scoring

This feature of the scoreboard keeps track of the number of points the player has earned in the game.

If you create a scoreboard with var scoreboard = new Scoreboard(), the following methods are available:

- scoreboard.score(42)—sets the current score in the game. This will replace any existing score. If no number is supplied, zero is used. If the score section of the scoreboard is not shown already, this will show it.

- scoreboard.showScore()—shows the score section of the scoreboard.

- scoreboard.hideScore()—hides the score section of the scoreboard.

- scoreboard.getScore()—returns the current score in the game.

- scoreboard.addPoints(10)—increases the score in the game by the specified number.

- scoreboard.subtractPoints(10)—decreases the score in the game by the specified number.

Timer

This feature keeps track of the total time that has gone by in the game.

If you create a scoreboard with var scoreboard = new Scoreboard(), the following methods are available:

- scoreboard.timer()—starts the timer in the game. If the timer section of the scoreboard is not shown already, this will show it.

- scoreboard.showTimer()—shows the timer section of the scoreboard.

- scoreboard.hideTimer()—hides the timer section of the scoreboard.

- scoreboard.stopTimer()—stops the timer from counting any more.

- scoreboard.startTimer()—starts the timer counting.

- scoreboard.resetTimer()—restarts the timer from zero.

- scoreboard.getTime()—returns the number of seconds that have elapsed in the game.

Countdown

This feature keeps track of the total time that has gone by in the game.

If you create a scoreboard with var scoreboard = new Scoreboard(), the following methods are available:

- scoreboard.countdown(60)—starts the countdown in the game with the number of seconds supplied. If no time is specified, then 60 seconds will be used. If the countdown section of the scoreboard is not shown already, this will show it.

- scoreboard.showCountdown()—shows the countdown section of the scoreboard.

- scoreboard.hideCountdown()—hides the countdown section of the scoreboard.

- scoreboard.stopCountdown()—stops the countdown from counting any more.

- scoreboard.startCountdown()—starts the countdown counting.

- scoreboard.resetCountdown(60)—resets the countdown to the specified number of seconds.

- scoreboard.getTimeRemaining()—returns the number of seconds left in the game.

- scoreboard.onTimeExpired('Time expired message')—sets the message to be shown when time expires.

- scoreboard.onTimeExpired(function()) "{ ... }"—if a function is supplied to the onTimeExpired() method, the function will be called when time runs out.

A2.5 Sounds.js

The Sounds.js JavaScript library contains the bare minimum of sounds for use in games. Full, up-to-date documentation is available at https://github.com/eee-c/Sounds.js.

To use the Sounds.js library, it must be sourced in a <script> tag:

```
<script src="http://gamingJS.com/Sounds.js"></script>
```

At the time of this writing, there were eleven sounds available: bubble, buzz, click, donk, drip, guitar, knock, scratch, snick, spring, and swish. Each sound can be played with code similar to the following:

```
Sounds.bubble.play();
```

To make a sound repeat, replace the play() method with repeat():

```
Sounds.bubble.repeat();
```

To stop the sound at a later time, call the stop() method:

```
Sounds.bubble.stop();
```

If you want a sound to repeat for a fixed amount of time, then start a repeating sound with a timeout to stop the sound:

```
Sounds.bubble.repeat();
setTimeout(function(){Sounds.bubble.stop();}, 5*1000);
```

The preceding would start repeated bubble sounds. After 5 seconds, the timeout function is run, stopping the repeating bubble sounds.

Index

Dynamic Audio and Cross-Platform Games

Add audio to your web, mobile, or desktop app. Learn how to create mobile apps for both iOS and Android in an easy language.

Sound gives your native, web, or mobile apps that extra dimension, and it's essential for games. Rather than using canned samples from a sample library, learn how to build sounds from the ground up and produce them for web projects using the Pure Data programming language. Even better, you'll be able to integrate dynamic sound environments into your native apps or games—sound that reacts to the app, instead of sounding the same every time. Start your journey as a sound designer, and get the power to craft the sound you put into your digital experiences.

Tony Hillerson
(200 pages) ISBN: 9781937785666. $36
http://pragprog.com/book/thsound

Develop cross-platform mobile games with Corona using the Lua programming language! Corona is experiencing explosive growth among mobile game developers, and this book gets you up to speed on how to use this versatile platform. You'll use the Corona SDK to simplify game programming and take a fun, no-nonsense approach to write and add must-have gameplay features. You'll find out how to create all the gaming necessities: menus, sprites, movement, perspective and sound effects, levels, loading and saving, and game physics. Along the way, you'll learn about Corona's API functions and build three common kinds of mobile games from scratch that can run on the iPhone, iPad, Kindle Fire, Nook Color, and all other Android smartphones and tablets.

Printed in full color.

Silvia Domenech
(220 pages) ISBN: 9781937785574. $36
http://pragprog.com/book/sdcorona

The Joy of Math and Healthy Programming

Rediscover the joy and fascinating weirdness of pure mathematics, and learn how to take a healthier approach to programming.

Mathematics is beautiful—and it can be fun and exciting as well as practical. *Good Math* is your guide to some of the most intriguing topics from two thousand years of mathematics: from Egyptian fractions to Turing machines; from the real meaning of numbers to proof trees, group symmetry, and mechanical computation. If you've ever wondered what lay beyond the proofs you struggled to complete in high school geometry, or what limits the capabilities of the computer on your desk, this is the book for you.

Mark C. Chu-Carroll
(282 pages) ISBN: 9781937785338. $34
http://pragprog.com/book/mcmath

To keep doing what you love, you need to maintain your own systems, not just the ones you write code for. Regular exercise and proper nutrition help you learn, remember, concentrate, and be creative—skills critical to doing your job well. Learn how to change your work habits, master exercises that make working at a computer more comfortable, and develop a plan to keep fit, healthy, and sharp for years to come.

This book is intended only as an informative guide for those wishing to know more about health issues. In no way is this book intended to replace, countermand, or conflict with the advice given to you by your own healthcare provider including Physician, Nurse Practitioner, Physician Assistant, Registered Dietician, and other licensed professionals.

Joe Kutner
(254 pages) ISBN: 9781937785314. $36
http://pragprog.com/book/jkthp

The Pragmatic Bookshelf

The Pragmatic Bookshelf features books written by developers for developers. The titles continue the well-known Pragmatic Programmer style and continue to garner awards and rave reviews. As development gets more and more difficult, the Pragmatic Programmers will be there with more titles and products to help you stay on top of your game.

Visit Us Online

This Book's Home Page
http://pragprog.com/book/csjava
Source code from this book, errata, and other resources. Come give us feedback, too!

Register for Updates
http://pragprog.com/updates
Be notified when updates and new books become available.

Join the Community
http://pragprog.com/community
Read our weblogs, join our online discussions, participate in our mailing list, interact with our wiki, and benefit from the experience of other Pragmatic Programmers.

New and Noteworthy
http://pragprog.com/news
Check out the latest pragmatic developments, new titles and other offerings.

Save on the eBook

Save on the eBook versions of this title. Owning the paper version of this book entitles you to purchase the electronic versions at a terrific discount.

PDFs are great for carrying around on your laptop—they are hyperlinked, have color, and are fully searchable. Most titles are also available for the iPhone and iPod touch, Amazon Kindle, and other popular e-book readers.

Buy now at *http://pragprog.com/coupon*

Contact Us

Online Orders:	*http://pragprog.com/catalog*
Customer Service:	*support@pragprog.com*
International Rights:	*translations@pragprog.com*
Academic Use:	*academic@pragprog.com*
Write for Us:	*http://pragprog.com/write-for-us*
Or Call:	+1 800-699-7764

CPSIA information can be obtained at www.ICGtesting.com
Printed in the USA
BVOW11s0056290115

385389BV00003BA/13/P